Michael

# HISTORIC FARM BUILDINGS

# BARN and CATTLE SHEDS at HOLKHAM.

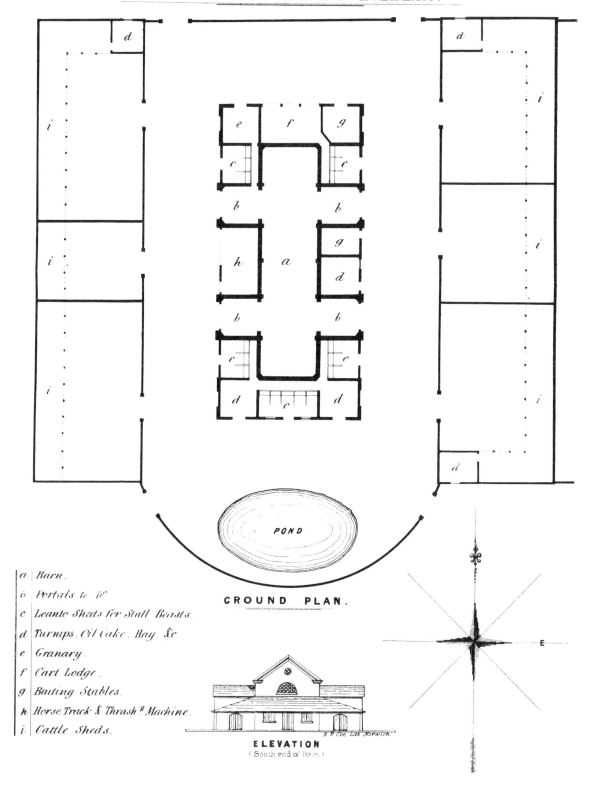

GROUND PLAN.

a | Barn.
b | Portals to do.
c | Leanto Sheds for Stall Beasts.
d | Turnips, Oil Cake, Hay &c.
e | Granary.
f | Cart Lodge.
g | Baiting Stables.
h | Horse Track & Thrash.g Machine.
i | Cattle Sheds.

POND

ELEVATION
(South end of Barn)

R B Coe Lith Norwich

# HISTORIC ❧ FARM ❧ BUILDINGS

*including a Norfolk survey*

Susanna Wade Martins

B.T. BATSFORD LTD London

*In memory of* Alan Carter, 1944–1988
*whose idea this project was but who sadly did not live to see*
*its completion.*

© Susanna Wade Martins 1991
First published 1991

Typeset by Lasertext Ltd, Stretford, Manchester
and printed and bound in Great Britain by
Butler & Tanner Ltd.,
Frome, Somerset
for the publishers
B.T. Batsford Ltd
4 Fitzhardinge Street
London W1H 0AH

A CIP catalogue record for this book is available from the British library

ISBN 0 7134 6507 7

Other titles by the same author

*A Great Estate at Work: The Holkham Estate and its inhabitants in
the nineteenth century*, Cambridge University Press, 1980

*A History of Norfolk*, Phillimore, 1984

*Eigg, An Island Landscape*, Countryside Publishing, 1987

*Norfolk, A Changing Countryside*, 1790–1914, Phillimore, 1988

*'Turnip' Townshend, Statesman and Farmer*, Poppyland, 1990

*A Year in the field, The Norfolk Historic Farm Buildings Project*
(ed. with Alan Carter), Centre of East Anglian Studies, 1987

*Frontispiece*
Plan of the Great Barn,
Holkham, published in
1843, showing the barn
surrounded by cattle yards.
Built in the 1790s, it was
the showpiece of the
Holkham estate, Norfolk.

# Contents

# List of Illustrations

# LIST OF ABBREVIATIONS

| | |
|---|---|
| **CPRE** | Council for the Protection of Rural England |
| **I & ESRO** | Ipswich and East Suffolk Record Office |
| *JRASE* | Journal of the Royal Agricultural Society of England |
| **MAFF** | Ministry of Agriculture, Fisheries and Food |
| **NRO** | Norfolk Record Office |
| **SPAB** | Society for the Protection of Ancient Buildings |
| **UEA** | University of East Anglia |

# Acknowledgements

The initial survey work for this book was undertaken by a Manpower Services Commission Community Enterprise Programme team working for two years. Without their very high level of recording this book could not have been written. At any time there were up to six people working, but the personnel changed over the two years. Both Laurence Mitchell, who took most of the photographs and directed the team in its second year, and Martin Leverington, who did much of the documentary research and was responsible for the perspective drawings reproduced here, worked with the project for most of its duration. The team was co-directed by the late Alan Carter whose knowledge of vernacular buildings and ability to ask the right questions was invaluable to its work.

The project was set up within the Centre of East Anglian Studies at the University of East Anglia and was based there throughout its duration. Without both the financial and moral support of the Centre, and particularly its director, Prof. A. Hassell Smith, the project would never have been begun or completed.

The survey team was also greatly assisted by the generous loan of a crew-bus from R. G. Carter (Holdings) Ltd, Norwich, and grants were also made by Anglia Television and Barclays Bank. The film taken by the survey team was developed and printed by the Royal Commission on Historical Monuments Historic Buildings Record.

The work of the project was overseen by a steering committee with members from both within and without the university. This included Dr R. G. Wilson, Dr B. A. Holderness, Dr P. Barnes, and Prof. A. Hassell Smith from the University of East Anglia, with Bridget Yates from Norfolk Museum Service, Robert Shorland-Ball, then Director of the Museum of East Anglian Life, Stowmarket, and Frank Meeres of the Norfolk Record Office. All of these busy people attended regular meetings and gave much helpful advice. Dr T. Williamson of the Centre of East Anglian Studies also gave the survey much encouragement. The staff of the Norfolk Record Office was helpful in pointing out relevant material we would otherwise have missed, and readily making it available for the team to use.

Michael Brackenbury and Stephen Heywood of the Historic Building Section, Department of Planning and Property, Norfolk County Council, have both shared their expertise on historic buildings and explained current planning policy. They have also drawn my attention to buildings of interest that I would not otherwise have known about. Similarly Edwin Rose of the Norfolk Sites and Monuments Record at the Norfolk Archaeological Unit and the Conservation Officers of the district planning offices, particularly John Denny and Peter Tolhurst, have given information and advice.

Further afield, Carole Ryan of the Shropshire County Planning Department was involved in the initial discussion setting up a recording system suited to our survey, and she also made her department's guidelines on conversion available to me while they were still in draft form. Work on Scottish farm buildings would not have been possible without the assistance of Mrs Elizabeth Beaton, and Dr Deborah Mays of Historic Buildings and Monuments at the Scottish Development Department introduced me to the department's photographs and records and allowed me to consult them. Dr John Shaw of the Royal Museums of Scotland took me to some of the most interesting farms near Edinburgh.

Dr R. G. Wilson and Mr N. Harvey have both read and commented on much of the text. My family have put up with farm-building-orientated holidays and my husband, Peter, has given constant help and encouragement.

I am very grateful to the British Academy for a grant towards the cost of producing the illustrations for this book. The line drawings, unless otherwise acknowledged, are the work of Phillip Judge.

Finally, the survey could not have been undertaken without the helpful co-operation of many farmers who allowed the team to inspect their buildings, lent their photographs, maps and documents, and patiently answered questions. We are indeed grateful to them for their help and also for their hospitality. Hot coffee and mince pies provided at one farm on a very cold pre-Christmas morning will always remain a vivid memory of an eventful and enjoyable project.

The following people and institutions kindly gave permission for their pictures to be reproduced in this publication. Norfolk Archaeological Unit (3 & 4), David Bartrum, Essex County Council (7, a & b), *Traditional Kent Buildings*, ed. Jane Wade, Kent College of Art and Design (6 & 11), Martin Higgins, The National Trust, North-West Region (9), The National Trust, North-West Region (13), Professor M. J. Jarrett and the Society of Antiquaries, Newcastle upon Tyne (5), Charles Carus (10), Eastern Counties Newspapers (123), Peter Messenger, *Cumberland and Westmorland Antiquarian and Archaeological Society* Vol. 75, (1975) (14), Royal Commission on Ancient Monuments, Scotland (17), Home Farm, Beamish Museum, Stanley, Durham (20), North Norfolk District Council (124), Carole Ryan, The Planning Department, Shropshire County Council (125).

Susanna Wade Martins
Centre of East Anglian Studies
University of East Anglia, Norwich

# 1
## Introduction

Interest in historic farm buildings and an appreciation of their value as evidence for agricultural change has increased in the last twenty years. Ironically, this is partly because of their rapid demolition and disappearance with the new 'agricultural revolution' beginning after 1945 and accelerating with Britain's entry into the Common Market. New-found prosperity has led to a wave of investment and reorganization not experienced since the 1880s; with it has come the demolition or abandonment of buildings unsuited to modern methods and machinery. More recently, with soaring house prices, buildings are being sold for conversion and consequently much of their historic value has been lost.

This book has been written to do three things; to provide a general introduction to the history of farm buildings, to present a detailed case study of one county and to assess the value of such a study for our understanding of agricultural history. In the first section, the state of our present knowledge of farm buildings, from the medieval period to the First World War, is summarized, whilst the final two sections deal in detail with a pilot survey carried out in Norfolk. This is of general interest, not only because a vital record has been made, but also as an example of the way such surveys can be carried out. It may provide inspiration for others trying to set up similar projects in their regions.

### WHY STUDY FARM BUILDINGS?

The history of agriculture in general has been written from the point of view of the publicity-seeking great estates rather than that of the typical farmer. The reason for this is obvious. The documentary

evidence that is available in numerous private muniment rooms and county record offices gives details of such things as farm rent and expenditure on improvement; cropping books and leases show how estate farms were managed; the local landlords themselves or their progressive tenants wrote in agricultural journals and were visited by writers such as Arthur Young. The typical farmer, however, working probably no more than 50 acres, rarely kept accounts or diaries. Transactions were mainly verbal and some farmers could not write: yet, if we are to understand the agriculture of a region and the rate of change within it, we must know something of the farming methods of the silent majority, and it is often only in their surviving farmsteads that this evidence can be found. All farms, however small, had buildings, and although they may not all survive, this survey has shown that in Norfolk at least, there is still a representative sample.

The buildings record the processes for which they were built, whether threshing with a flail in the barn, intensive cattle feeding in loose boxes, or manure production in yards. Building materials and techniques demonstrate the gradual breakdown of regionalism through the introduction of mass-produced components and materials. Conversions and adaptations show changing farming methods and the need to minimize expenditure, while large-scale new building may represent high expecta-

1 Barn with farm machinery at Hook's Farm, Letton, Norfolk. The half-timbered early eighteenth-century barn has been weatherboarded, probably this century.

tions rather than immediate real needs.

One of the aims of this book is to strike a better balance between the great estates and their neighbours and present a truer picture of agricultural change as represented in farm buildings.

There is also the question of regional variations, which may well be best defined through the study of buildings. In Norfolk, the half-dozen quite distinct agricultural regions were defined by Arthur Young in 1804 and accepted by later agricultural writers. These divisions are in general confirmed by the early agricultural statistics. It is only the buildings, however, that allow us to study and define the regions farm by farm and so test the long-accepted regional pattern. It is evident from this survey that the natural prejudices of Young and others against the small owner-occupier farms of the south of the county have resulted in too sweeping a condemnation of their agriculture. Faith in enclosure and 'The Norfolk System' made the improvers too dismissive of previous farming methods. Certainly the existence of large barns dating from well before the enclosures, particularly in the light soils of north-west Norfolk, suggests that there was more grain being produced there before 1750 than they would have us believe. For far too long their propaganda for 'The Norfolk System' has been accepted as sound historical evidence. It certainly was not written as such and it may be

2 Buildings at Blye's Farm, Sedgeford, Norfolk. The roofs of these particularly attractive traditional buildings are deteriorating and will soon be beyond repair.

that the buildings rather than the literary evidence give us a more accurate picture of the different farming achievements, both in the regions of Norfolk and the country as a whole.

There is a final and important reason for studying farm buildings. They are an essential ingredient in the man-made rural environment, which is at the moment being subjected to devastating change. In Norfolk in 1951 there were 13,132 separate farm holdings. Now there are less than 5,500. Farm amalgamation inevitably means that buildings become redundant. At the same time farm technology has changed. Cart horse stables are of no use to the modern farmer. Cart lodges are too low to take modern tractor cabs and tractors cannot negotiate the narrow entrances to old cattle yards. There is nothing new in this obsolescence and inevitable adaptation. Now, however, the pace of change is much faster than in the past and our capacity for destruction greater. Every year this source of historical evidence, only recently appreciated, is diminishing at an alarming rate.

It is to be hoped that an understanding of the buildings that have contributed so greatly to the traditional landscape will increase our appreciation of their value so that decisions to alter, convert or demolish will not be so lightly made.

## THE DEVELOPMENT OF THE SUBJECT

Increasing interest in farm buildings has been part of our developing understanding of the value of reading buildings and landscapes as historical documents. Subjects such as vernacular architecture and landscape studies are now attracting much attention, and the techniques of industrial archaeology are being used by agricultural historians. In all fields, the value of the typical and ordinary in our past is being recognized as just as worthy of study as the work of the political and social elite.

The recognition of the importance of farm building studies can be dated to the publication of two very different books: *The development of farm buildings in west lowland Staffordshire up to 1880* (1969) by J. E. C. Peters, and *The history of farm buildings in England and Wales* (1970) by N. Harvey. The first is a detailed study of a small area carried out from the University of Manchester, showing how much can be learnt from a close analysis of the architecture. The second, a more general but nevertheless pioneering work, indicates the value of farm building studies and draws attention to buildings as a source of evidence. It is from these two studies that most of those working in the field have drawn their initial inspiration. Since then, the number of publications has increased rapidly. There have been several more general works, and of these R. W. Brunskill, *Traditional Farm Buildings in Britain* (1982) and J. Lake, *Historic Farm Buildings; an introduction and guide* (1989) are the most comprehensive. The increasing volume of literature, particularly since 1980, plus the founding in 1985 of the Historic Farm Buildings Group is an indication of the degree to which the subject is recognized today.

Interest has also been stimulated by the ever-increasing rate of destruction and conversion. This has resulted in a whole body of literature concerned with alternative uses and conversion of farm buildings. Many local planning departments have produced their own guidelines for conversion. Both the Ministry of Agriculture, Fisheries and Food, and English Heritage are becoming involved, and for the first time there are now (1989) Ministry of Agriculture, Fisheries and Food grants towards keeping traditional buildings sound and weatherproof. Concern for their future has reached such a height in Norfolk that the need for 'carefully converted farm buildings' for light industry was even mentioned by one candidate for the 1989 County Council elections in her letter to voters.

The threat of imminent loss has led to some of the finest examples being taken over by farm museums, local trusts, the local authority, English Heritage and the National Trust. As a last resort, some are moved to new sites in open-air museums (for a list of such sites see Appendix II).

It was against this background that the Historic Farm Buildings Project was set up at the Centre of East Anglian Studies in the University of East Anglia. Norfolk has long been regarded as 'the cradle of the Agricultural Revolution', and it seemed appropriate, therefore, to begin here. Little was known about the development of farm buildings outside the great but untypical Holkham estate,[1] and it was as an attempt to explore the rest of this important agrarian county that this survey was undertaken.

There is no doubt that interest in the subject is growing, and it is becoming abundantly clear that if the stock of surviving evidence is not properly recorded and representative examples conserved over the next few years, it will be too late, and a valuable source of historical information will be lost. A landscape without farm buildings of traditional size and shape and built of local materials will lack the vitality and variety that gives the British countryside its own very individual character.

# 2

# Farm Buildings before the Agricultural Revolution

## THE EARLIEST EVIDENCE

Farm buildings present a very varied picture, resulting not only from types of building materials available locally, but also from differences in agricultural progress and the stage of development during which they were built.

The earliest evidence for farm buildings comes, not surprisingly, from archaeological excavations. Confining our attention to the post-Roman period, they show that even by the early Middle Ages regional differences in layout and building technique were clearly defined. Excavations on deserted medieval village sites have occasionally produced evidence of non-domestic buildings which were most probably agricultural. These fall into two distinct types.

In the lowlands of the south and east a courtyard layout is discernible from an early date. For instances at Grenstein, Norfolk, a complete 'toft' or single occupation site was excavated and, although remains were often slight, the house and several other buildings were identified. A long range opening onto a yard may have been used for livestock, whilst another large rectangular building of 5 m × 12 m (16 ft × 39 ft) may have been a barn. There were no seed remains to support this suggestion, nor is there any evidence for a threshing floor between opposing winnowing doors. The main reason for the uncertainty of the evidence is that the buildings were clay and so are only indicated by clay stains and gaps in the cobbling that covered the yard area. However, even from this slim evidence we can assume that the typical peasant on his small toft by the village street had a collection of buildings to house his crops and livestock, ranged around a yard beside

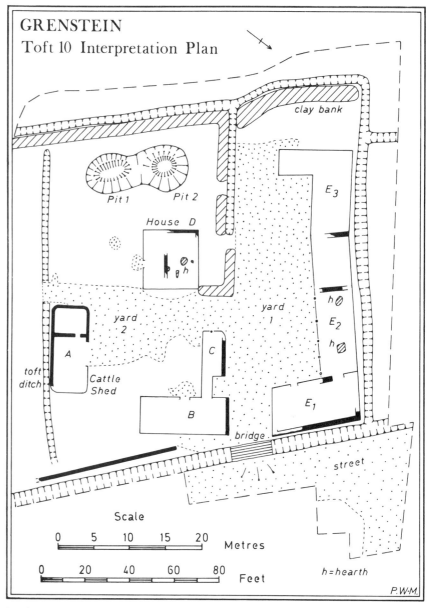

**GRENSTEIN**
**Toft 10 Interpretation Plan**

clay bank

Pit 1    Pit 2

House D

E₃

yard 2

yard 1

A

Cattle Shed

toft ditch

B

C

E₂

h

h

E₁

bridge

street

Scale

| 0 | 5 | 10 | 15 | 20 | Metres |

| 0 | 20 | 40 | 60 | 80 | Feet |

h = hearth

P.W·M.

3 Plan of a late medieval farmstead at Grenstein. The farmstead contained several buildings arranged around a yard. Building A has been interpreted as a cattle shed, while E1 may well have been a barn. The house, D, is divided from the cobbled yard by a ditch.

his house and within his own boundary ditch.[1]

A rather incomplete series of accounts for the Prior's manor at North Elmham, Norfolk, remains from 1255–6 to 1410–11 and they confirm the variety and superior quality of the buildings to be found on manorial as distinct from tenant farms. These records list in detail the repairs carried out, and they show that the barns were all timber-framed and thatched with reed straw. Separate barns were provided for wheat, barley and rye crops. The granary was adjacent to the barn and there was a partition between it and the stable which was carefully kept in good repair. There was also some evidence for housing for stock with scattered references to a cow house and piggeries. New cart sheds were built in 1272.[2]

Similarly, in the fourteenth and fifteenth centuries, the farm buildings on the Bishop of Winchester's grange at Adderbury, Oxfordshire, included a malt house, brew house, granary, hay barn, pig house, ox house, dovecot and sheep cotes.[3] Dovecots were important as housing a source of fresh meat during the winter and were found on all medieval manors.

The manorial accounts of Cuxham, Oxfordshire, for the years 1276–1359 refer to the cost of repairing old buildings and putting up new ones. The entries are often very detailed; for instance, a hay house was rebuilt between 1320 and 1323 with stone walls, a wooden stairway and a door fitted with a lock. A new wheat barn was also built in the 1320s.[4] Manorial accounts for some 200 farms in Norfolk survive and this rich source of information on medieval farm buildings remains largely unexplored. Their erection and repair is usually listed in the expenses sections of the accounts (information from Dr Bruce Campbell). For instance, the account roll of the manor of Forncett from 1272–3 includes at least three stables, a cattle house, granary, hay house, goose house, hen house and pin fold. They were built of clay with thatched roofs and were placed around courtyards. One hundred years later many of the farm buildings had fallen into decay and between 1376 and 1378 the accounts show considerable repairs and additions being undertaken. 'A stable and cow house 84 feet long' was built and the 'hay-house, granges and stables' were repaired.[5]

Maps provide valuable evidence for farm building study, and they survive for many estates from the sixteenth century. Often the buildings are drawn and it is possible to guess at their original use. One late seventeenth-century example from Longham, Norfolk, clearly shows farm buildings at Longham Manor.[6] Two long buildings may have been barns, and a third a stable or other livestock accommodation. A circular structure may have been a dovecot although it could equally well be a hay or straw stack.

An interesting group of buildings is shown in great detail on a map of 1640 of the Channonz estate in Tibenham.[7] A drawing on the map shows the buildings near the hall and here for the first time we can see the barn with ventilation slits beside the doors and two pairs of double doors indicating two threshing floors behind. The buildings are shown on their medieval site beside the moat, while a new house has been built outside the moat to one side of the buildings.

It appears that Channonz Hall, like many others, was served by a variety of buildings suggesting a highly capitalized mixed farming system existed in much of lowland Britain by the end of the Middle Ages. Whilst it is often only the barn that survives from the seventeenth century, there were certainly other substantial buildings on the late

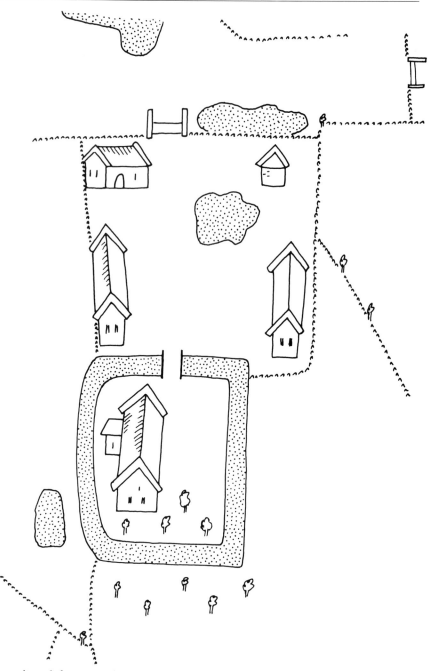

4 This redrawing of the Longham Hall area from the sixteenth-century map of Longham shows the hall in its moat and, behind, three or four farm buildings arranged around a yard and pond. The two largest may be barns, while the smaller building in the left-hand corner may be a stable. In the right-hand corner stands what may be a hay or corn rick, or a dovecot.

medieval farmstead.

In the west and north of Britain the arrangement of individual buildings around a courtyard gave way to a longhouse layout. In the early Middle Ages longhouses were to be found as far south as Sussex and east as Northamptonshire. Thirteenth-century longhouses are found in excavations as at Upton in Gloucestershire, but by 1350 they were becoming a rarity.[8]

Building agreements become available from about 1350 and a Worcestershire example describes the building of a longhouse at an unusually late date; a tenant agreed to build 'a hall..and a chamber at the front end of the hall, with a byre at the rear end'.[9] Gradually, however, they were replaced by a house with a separate byre or barn arranged around two sides of a yard.

By the sixteenth century longhouses proper were confined to upland Britain with sixteenth-century examples being found in Devon and seventeenth-century survivals in the Lake District, south and south-east Wales.[10] However, even here the peasant farmstead might well contain a number of substantial, permanent structures, including one or more of 'longhouse' type.[11] In the simplest longhouse, people and animals shared one entrance to a long building in which animals were housed at one end and people at the other. Longhouses have been excavated at sites such as Wharrham Percy in Yorkshire and West Whelpington in Northumberland.[12] At West Whelpington in the fifteenth century the humans and animals were initially separated only by a paved way, which was later replaced by partition walls. The buildings were only one storey and built of stone rubble with cruck frames and heather-thatched roofs. By the time the village was deserted in about 1720 the internal access between the living room and the byre had been blocked up, but there was no sign of cattle being housed in separate ranges of outbuildings as in the south-east, although there were outbuildings, possibly barns or stables, elsewhere on some of the crofts.

At Gomeldon, Wiltshire, the change is taken further and the move

5 Plan of a longhouse excavated at West Whelpington, Northumberland. Animals and humans shared the central entrance. The humans lived to the left, as indicated by the remains of the hearth and ovens. The animals were stalled facing the wall along the byre on the right. The central drainage channel can be seen on the plan.

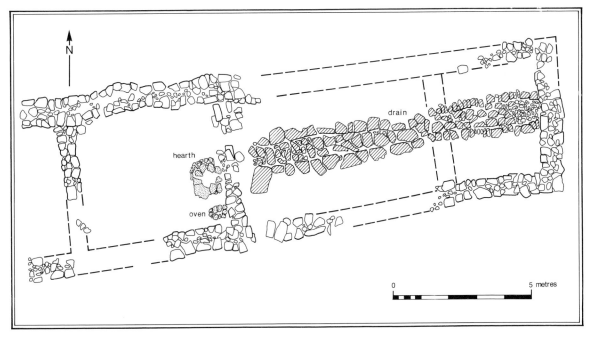

by the end of the thirteenth century from longhouse to separate byre built at right angles to the house can be traced. At Hangleton in Sussex both longhouses and houses with separate byres were in use on the same site in the thirteenth century.[13]

By the seventeenth century the building of longhouses was confined to the South-West Peninsula, particularly Dartmoor, Wales and the border counties, and the north. At the end of the sixteenth century Henry Quick of Wicca farm at Zennor, near St Ives, built a chimney in the top gable wall of his house to replace the open hearth, and the cows were moved out of the lower part, to another building, and their former byre became a dairy. The floor above remained a children's bedroom.[14] In Wales up to 1560 most farms were longhouses, although later the byre became part of the house, forming a large outer room.[15] The tradition of house with cow byre attached to give a longhouse appearance persisted in Wales into the nineteenth century.

Longhouses provided shelter for animals and people, but not crops or animal feed. At West Whelpington, hay and corn were stacked on stone bases and grain could be stored either in some of the small outhouses or in the house itself. Where threshing was carried out is not clear. At Cregneash (Isle of Man) the through passage in the house was used for winnowing out the chaff from the grain until the nineteenth century, and perhaps this was also true in mainland longhouses.

A two-storey variation that allowed for the storage of hay above the cow byre, often with a stable and barn all under the same roof, was the laithe-house, built from the 1650s into the nineteenth century. Its distribution was almost entirely restricted to the Pennine slopes of Lancashire and West Yorkshire, and it became the standard form of house for those farms created by the eighteenth-century enclosure of uplands; the latest dated example known in West Yorkshire was built in 1880. They were well built of ashlared stone with walls decorated with carved finials, moulded kneelers, string courses and mullioned windows, suggesting a prosperous, yeoman type of farmer.[16]

A third type described by the Northumbrian historian J. Hodson in his *History of Northumbria* in 1827 as being the 'principal farm house in Northumberland 100 years since', is the peel house, consisting 'of a byre or cow-house below, and the family apartments above...approached by stone stairs on the outside.' Ruins and remains of peel houses incorporated into later houses and farm buildings can be seen across northern Northumberland and were supposed to provide some sort of protection against cattle rustlers and border raids.

The reasons for this contrast between linear farmsteads in the uplands and a scattered or courtyard layout in the lowlands are many. A linear arrangement is more suited to the small-scale farming typical of upland areas. It was also more practical than a courtyard arrangement on sloping ground. In the wetter uplands, cattle were more likely to be stalled all winter than in the eastern lowlands where yards surrounded by cattle sheds were more suitable.[17]

Longhouses or blackhouses continued in use in the poorer parts of north-west Scotland and Ireland into this century, but in the Middle Ages they were not confined to the lower levels of farming society. Some much larger and prestigious houses maintaining the longhouse principle survive from about 1500 in Devon, the Lake District and Wales. One fine late example in Westmorland is dated 1735, by which date many were substantial two-storey houses.[18]

A small building often found on medieval farms but not generally used in England after 1500 was the corn-drying kiln. These were particularly common in the south-west and the highland zone, but may well have been usual in other areas during the climatic deterioration of the fourteenth and fifteenth centuries. They could be used for drying peas, beans, flax and hay. They were similar to pottery kilns in construction, except that the flue was usually longer.[19] In northern Scotland and parts of Wales they were used into the nineteenth century, when the process of drying was transferred from the farms to the corn mills.[20]

The scattered written and archaeological evidence shows, therefore, that a great variety of buildings served the activities of the medieval farmer. Cattle and pigs were often housed; corn, both threshed and unthreshed was stored; horses were carefully cared for and carts, too, were kept under cover. Regional differences were very clear with certain types of building, such as longhouses, never occurring in the arable south-east. Although it is undoubtedly true that the medieval farm had to be self-sufficient, the regional variations suggest that specialization in either livestock or cereals was already developing.

When we look at standing medieval farm buildings, we are obviously only looking at the very finest examples, which have not needed replacing over the last 500 years, although they may well have been altered and modified many times. Not surprisingly, it is mainly barns that survive and then only those serving a large manorial or monastic estate. These great barns therefore reflect aspects of feudal and ecclesiastical tenure of the area rather than wealth generated solely from local agriculture.

## AISLED BARNS

This is particularly true of the great aisled barns of south-east England, an important arable area where, from the early Middle Ages, the religious institutions owned much of the land, and had the capital to put up these massive structures.[21] They were found on monastic estates from the twelfth century[22] and most of those surviving are prestige buildings associated with monastic or collegiate ownership.

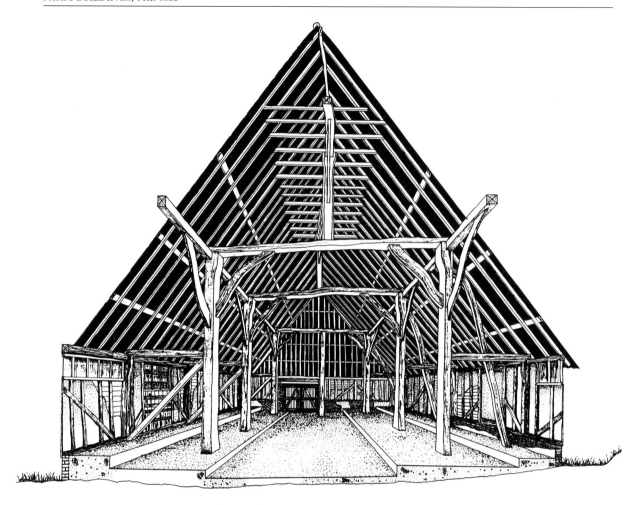

6 The major barn, Abbey Farm, Faversham, Kent, looking west is a fine example of a late medieval aisled barn with a crown post roof. As its name suggests, the farm was owned by the Benedictine abbey of Faversham and this helps to explain the barn's great size 43 m (130 ft) × 14 m (40 ft) and quality.

The earliest known aisled barns date from the early thirteenth century. The barn at Grange Farm, Coggeshall, Essex, has been carefully restored by the National Trust whilst those at Cressing Temple, also in Essex, have been preserved by Essex County Council, and Abbots Hall barn, Stowmarket, Suffolk, is part of the Museum of East Anglian Life. They all date from the thirteenth century. One of the finest Norfolk examples must have been the Grange barn at Castle Acre, demolished in 1836, but drawn previously and illustrated in J. H. Bloom's account of the antiquities of Castle Acre, written in 1843. Originally 11 bays long, with about 6 metres (20 feet) in each bay, the aisle posts were set in 2.5 metres (8 feet) from the outside walls. The great thatched roof swept down from a 11.5-metre (38 feet) ridge to within 3.7 metres (12 feet) above the ground at the eaves. The gaps in the timber framed walls were lined with chalk internally and rough flint externally.[23] The illustration shows this barn as having only one pair of double doors, with no opening in the far wall to provide the draught needed for winnowing. This suggests that it was not built as

7 The Wheat Barn, Cressing Temple, was built in the mid-thirteenth century by the Knights Templar: (*above*) exterior, (*left*) interior.

8 Etching of the Grange Farm aisled barn at Castle Acre, by J.H. Bloom, made shortly before it was demolished in 1836.

a working barn in which corn was threshed and winnowed, but rather for storage, perhaps of monastic tithes.

Aisled barns were not found west of the Cotswolds, but one of the finest stone examples is only a little to the east of this boundary, at Great Coxwell, Oxfordshire. Built between 1275 and 1350 for the Cistercian monks of Beaulieu Abbey, it is of cathedral-like proportions and built to cathedral standards of craftsmanship with stone copings on the roof gables and ashlared stone buttresses. Beaulieu Abbey's own barn at St Leonard's in Hampshire is another stone built aisled barn with the largest storage capacity of any known barn, 14,913 cu. m or 526,590 cu. ft.[24]

There is another substantial group of aisled barns in the Pennine region of the West Riding of Yorkshire and east Lancashire, mostly built between 1570 and 1650. Although they now mostly have stone walls, they were originally timber. The size of these barns suggests that more corn was grown in this traditional sheep country than was once thought to be the case. Some of these farms are on what would now be considered marginal land above 250 m (800 ft).[25] The late sixteenth century was a time of climatic improvement, a growth in population, and a rise in grain prices that made the growing of corn even on marginal lands profitable. The older, smaller, cruck barns were therefore replaced, and their timbers sometimes reused in larger, aisled constructions.[26] An early example has recently been carefully restored by Leeds County Council at Beeston, on the outskirts of Leeds. It was built by the Beeston family in the late fifteenth or early sixteenth century as a great manorial barn, and in the seventeenth century a stone cross wing was built on one end, containing stables below and a manorial court room above.

In his book, *Treatise on Building*, written in 1698, Roger North of Rougham, Norfolk, advocated the practice of increasing the width rather than the length of the barn. A long barn needed 'many great doors and threshing floors; and the roof being so much extended is often out of order, and a great charge to maintain'.[27] The problem with an aisled barn was it 'swallows a world of timber and hath a vast roof.' He suggested an unlikely construction 60 feet square that needed strengthening at the corners to take the thrust of the walls and roof. No such barns survive, but Roger North's barn at Rougham has an aisle on one side, perhaps the best compromise he could devise: gaining width, but not using as much timber as a fully aisled building.

Grain prices were rising fast in the fourth quarter of the sixteenth century, and it would not be surprising to find more barns being built at this time. If long timber for wall plates and ridges was not easily available, aisling was one solution to the problem of providing extra space, and this method of building continued for a long time. There is an aisled barn built of machine-sawn timber and dated to about 1880 in Trunch, Norfolk, and another nineteenth-century flint barn in Letheringsett has cast-iron aisle posts. Most of the other Norfolk examples have been conservatively dated to the sixteenth and seventeenth centuries, although they may well be older. This is an indication of large-scale estate farming producing a sizeable cereal surplus for sale.


## CRUCK BUILDINGS

A medieval type of structure, confined to the Midlands and the north-west of the British Isles, is the cruck building, which survives in these areas in large numbers (over 3000 identified in 1980).[28] It is a strong construction, consisting of a series of pairs of curved timbers, set up to form an inverted V. The apex of the V takes the ridge, and the roof with its purlins and rafters is supported by the crucks rather than the walls of the building. The crucks may extend to the ground, rest on a stone foundation or wooden sill, or they may spring from higher up the wall. It is the strength of this construction that probably explains

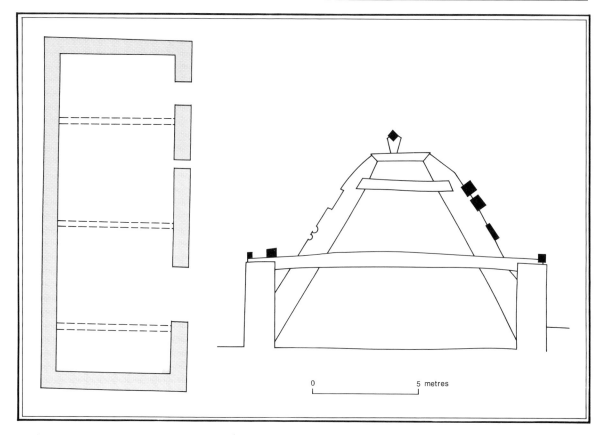

9 This small cruck building in Langdale, Cumbria, is of a very primitive design, but probably dates from the seventeenth century.

its survival, even in fairly humble buildings, when other less sound structures have disappeared.

The structure had gone out of favour for domestic buildings by the sixteenth century because it was difficult to insert an upper floor, but this problem did not arise in most farm buildings where the technique may well have been used into the eighteenth century. It was described by Robertson as being used 'formerly' in Midlothian. He described the typical layout of a traditional farm; 'On the other side stood the barn, in which the roof timbers, from the idea of giving more strength, were built into the wall from the foundations'.[29]

Of the 3000 recorded cruck buildings, nearly 800 were constructed for agricultural use. Most of them are barns, but they do include a few stables, byres and granaries. The proportion of agricultural to domestic buildings varies greatly across the country, from under 1 per cent of the surviving crucks in the south-western counties of Somerset and Devon to between 50 per cent and 70 per cent in the northern counties of South and West Yorkshire, Cumbria and Derbyshire.[30]

## THE SIXTEENTH CENTURY

No surviving Norfolk farm building can be dated definitely to a pre-sixteenth century date, although the huge flint and stone barn at West Acre Priory must predate the Reformation and could well be fifteenth century. Although its length has been reduced by 15 metres (49 ft) it would originally have been about 45 metres (147 ft) long, making it one of the longest in the county. Two sets of double doors open onto threshing floors, although in both cases the opposing door is only single width – wide enough to provide the necessary draught for hand flailing and winnowing, but not to allow wagons to pass through.

Another early barn, this time for secular use, survives on the Shotesham estate near Newton Flotman. A timber-framed building with massive wall posts and arch braces and a magnificent two-tier queen post roof, it may well date from before 1500. A very fine barn over 60 metres (197 ft) long was built at Hales at the same time as the hall was built and the church restored, in the years after 1480. It is unusual in that it was built with living quarters at the east end, presumably for servant accommodation.

A common feature of pre-seventeenth-century barns such as those at West Acre, Norfolk, and Abbot's Hall, Stowmarket, Suffolk, is the lack of opposing double doors; instead there is only a single 'winnowing' door opposite the main double ones. This would have been enough to create a draught, but would not allow a wagon through. This can be explained by the fact that carts rather than wagons were used before the eighteenth century and these two-wheeled vehicles could be turned on the threshing floor and taken out the way they came in. That carts and not wagons were used for hay and presumably for corn carting in the sixteenth century is shown by Thomas Tusser, writing of East Anglia in 1557,[31]

> 'Let cart be well searched without and within
> Well clouted and greased ere hay time begin.'

More barns survive from the sixteenth century. In the north-east of Norfolk are two enormous brick thatched barns at Paston and at Waxham. The Paston barn is dated 1581 (illustrations 123 and 124) and that at Waxham was built about the same time. Both over 50 m (164 ft) long, they are amongst the largest historic barns in the county.

## TITHE BARNS

Perhaps the most well-known type of farm building is the so-called tithe barn. Until 1836, the rector, or in some cases before 1530, a monastery, was entitled to claim a tenth of the crop and this would be kept in the barn. The rectorial tithe barn, which would have contained

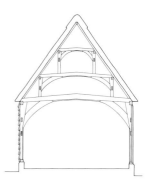

10 Cross-section of the barn at Dairy Farm, Newton Flotman, Norfolk. This unusual timber-framed building probably dates from the late fifteenth century.

the produce of the glebe and the tithes of a single parish, was often no larger than those of the parishioners and many were demolished at the time of the Tithe Commutation Act of 1836, which finalized the change from the payment of tithes in kind to one in money. Many of the largest surviving medieval barns were tithe barns owned by monasteries but not all tithe barns are medieval or monastic; they continued to be built until the 1780s. In Norfolk, the one at Great Snoring is late sixteenth century, while that at Dersingham is dated 1671. Usually these barns are not typical agricultural buildings, not only because of their size, but because they were intended for storage rather than the processing of the crop. They are the warehouses rather than the factories of large-scale medieval farming.

It is clear that, for this early period, surviving farm buildings provide only very patchy evidence for farming practices. They do however emphasize the gap between the peasant farmer in his longhouse or small group of mud and thatched buildings, and the great ecclesiastical and aristocratic estates, with their huge barns and extensive buildings, producing large surpluses for sale. Documentary evidence makes it clear that there were many different types of building on the manorial farms and yet very rarely do any but the barns survive. Other buildings, presumably not so substantial, have had to be replaced since the Middle Ages.

# 3

# The Early Years of Improvement, 1600-1750

## THE BEGINNINGS OF CHANGE

Although new crops were being introduced into Britain from 1500, their impact up to 1650 was limited. However, by 1650, there had come into existence a generation of literate farmers who were reading and discussing new ideas put forward in an ever-increasing number of practical farming books.[1] This group, blending together scientific and practical interests, were at the forefront of agricultural change, while others were prepared to watch and take on their more successful projects. This flurry of activity was spurred on after 1660 by the need to diversify in a period of declining grain prices.

Increasing urbanization and the rise of a wealthy commercial group encouraged the growth of market gardening from the late seventeenth century, particularly in Kent and the Vale of Evesham, supplying London, Birmingham and Bristol. Dairy and meat production in Northumberland and Durham expanded to serve the miners of Tyneside. Other exotic crops were also tried for the new urban market, particularly on small farms with a ready labour supply.

The fall in grain prices (25 per cent between 1640 and 1750) was not mirrored by livestock prices, where cattle values increased by 13 per cent in the same period. There was therefore an incentive to improve pastures and cattle feed, and it was in this field that much of the early interest was concentrated. This was particularly so after the poor summers of the 1640s when hay rotted in the fields and winter fodder was short. 'Improved' grasses such as clover and sainfoin were increasingly grown and they spread across the country from the 1660s to the 1680s. Turnips were grown in East Anglia from the 1650s, but

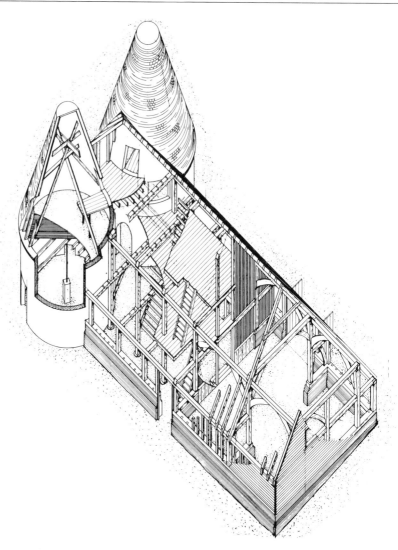

11 Vale farm, Broadoak, Sturry, Kent. Nineteenth-century oast houses and three-storey storage area replacing the south end of a late medieval barn, only two bays of which remain (in the foreground of the drawing).

spread more slowly and were not regularly grown elsewhere until the 1720s and '30s.[2]

Another new crop was hops, which became firmly established in Kent and parts of Sussex by 1700. The increase in beer drinking made possible by the low price of grain encouraged an increase in hop growing. Artificial drying of hops in a kiln was recommended by Reynolde Scott who wrote in 1574, 'A Perfitte Platform of a Hoppe Garden' in which he described an oast house. It was mainly a timber-framed building with a brick wall adjacent to the furnace. The kilns were square or rectangular and there is no indication that at this early date they had a roof vent. The fact that kilns were frequently demolished and replaced as technology advanced means that very few examples from before 1750 survive.

The industry began to expand after 1760 when larger and more efficient kilns were needed to cope with the increased acreage of hops. Bricks gradually replaced timber-framing and the familiar metal cowl that can be set against the wind by a horizontal vane to increase the flow of air was introduced in the 1790s. After 1815, the circular brick cone replaced the square lath and plaster inverted pyramid kiln. 'It contained,' wrote Loudan in 1833, 'a greater area than any other figure with the same quantity of external walling'.

During the nineteenth century kilns were rebuilt and enlarged. Improvements continued into the 1880s, and hop production remained profitable into the twentieth century. The installation of new kilns involved alterations and modifications to old buildings, providing 'vital clues to the successful unravelling of the history and archaeology of the building'.[3]

Whilst grain was cheap the keeping of pigeons thrived, and the period 1640–1750 was the heyday of the dovecot with many being built across the country. The birds were either consumed at home or sold at local markets; while their dung was also greatly valued.[4]

One way to combat the fall in grain prices in the mainly corn-growing areas, was to produce more, particularly for export. The survival of many late seventeenth-century barns in Norfolk suggests that this was a solution favoured on many East Anglian farms. Norfolk was already an important producer of high quality malting barley, and this crop too would be stored and threshed in the barns.

## A PERIOD OF YEOMAN FARMER BUILDING

By the late seventeenth century more evidence from farm buildings is available. Maps show groups of farm buildings, and seventeenth-century barns survive on farms of all sizes. There were 22 within the Norfolk survey area. The income of many English yeoman farmers probably doubled between 1500 and 1640 when grain prices increased more than six-fold prior to their fall.[5] Many of these were substantial freeholders with money to invest in prestigious high quality buildings; a group 'close enough to the land to understand how it should be farmed, large enough to handle sufficient capital to ensure what was, for the time, efficient farming'.[6]

Many examples of their fine substantial houses and barns survive in areas away from improving estates. In the clay lowlands they were often of brick rather than timber-framing with wattle and daub, while stone was the building material of the uplands.

Some of the finest brick building to be found in Norfolk is in the owner-occupier parishes bordering on the Norfolk Broads. A combination of lush grazing and good loam soils resulted in prosperous farming from the seventeenth century, and huge barns are typical of

12 At South Burlingham a unique group of early eighteenth-century buildings survives on the rich loam soils of the broadland edge, to the east of Norwich. The early eighteenth-century barn has a very fine brick gable, built for display to be seen alongside the house front.

the region. A particularly impressive group of brick buildings, which exhibit all the characteristics we would expect in this area, is to be found in South Burlingham. The large one-threshing-floor barn is early eighteenth century and a superb example of the brickwork of this period. It stands near the impressive seventeenth-century house with its east gable visible from the road. The steep gable with decorative brickwork forming a ventilation grid was designed for a roof thatched with reeds. Nearby is the stable, of a slightly later date, but still built to a high standard with decorative black brickwork on the south side and east gable to relate it to the barn and house. Above the stables is a hay loft, with pitching holes in the gable and a ladder from the stable below. Internally the hay racks, mangers, partitions of wooden panelling and cobbled floor survive as well as a tack room in the east end. A third fine brick building is the granary, dated 1749 on a tie beam. These three free-standing buildings make up a typical early eighteenth-century group, indicating the prosperity of these small, often one-farm estates on the good soils of north-east Norfolk in the period before the great estates as a whole began taking an increased interest in agriculture.

On some estates, landlords were beginning to become involved in capital investment in the early eighteenth century, although from estate accounts it is difficult to be sure to what extent this happened. Materials produced on the estate, such as wood, bricks or thatch as well as estate labour, is often not included in accounts; nor is compensation to tenants for their own improvements. 'In general landlords probably ploughed back more into their estates than they have generally been given credit for'.[7] The Windhams at Felbrigg, and the Hobarts at Blickling, both in Norfolk, were becoming involved in estate repairs from about 1600, sharing the costs of building and repairs with their tenants.[8] In Wales date stones became common in the last quarter of the seventeenth century and these indicate the first 'clearly discernible wave of agricultural building', confined mainly to the prosperous east. On the other hand, very few buildings in the west can be dated before 1800.[9]

In the Lake District, it was a group of independent, small-scale pastoral or 'statesmen' farmers who benefited most from the dissolution of the monasteries and the subsequent sales of ex-Church land. Instead of squire-dominated villages, Lakeland communities consisted of small groups of statesmen farmers scattered along the valley bottoms, and it was the period 1600–1750 in which they prospered and frequently rebuilt their farmhouses and steadings, usually including a decorative initial and date stone in the fabric.[10] A type of building dating from this period found particularly in that region is the bank barn. These buildings, suited to the steep terrain and the mixed farming of this upland region, were of two storeys and built into the hillside. Below, with entrances along one side or at the end, were the cow byres, often for twelve beasts, and sometimes a stable or cart lodge. Above, and entered from the other side, was the barn, with double doors on the hillside and a separate winnowing door above the byre opening out across the valley to provide a draught. The fact that this threshing floor was provided shows that these were grain rather than hay barns.[11] They date from the late seventeenth century and were still being constructed at the end of the nineteenth. They replaced the earlier, single-storey cruck barns and byres of the area. The earliest bank barns were found on the farms of the larger gentry. Later, this method of construction filtered down to the smaller freeholders.[12] Two-storey barns of a similar design are found throughout much of western upland Britain.

Farm buildings other than the barn survive from the early 1700s onwards, the most usual being the stable, and sometimes a granary over a cart shed. These early stables were often either abutting the barn or part of it, and in many cases their interior fittings still survive.

Horses were the farmer's most valuable possession and might well have been a status symbol, so the stables were often very well fitted out. Interest in horse breeding predated that in sheep and cattle and can be traced back to the seventeenth century. The elaborate seventeenth-century carved wooden pediment over a stable door in Shelfanger, Norfolk, until recently in what appeared to be its original position, is an indication of this.

13 Carved wooden pediment over a stable door, Shelfanger, Norfolk.

14 Bank barn at Low Tewdale, Coniston. The barn is built into the hillside and cattle were kept below whilst the grain was stored above.

It is from the period 1750–1820, when grain prices began to rise again after 100 years of depression, that nationwide interest in the design of farmsteads began to increase. Plans of model farmsteads and advice on farm buildings were published from 1770 and increased in volume throughout the prosperous Napoleonic War period. It may seem surprising that interest in improving the farmstead was so long delayed when we know that many of the improvements associated with the 'Norfolk Husbandry' were well established a generation before. Corn was being exported from East Anglian ports throughout the eighteenth century and corn production in England as a whole rose by 43 per cent during the eighteenth century,[13] suggesting that farming was becoming more intensive throughout the century; yet the period of great farm building was delayed until its end.

Arthur Young wrote of Norfolk that farming had 'undergone two pretty considerable revolutions', the first between 1730 and 1760 when the four-course rotation including turnips and grasses had been introduced, mostly in the newly enclosed strip fields. This allowed both the elimination of the fallow year and the keeping of more cattle during the winter. With little in the way of artificial fertilizers available, enough manure to keep the land in good heart had to be produced. As the value of animals, and particularly their manure, became fully appreciated, methods of keeping them so that their manure could be collected and preserved had to be developed.

There then followed 30 years when farmers 'had reposed upon their laurels'.[14] The second phase was that associated with the enclosure of the commons and the great increase in farm incomes and rents that accompanied the Napoleonic Wars. Landowners were suddenly much better off and farmers were keen to co-operate in improvements. Interest in rebuilding farms increased. The development of farmstead design seems to have been part of this rather than the earlier phase.[15]

The enclosure of large areas of commons and open grazing necessitated the provision of a new type of building from the late eighteenth century. With enclosure, many farms gained new land at some distance from the home premises, and so buildings were built in the middle of the new fields to serve them. These buildings, called field barns, provided housing for both crops and livestock. Hay and other fodder crops, and cereals cut in the nearby fields were stored there. The grain would be threshed out and the straw used on the spot. Hay and turnips would also be consumed and manure produced that could then be spread on the neighbouring land. At the end of the winter the fattened calves would leave either for market or finishing on grass. These field barns could therefore be regarded as out-factories of the farm for manure and beef production. In the more pastoral, upland areas of Britain, field barns are two-storey with a hay loft above and animal housing below. The hay might be stacked alongside the barn rather than lofted above the cattle; sometimes the hay was stored at ground floor level under cover beside the loose boxes. Buildings of this type are particularly common in the Yorkshire Dales as well as Derbyshire and Devon.[16] Somewhat similar are the field cow-houses found at a distance from the main farm in Snowdonia and the adjacent hilly districts.[17]

In the arable lowland areas, field barns consisted of a threshing barn, turnip house and cattle sheds and one man might be employed all winter threshing out the crop to keep the cattle yard supplied with straw.

Gradually, as agriculture improved and productivity increased, new buildings were needed. It is clear that there were many prosperous owner-occupiers who were able, from the seventeenth century onwards, to erect substantial, functional buildings on their farms. Although it is still mainly barns that survive, there are also some examples of stables and livestock accommodation, especially where they are an integral part of a barn-type building.

# 4

# The Rise of the Great Estate, 1750-1820

## INCREASING LANDLORD INVOLVEMENT

The depressed prices of the early eighteenth century had resulted in many smallholders selling out to the owners of larger estates, who were only too ready to avail themselves of the prevailing low land values, often buying out intermingled holdings and thus consolidating their estates. Estates were also enlarged by intermarriage and inheritance as the total number of aristocratic families tended to diminish in the late seventeenth century. As a result, the amount of land in estates of less than 300 acres declined from somewhere between 11–13 million acres in 1650, to 2.5–3.5 million acres a hundred years later.[1] It was not until the beginning of the nineteenth century that Welsh estates were expanded and amalgamated to an extent that shows their new owners had enough capital to improve their buildings.[2]

From about 1750, agricultural fortunes began to rise again as the population increased. The possibility of increasing rents was again a real one for landlords whilst higher prices encouraged farmers to look for improved methods.

At the same time the division between landlord's and tenant's capital was becoming more clearly established. Although the landlord usually continued to run a home farm, he was now primarily interested in increasing his rent role and attracting good tenants. For this reason it was the improvement of the land and the layout of the farm as well as the provision of adequate farm buildings that was his concern. On the other hand, it was up to the tenant to stock and run the farm.[3] Enclosure and land improvement was the most expensive if potentially the most profitable investment for the landlord, but farm buildings could also be a major outlay.

The reasons for this great interest are many, but underlying them all was the landlord's desire to increase rent. Prices rocketed in the Napoleonic Wars, when grain prices, which had been about 25 shillings a quarter in 1790, were occasionally as high as 130 shillings between 1796 and 1815 and frequently above 100 shillings. As a result of intensive farming, based on increased grain output and relying on an abundant supply of farmyard manure, the rents on many estates doubled. Good buildings were designed to attract improving tenants who would increase the productivity of the farm, so allowing for the rent to rise even higher. However, it was not just the lure of financial gain that made farm building a gentlemanly and respectable pursuit. Robinson identifies the classical, romantic and biblical associations that went with a concern for rural improvement, as well as a patriotic duty and passion for field sports.[4]

With this increase in landlord involvement the style of building was likely to change. More capital was available to the large landowners than to the yeoman farmers, so substantial long-lasting buildings, perhaps patterned after the architectural styles of their houses, were likely to be erected. The larger landowner, too, was more likely to be educated and well travelled. He would have seen and read about agriculture on the Continent and would have studied the elements of architecture. He had social, political and financial connections throughout the country. He might well employ non-local agents and architects and all these men, too, were likely to be widely read. The distinctive local styles, so typical, for instance, of the 'statesman' farms of the Lake District, were to be displaced by the pattern-book architecture of the agricultural architects and improvers. The traditional linear arrangement of cow byre and house gave way, as elsewhere, to a courtyard with the house on one side and cattle, barn, stables and stores around it.[5]

The late eighteenth and early nineteenth centuries saw the publication of a flood of books on farm buildings, but much of the advice contained in them was contradictory. There was much disagreement over whether the layout should be circular or square. The advantage of the circle was that there were no awkward corners for animals to get into, or to be cleaned out. The circular layout seems to have been particularly popular in Scotland; the most spectacular surviving example, which was only half completed, is that at Maam Steading, Inveraray, built for the Argyll estate.[6] William Marshall suggested a compromise between the circular and rectangular layout that would overcome the problems of the corners. He thought buildings could be arranged on a polygonal plan, 'although a complete set of buildings has not yet been erected on such a plan'.[7] A variation on this theme had in fact already been built in the 1790s at Leicester Square Farm, South Creake, on the

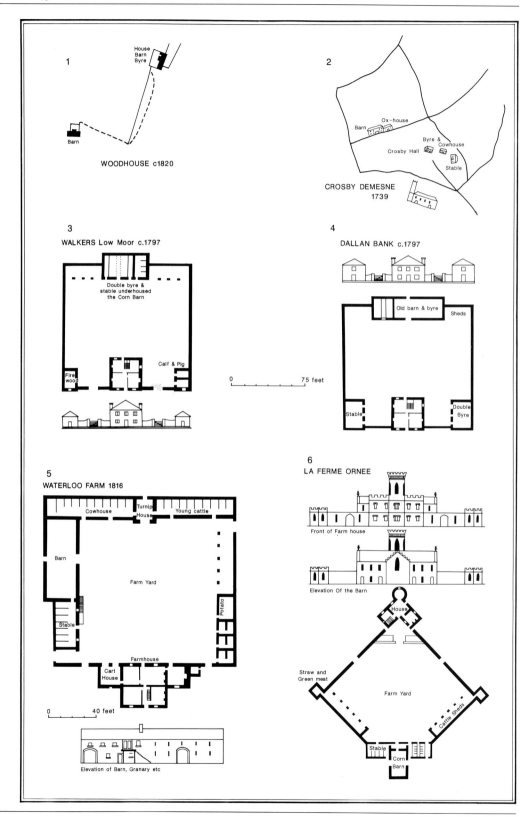

1 WOODHOUSE c1820

House
Barn
Byre

Barn

2 CROSBY DEMESNE 1739

Barn
Ox-house
Byre &
Cowhouse
Crosby Hall
Stable

3 WALKERS Low Moor c.1797

Double byre &
stable underhoused
the Corn Barn

Calf & Pig

Fire
wood

4 DALLAN BANK c.1797

Old barn & byre
Sheds

Stable
Double
Byre

0            75 feet

5 WATERLOO FARM 1816

Cowhouse
Turnip
House
Young cattle

Barn

Farm Yard

Potato

Stable

Farmhouse

Cart
House

0      40 feet

Elevation of Barn, Granary etc

6 LA FERME ORNEE

Front of Farm house

Elevation Of the Barn

House

Straw and
Green meat

Farm Yard

Cattle Sheds

Stable
Corn
Barn

Holkham estates, where the angle of the gateway connecting the barn and the livestock blocks would have been more than 90 degrees. There was also a battle of styles between Gothic and Classical, utilitarian and ornate, all of which is fully discussed in the literature.

Daniel Garrett's *Designs of farm houses, etc. for the County of York, Northumberland, Cumberland, Westmorland and the Bishopric of Durham* was published in 1747 and provided model farm plans for the 'gentlemen' of the district,[8] and influenced the work of the York architect John Carr, who built several model farms in the middle years of the eighteenth century. The most impressive of these were on the Harewood estate where stables, workshops, pigsties and an eye-catching tower containing a granary and dovecot were built. In 1805 Carr's successor designed a new Model Farm, built of stone and in the classical tradition. An impressive symmetrical stable block has a central pediment and accommodation for farm workers above. Other ranges enclosing the courtyard include barns, a dairy and open cart sheds.

One of the earliest practical books of advice on farm buildings that saw agricultural improvement 'not as an amusement, but as a science'[9] was *Hints to Gentlemen of Landed Property* by the land agent Nathaniel Kent, published in 1775. Its very title suggests that interest in the improvement of farm buildings had passed from the farmers into the hands of the owners of estates. Kent wrote that buildings should be on a 'small compact scale and as much as possible upon squares or parallelograms, not in angles or notches'.[10] In 1804 Marshall laid down the general principles for building; firstly the barn, stables and granaries should be readily seen from the farmhouse and secondly the farm buildings should form a rectangle, enclosing a yard, which could either be used for cattle, or, where cattle were usually stalled, simply as a receptacle for dung. A third consideration, not so important where labour was cheap, was the arrangement of the buildings to allow for the efficient movement of feedstuffs, animals and produce for market. In better planned farms, much consideration was given to the arrangement of barn, livestock sheds, feed stores and manure collecting yards, to allow for efficient movement between them. This involved the gradual adoption throughout lowland Britain of a courtyard plan or, failing that, a U-shaped plan open on one side. With the gradual abandonment of flail threshing and the increasing importance of stock and their manure within the farming economy, the barn began to occupy a less dominant position relative to cattle accommodation.

One of the late eighteenth century's great improvers was unusual in that he was also his own architect. Christopher Sykes of Sledmere in the Yorkshire Wolds sold his shipping interests and government stock to finance his improvements. Between 1775 and 1800, he was responsible for reclaiming and laying out new farms.[11] The rediscovery of the art of constructing dew ponds enabled stock to be yard fed and watered

15 *opposite* The development of the farms of the Lowther estate. 1 Woodhouse, Lowther estates, about 1820. 2 Crosby Hall, Ravensworth, estate map of 1739. 3 and 4 are two late eighteenth-century drawings 3 'sketch for farmhouse, etc. at Walker's Low Moore' 4 'sketch for a farmhouse at Dallan Bank'. 5 plan of Waterloo Farm, drawn in 1816 to be a more elaborate layout than that of the two earlier ones. A long cattle range for tying up young cattle makes up the side of the yard opposite the house. The final drawing. 6 shows an ornamental farmstead planned for the Home Farm at Lowther Hall, designed for landscape and picturesque reasons rather than merely as a food producing unit.

on thin chalkland soils, and in 1778 as many as fourteen farmsteads were being rebuilt at once. Their designs are very similar to those built 20 years later by Samuel Wyatt on the Holkham estate. We know that he knew Sledmere well and he must have been influenced by what he saw. Although there is ample cattle accommodation around yards, there is a puzzling lack of threshing barns, perhaps reflecting the difficulties of growing grain on these dry upland farms.

Syke's new house (Sledmere Hall) was also built to his own design and his interest in farms is shown in that from his upstairs library windows he could see three of them at the end of carefully laid out vistas.

## THE SCOTTISH EXPERIENCE

Agricultural change after 1750 was far more sweeping north of the border than in England. Roy's map of Scotland, surveyed after the 1745 rebellion, shows that in all but the most progressive parts of the Lowlands, strip fields were the normal system of tenure. They had disappeared from the Lowlands by 1800 and the Highlands by 1850. After the last Jacobite rebellion of 1745 a wave of systematic enclosing, draining, tree planting and farm building transformed the Lowland landscape into a region of improved farming. As a result very few agricultural buildings built before then survive, although they are described in Robertson's report on Midlothian, published in 1793:

'A farmer's main as they are here called consisted formerly of a set of low buildings, in the form of a square. One side was occupied by the master himself, whose habitation was composed of two or three dismal apartments, on an earthen floor, having a low ceiling, and a few diminutive lights. On another side stood the barn . . . the wall itself not being more than five foot in height. Opposite the barns were the stables and the byre or cow house. The stables were totally without division, and the horses fed in common, but the neat-cattle, less passive, were each confined to their stakes. The cottages occupied the remaining side: in the midst of all lay the dunghill. These buildings were made of turf and stone alternately, or with stone with clay for mortar; – the roof of thatch or of thatch and divot (turf or sods) intermixed.'[12]

The reports of the Board of Agriculture at the end of the eighteenth century give a universal picture of newly-built farms. The English market for cattle increased and by the 1780s the Aberdeen Angus and Ayrshire cattle were established breeds, and cattle housing improved. By 1794 most cattle in East Lothian were stall fed in byres.[13] The old one-storey houses with byres alongside were replaced by two-storey houses with cattle sheds around a courtyard. In East Lothian 'It was not until about the year 1750 that the gentlemen and tenants began to

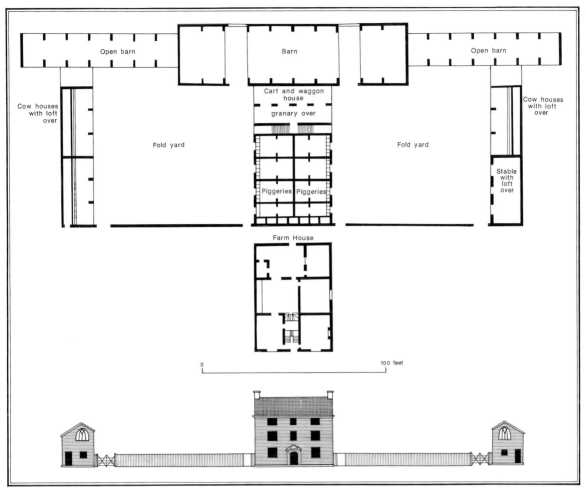

emancipate themselves from the fetters of ancient usage and to think and act upon their own judgement.'[14] Progressive farmers had visited England. The Marquess of Tweedsdale employed an English agent and Sir George Suttie of Balgae visited Norfolk and soon after 1750 introduced the 'regular Norfolk system'.[15] Further north, in Perthshire, Lord Kinnaird granted leases over much of his estate in 1775, letting his farms to 'substantial and intelligent farmers', who replaced old single-storey mud and straw houses and buildings with good two-storey stone and slated houses and well laid-out farm buildings.[16] Even north into Morayshire, stone slated buildings were replacing those of turf and clay with earthen floors and thatch or turfed roofs. 'A tenant of Lord Fife's at Moneton near Elgin, was the first who built a regular set of farm buildings in the district'.[17] Because of this great interest in rebuilding, little survives from before the middle of the eighteenth century. This is borne out by Bruce Walker's survey of Grampian, which showed that none of the buildings surviving in the region can be dated to before 1770.[18]

16 An early model plan was that drawn by W. Pitt and published in *The Annals of Agriculture* in 1788. The huge two-threshing-floor barn is flanked by open-sided sheds to house more of the crop. In contrast the cattle sheds are small and there are no subdivisions between the fold yards. The wagon shed is strangely placed within the yards.

The change from longhouse to the courtyard arrangement was almost complete in lowland Scotland by 1800, whilst the Napoleonic Wars encouraged the cultivation of marginal land and the building of improved farmsteads in the most inhospitable of regions.[19]

The most advanced farming in Scotland in the eighteenth century was found on the fertile East Lothian plain, stretching along the Firth of Forth to the east of Edinburgh. Here on rich, deep, well-drained soils, in a region where the climate was dry and the slopes gentle, a period of peace and prosperity had commenced by the 1660s and agricultural improvements began.

In 1699 Lord Belhaven, who owned an estate near Dunbar, wrote a book entitled *The Countryman's Rudiments*. In it he advocated a courtyard layout for the farmstead with the barn on the western side. The farmhouse should face south across the courtyard with the stables and byres opposite and the dunghill in the middle. However no surviving steadings can be dated to this early period and most went through several periods of alteration or rebuilding in the generations that followed.

Unlike much of eastern England, where it was large estates that led improvement, East Lothian was dominated by small estates, many owned by influential and improving landlords. Edinburgh merchants and lawyers bought holdings in the area, often consisting of one home farm or 'Mains' and up to half a dozen tenanted farms. The division between small landowner and large tenant could become rather blurred. Although much of the effort of improvement was concentrated on the Mains, the tenant farms were also added to and modified to meet the standards of each succeeding age.

At Eaglescairnie Mains, near Haddington, much of the earliest phase of farm improvement can still be seen amongst the later developments. A stone barn built in the days of hand threshing is an unusual survival. It has two opposing doors, neither large enough to drive a cart through. (Wagons were unknown north of the border.) The sheaves must have been brought in by hand from the stack yard for threshing. In the late eighteenth century the building was heightened and a wheelhouse for a horse gin incorporated. The old single-storey farmhouse remains on one side of the courtyard and the stable on another. During the nineteenth century a new house was built a short distance away and the old house became a stockman's cottage. At about the same time the open courtyard was divided up into cattle courts.

A common early nineteenth-century development was the rebuilding of the house away from the steading and the total enclosure of the court with four sides of farm buildings. The early introduction of, first, the horse gin, swiftly followed by the stationary steam-engine, meant that the threshing barn was not the dominant building it was elsewhere. Instead, in the centre of the front range was the gatehouse, often two-

storey with a dovecot or granary above. This gatehouse with its double doors allowed the court to be completely enclosed. Cart sheds with granaries above were sometimes in separate blocks opening on to a hard road. Nearer the Berwickshire border, in an area where the tradition of raids across the border with England, and defensive steadings, was stronger, cart sheds tended to be inturned, comprising one side of the court and facing in to the central yard. Here there would be a driveway between the cart sheds and cattle court in the centre.

Other nineteenth-century changes included the replacement of the wheelhouse for housing the horse gin, which had spread rapidly after Meickle's invention of the threshing machine in 1786, with steam-engine housings. The proximity of the mines meant that labour was scarce, and therefore expensive, whilst coal was cheap. East Lothian's rural landscape still features compact, square groups of buildings dominated by a tall industrial-type chimney rising above even the modern buildings of the farmstead.

Cattle fattening played an important part in the East Lothian farming system. In the late eighteenth century this would have been in the byres around the central yard which would have contained the dung heap. Soon, however, small cattle courts with shelter sheds or 'shades' around, each to contain between twelve and fifteen cattle, were built within the court. Here the muck would have built up over the winter. This system became more sophisticated through the nineteenth century. Covered

17 The steadings at Eastfield Farm, East Lothian (built *c.*1850), served the 200-acre home farm of the Balfour estate. The barn is dominated by the chimney for a steam-engine, built in 1880. In the foreground is the stable block with hay loft above. A long range of cart sheds face out onto the hard road, with a central gateway and granary running the full length of the upper floor.

18 Wattle-ended barn, Kirkton of Lochalsh, Ross and Cromarty. The wattle allowed for good ventilation through the barn.

feeding passages divided the courts, often with small hatches opening from the passage above the feeding troughs around the yard. The farmstead at Thurston was built as a home farm in the 1840s for James Hunter. He was a president of the Highland Society for Science and Technology and one of the first to buy a McCormick reaper after its initial appearance at the Great Exhibition of 1851. The buildings are full of ingenious devices that were his own design. There are four cattle yards with feeding passages between the yards and loose boxes. Along one feeding passage is a tramway with a truck for taking the skeps of turnips to the livestock.

By the second half of the nineteenth century the central open court was frequently roofed over. The steading for the 200-acre home farm of the Balfour estate at Eastfield was altered in 1880. A covered yard for 50 cattle as well as a central turnip store and byres for a dairy herd were constructed.

Although some home farm steadings had ornate Gothic or Classical façades with the central gateway treated as an architectural feature, many were plain functional buildings, well built of local red sandstone and roofed either with slate or pantile. The quality of their design and construction, as well as the care taken over detail, indicates the prosperity of these farmers and landlords until the agricultural depression of the 1880s.

In the west and south, conditions improved more slowly. Some progress had been made in Dumfries with E-shaped layouts consisting of a central dwelling house with two wings containing stables and byres on one side and a barn on the other. The fourth side was sometimes also closed by sheds. The problem was that square-shaped farms were vulnerable to the wind, and so a linear arrangement with the house at the east end away from the prevailing westerlies was sometimes thought more suitable.[20] The linear arrangement still prevailed in Galloway but here the one-floor thatched buildings with the 'offices a piece with the house' were described as 'still bad'.[21]

In some areas, particularly in the remote regions away from the influence of mainstream improvers, very distinctive types of building survive. In the Kintail of Lochalsh, area of Ross and Cromarty there are cruck-framed barns with wattle infill, built to allow for plenty of ventilation through a possibly damp unthreshed cereal crop and similar to those found in other regions of heavy rainfall such as parts of Wales and the West Midlands. For the same reasons, grain-drying kilns were installed in some of the larger Caithness and Banffshire farms in the early nineteenth century.[22]

## THE MODEL FARM AND THE BEGINNINGS OF MECHANIZATION

The more extravagant buildings resulting from this burst of enthusiasm on both sides of the border are limited to a few of the largest estates, mostly concentrated in the grain-growing Midlands and East of Britain from Norfolk to East Lothian, and it was their work that received the greatest attention.

Although much was written about the courtyard plan, it was only suited to farms over 150 acres, and so was only adopted on larger estate farms, or, more particularly, on the home farms of the landlord. An analysis of the total Norfolk sample studied in this survey, showed that it was by no means universal by 1840.

Many of the famous architects of the day dabbled in farm building design, often including model farms in their plans for country houses and environs, but there were wide differences in detail. The problem of how to reconcile two seemingly contradictory currents of thought: the rational search for improved agricultural buildings and the romantic rural idyll, were solved in a variety of ways. Two of the most important architects involved were Sir John Soane and Samuel Wyatt.

Sir John Soane was able to indulge his interest in so-called 'primitive' architecture in his dairy designs for his patron, Philip Yorke, 2nd Earl of Hardwick, which were based on the 'primitive hut', with pillars made of unbarked tree trunks. The dairy at Hammels, Hertfordshire, was built in 1783 by Philip Yorke for his wife. The supervision of dairies was a fashionable occupation for ladies, who would visit and inspect the work before partaking of strawberries and cream while reading rustic novels.

A far more ambitious project was the building of the Home Farm at Wimpole in Cambridgeshire in 1794. The conventional courtyard plan, dominated by a huge barn, survives intact and forms the centre of the National Trust's Home Farm at Wimpole. Although the layout conforms to the best farming practices of the day, Soane's interest in rural simplicity is shown in the use of traditional building materials such as thatch and weatherboard on a brick plinth.[23]

In contrast, Samuel Wyatt's style was simple neo-classical. Through this he was able to indulge his interest in geometrical construction and try out new building materials such as slate. Even the feeding troughs at Penrhyn were made of slate. Many of his designs allowed for the latest in technological advance, such as the water-powered threshing machine at Shugborough. Some of the most important examples of his work are at Holkham and are described later in this chapter.

Whilst the acceptance of the courtyard plan by the great estates across the country was almost universal, the adoption of mechanization was not. On the whole it was a change in husbandry techniques, encouraged by the changes in farm layout brought about by enclosure, rather than mechanical innovation that was at the heart of the early

19 The central feed store at Shugborough Park Farm, Staffordshire. A tram line runs from the water-powered mill opposite into the store.

stages of the 'agricultural revolution'. But there was only one technical development of the late eighteenth century, the invention of the threshing machine, which was to have a profound influence on farm building design.

Although there had been previous attempts to replace hand systems of threshing by machine, George Meickle, a Scot from East Lothian, was the first to construct an effective threshing machine, at Kilbogie in Clackmannanshire, in 1786. Meickle's original machine was horse-powered, but by the 1790s several water-powered examples were to be found in Scotland and in 1800 one was built at White Barn on the Shugborough estates, Staffordshire,[24] and at Shugborough Park Farm, designed by Samuel Wyatt in 1805, a mill pond was constructed that provided the head of water to power a wheel to work barn machinery. The Marquis of Stafford's farms in Staffordshire, Shropshire and Sutherland were all rebuilt between 1800 and 1830 and were provided with water-powered threshing machines built into the structure of the barn.

Wind power was also tried at an early date, but it was twice as expensive to construct and was also unreliable. In 1814, Gray illustrated a 'combined wind and horse-powered threshing mill' in a publication about the 'important implements of husbandry used in Scotland'[25] but none have survived.

Steam-powered threshing machines were introduced more slowly

20 Wheelhouse at High Staward Farm near Heydon Bridge, Northumberland.

because of their expense, but by 1800, they were to be found where coal was cheap, near the coalfields of East Lothian and Yorkshire. One, surprisingly, was found on the innovative Holkham estates in Norfolk, far from any coal supply.[26] Steam-engine chimneys, giving farms a distinctively industrial look, survive on some of the largest farm complexes, particularly on the home farms of the great estates.

By far the most usual source of power was horse power, and the earliest horse gins consisting of a large wooden crown wheel with wooden gearing and shafts, needed a completely new type of farm building. From the 1780s round houses, which became so typical of the farming landscape of Northumberland, eastern Scotland and the south-west peninsula, began to be built. They indicate areas in which the threshing machine became immediately popular. The evidence of the Board of Agriculture reports, although patchy and subjective, suggests that it was in these areas that threshing machines 'were in general use' by the early 1800s.[27] This distribution is borne out by Keith Hutton's map showing the distribution of surviving wheelhouses in the British Isles.[28] They are shown concentrated in north-east England, through Yorkshire, County Durham, Northumberland and the eastern lowlands of Scotland, with scattered examples up the east coast and on Orkney. A few are scattered across the southern lowlands of England, with a concentration along the Welsh borders. To the west they are found in Cornwall and Devon with a very few in Wales, and both sides of the Scottish border, with several on Islay and the Mull of Kintyre.

The spread of threshing machines in Scotland was rapid, reaching even the Hebrides by 1811. In contrast, throughout much of the lowlands of England it was slow. Whilst we know that there were 386

**21** Home Farm, Beamish, County Durham, has changed little in layout since 1790. The wheelhouse containing the horse engine was added in 1799, providing power for mechanical threshing.

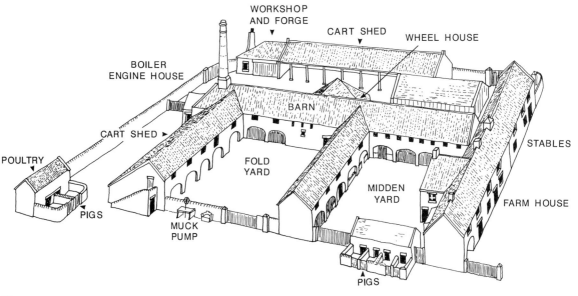

WORKSHOP AND FORGE

CART SHED

WHEEL HOUSE

BOILER ENGINE HOUSE

BARN

CART SHED ▶

STABLES

POULTRY

FOLD YARD

MIDDEN YARD

FARM HOUSE

PIGS

MUCK PUMP

PIGS

in East Lothian (7 wind, 30 water, 80 steam, and 269 horse) in 1845, with hardly a farm in Scotland over 50 acres without one,[29] there were many large and progressive farms in Norfolk where at least part of the crop was still threshed by hand. The reason for this was given by one Norfolk farmer in 1844, who had a threshing machine, but powered it with men rather than horses, it 'costs as much as to flail – we are too many men so I do not use horse powered.'[30] In areas where there was a surplus of labour the installation of machines was an incitement to riot and machine burning. Threshing provided much sought-after winter employment and to throw men out of work only increased the burden of the poor-rates paid by the farmer. This was the situation throughout much of the rural south-east, too far from the pull of the industrial towns. Here there was little mechanization until the 1850s when the portable steam-engine and threshing tackle began to take over.

In Northumberland, however, there was a shortage of labour as the men found work in the mines. In 1808 William Marshall, commenting on the region, called the threshing machine, 'the most valuable machine of agriculture that has been discovered for ages past.' As late as 1890, a quarter of the agricultural labourers in Northumberland were women, because the men were at work elsewhere.

A further point of interest about Northumbrian wheelhouses came to light when their distribution was studied in detail: 575 sites were identified on the second edition 25-inch Ordnance Survey map (1896–8) and it was noted that they were located not only on the better soils, but also on the margins of cultivation on the moorland fringes, particularly north and south of Hexham, and in the upper reaches of the rivers Aln and Coquet.[31] Their location is an indication of the expansion of arable farming into marginal land during the early years of the nineteenth century.

## 'COKE OF NORFOLK' AND THE HOLKHAM FARMS

A name that, more than any other, is associated with the late eighteenth and early nineteenth-century phase of the 'agricultural revolution' is that of Thomas William Coke of Holkham Hall, Norfolk (owner of the estate 1776–1842). By well-targeted publicizing of his agricultural achievements he managed both to improve his political standing and increase the fashionable image of farming. By the 1860s his estate had reached 42,000 acres; an enormous extent, divided between the light chalky soils and heavy clays of west and central Norfolk. It contained 70 farms, a third of which went through a period of major rebuilding between 1780 and 1820. This work always included rebuilding or refurbishing the house and building a barn and often a stable block on one side of a yard, with shelter sheds for cattle and a turnip house

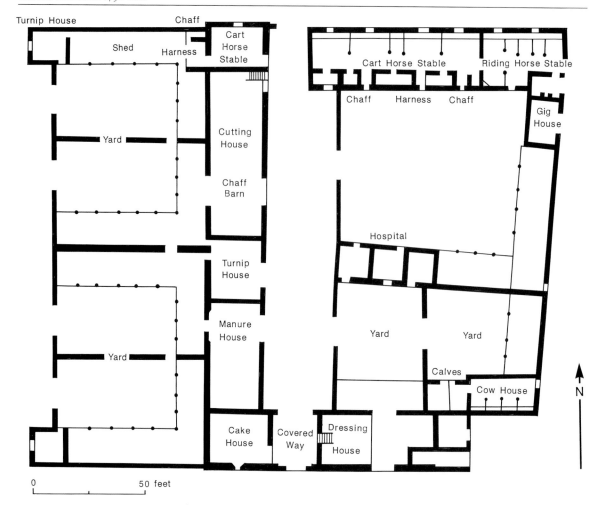

**0          50 feet**

**22** Waterden Farm was one of the earliest 'model' farms on the Holkham estates and was visited by Arthur Young in 1784. This plan was drawn in 1870 when there was some rebuilding, but the general plan is that of nearly 100 years before.

making up a third and sometimes a fourth side. The house either backed onto the yard or was nearby. Most of these farmsteads were of a plain functional style, built out of local red brick with pantile roofs. The houses were frequently of the more fashionable white brick produced in the Holkham kiln.[32]

The farm buildings at Waterden on the Holkham estate are perhaps the earliest set of 'model' farm buildings to survive as a whole. They were described by Arthur Young in 1784 in the *Annals of Agriculture*: 'Nothing in this style can exceed the buildings that Mr Coke has raised at Waterden. Every convenience to be imagined is thought of and the offices so perfectly arranged as to answer the great object, to prevent waste and save labour'. What buildings existed in 1780 is not clear, but certainly the two huge L-shaped barns were there. The stables too may be eighteenth-century, and form the third and south side of a yard. The present cattle sheds, abutting the barn to the east, are dated 1871, when £721 was spent at Waterden, but they may well have replaced earlier ones as the buildings described by the land agent William Keary in 1851 were similar in layout and capacity to those that survive.[33]

Samuel Wyatt was employed by the Holkham estate in the 1790s and is the only architect known to have worked on agricultural buildings for Thomas William Coke. A complete farm as laid out by him survives at Leicester Square Farm, South Creake (illustration 120a and b). The house was very much part of the original design with the 'back' door aligned on the central door of the huge three-threshing-floor barn. The barn, stables and cattle sheds are arranged in a U-shape, open towards the house so that the barn would have been clearly visible from it. The link between the house and buildings is emphasized by the curving wings of domestic 'offices' stretching from the house towards the farm buildings.[34] The advantages of the rectangular and semi-circular layouts are combined in this farmstead by overcoming the problem of corners in the yards by truncating them to create an irregular polygon.[35] The buildings are now going through another phase of alteration in which the Wyatt yard is being opened up and central cattle yards of the 1870s demolished. The stables and cattle sheds are being converted to residential use. On the other hand, the barn restored to its former glory will again be visible from the house.

Perhaps the most famous of the farm buildings of the 'Agricultural Revolution' is the Great Barn at Holkham. It was one of the most impressive buildings designed by Samuel Wyatt and was built in the 1790s to serve Coke's home farm. It provided the backcloth for the annual sheep shearings – predecessors of the modern agricultural show – and run by Thomas William Coke from 1776 to 1821. The barn, orientated east-west, contained two threshing floors, with porches over the double doors on both sides. Stables and granaries were in lean-tos around the barn. This is the only example on the Holkham estate where the enclosing of an open space to form a courtyard layout is abandoned for a nucleated arrangement around a central building. The advantage of arranging the cattle sheds around the barn across a yard was that distances over which fodder and straw from the barn had to be carried to the yards were reduced. It was much praised at the time of its construction for the functional arrangement of the buildings.[36]

The only plan we have of the barn is one drawn for R.N. Bacon's book on *Norfolk Agriculture*, published in 1844, which appears to correspond with Arthur Young's description in his county report of 1804, 'built in a superior style, 120 feet long, 30 feet broad and 30 feet high surrounded with sheds for 60 head of cattle.' It was clearly intended that the barn should be seen from the house and so it was built of the white brick and slates of polite architecture rather than the more usual red brick and pantiles. Not all comers were impressed by the barn. Loudan complained of the needless expense and described the barn as 'ostentatious'.[37]

## JAMES LOCH AND FARM IMPROVEMENTS

Whilst only a minority criticized the work of Coke at Holkham, the changes wrought for the second Marquis of Stafford, later first Duke of Sutherland, by his agent, James Loch, were almost universally condemned. The Marquis of Stafford married the heir to the enormous Sutherland estates, thus combining two of the greatest fortunes in early nineteenth-century Britain. It was wealth derived from the Bridgewater Canal, also controlled by the family, that paid for the grand schemes of agricultural improvement that involved the re-ordering of society on a massive scale.

**23** Lilleshall, 1810.

The project, both in Shropshire and Staffordshire, and in Sutherland,

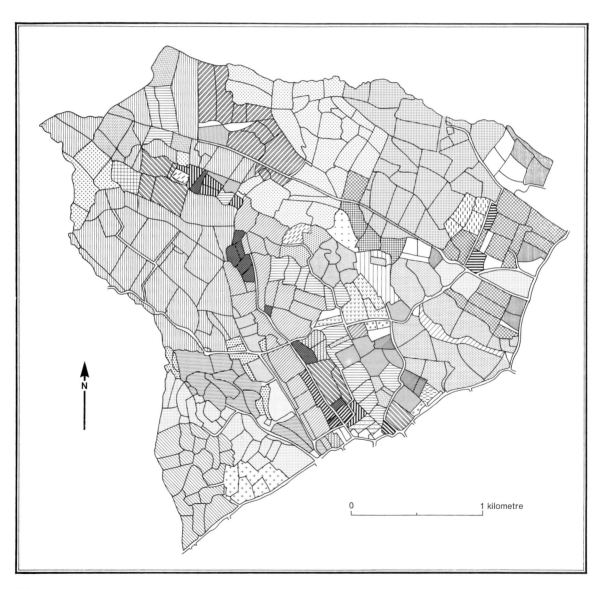

was masterminded by James Loch, who became chief agent to the Marquis of Stafford in about 1812. He was a student at Edinburgh University in the late 1790s studying law, and became one of an eminent intellectual group of economists and political philosophers working there at the time. His experience of estate management came from his work on his uncle's property at Blair Adam, near Kelty in Fife, before entering the service of Stafford.

As agent for the largest aristocratic fortune in Britain, he was able to put his economic theories into practice. He wrote in 1816, the 'property of a great English nobleman must be managed on the same principles as a little kingdom, not like the affairs of a little merchant.'

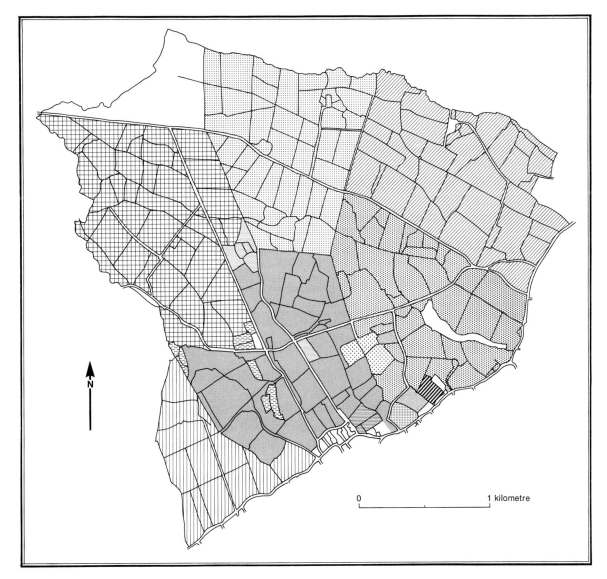

24 Lilleshall, 1820. This and the preceding plan show the parish of Lilleshall in Staffordshire before and after the rearrangement of the farms. Comparison shows how the farms were rationalized into large, compact holdings with regular fields which accompanied the new buildings and drainage systems.

0       1 kilometre

To one of his sub-agents he wrote, 'You must look forward 50 years so that you may make the most of the present.'[38]

The result was the complete reorganization of both the Midland and the Scottish estates. In Staffordshire and Shropshire, often as many as five farms were amalgamated and rearranged to form compact holdings with large new steadings. Although the estate paid for the new buildings, the tenants were frequently expected to pay for massive fencing and drainage schemes. Those who were wealthy enough to take them on were often outsiders, leaving the local rural population dispossessed. Some local tenant families, often incumbent for over 200 years, did remain. Between 1813 and 1820, 37 new sets of farm buildings were built and eight thoroughly overhauled on the Midland estates.[39] Loch took an intimate interest in every detail of the farm designs and wrote long letters of criticism to the architects involved.

The soils of the Midland estate varied greatly from heavy land, which even after drainage was most suited to dairying, to good turnip and barley land. Loch was critical of farmers who tried to get too much out of the land and often recommended leaving fields under pasture longer. The buildings Loch erected were in what he described as a 'common country style' with little in the way of architectural embellishment.

Many farms were provided with a water-wheel or steam-engine house, while one had a roundhouse for a horse gin. A few still had a barn with double doors and a threshing floor. Although all but one farm were laid out on a courtyard plan with one or two fold yards, only one had shelter sheds around the yard. Instead there were sheds

**25** Plan of a farmstead for the 400-acre farm at Stallington Grange, Staffordshire, built between 1811 and 1813. The cattle were mostly tied up with only a few being kept in the open yards. The threshing was done by horse power working a threshing machine in the small barn.

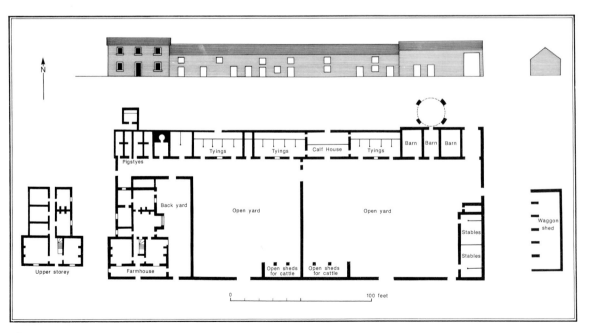

for tying up cattle, which implies that the yard was more of a midden for storing manure from the cattle sheds than for free ranging stock. Several examples included the northern arrangement of a paved walkway inside the U formed by the buildings, with the fold yards in the middle and inward-facing cart sheds. At Honnington Grange, Lilleshall, Staffordshire, there was a tramway with trucks in which fodder could be taken to the cattle.

Almost the whole of Sutherland was owned by the Marquess and so Loch was able to operate on an even larger scale than in England. The traditional multiple tenancy communal farms based on the township (or *baile*) were already disappearing over much of Highland Scotland as the commercial interests of the landlords replaced the customary relationship between the clan chief and his kinsmen. As early as 1730 the clearance of the old townships and their replacement by single tenanted farms, concentrating on black cattle or sheep, had begun in Argyll.[40] Loch had plenty of examples to follow when he began his programme of resettlement in Sutherland.

Twenty-seven new sets of farm premises were built between 1809 and 1820, mostly along the coast. These farms contained both arable on the thin coastal strip and huge areas of upland grazing, intended for sheep. The upper glens and coastal strip were cleared of people who were moved to the new fishing communities along the Moray Firth where other industries, such as flax mills and distilleries, were also established. The cleared upland was then either let as huge sheep farms or as summer grazing for the new large coastal farms.

The area around Culmainly was typical of much of the coastal area before reorganization. 'It was covered with black huts and cultivated in detached patches. The pasture, which lay intermixed with the arable land, was destroyed by being pared from time to time in order to build or cover their huts.' By 1820, however, the new farm presented 'one uniform scene of the most beautiful husbandry, extending from the mountains to the newly formed plantation near the coast...it is regularly divided into fields of a rectangular shape.' The tenant, Mr Sellar, notorious for his part in the clearances, had 'actually torn out of the mountain, and otherwise brought into cultivation, above 100 acres, now bearing the best crops of every species of grain with excellent turnips...though at an expense of labour and of money which would astonish and probably deter any farmer from the south from undertaking such an improvement.'[41]

Much of the coastal strip was suited to cereals, and Dunrobin main farm, tenanted by a Roxburgh farmer, grew crops of barley and turnips that were 'the admiration of every stranger travelling through'.[42] All the farms were provided either with a horse gin or water-wheel for threshing.

The main emphasis, however, was on stock farming. There was

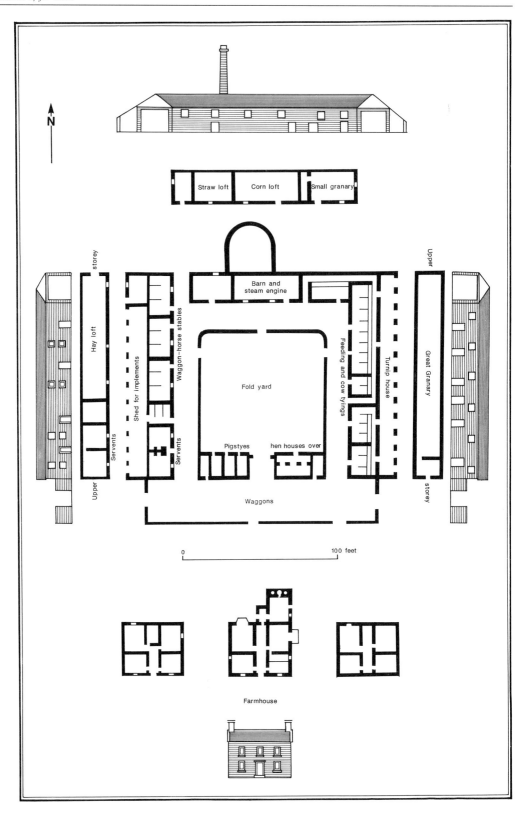

Straw loft    Corn loft    Small granary

storey    Upper

Hay loft

Barn and
steam engine

Shed for implements

Waggon-horse stables

Feeding and cow tyings

Turnip house

Great Granary

Servents

Fold yard

Upper    Servents

Pigstyes    hen houses over

storey

Waggons

0                    100 feet

Farmhouse

accommodation at Dunrobin for 60 West Highland breeding cows, and young stock always found a ready market further south. The Sutherland farms, unlike the Midland farms, all had shelter sheds around the yards. There was always also a long range of stalls for tethered stock.

More typical are the tenanted farms, at a distance from the Mains at Dunrobin. The buildings at Craikaig were completed in 1829 and consisted of a courtyard arrangement with a central gateway and dovecot above on the west side, and byres, stables and open sheds for stock on the others. The buildings are far simpler than those in Staffordshire, using local undressed stone. The buildings at Lothbeg are similar, making use of the same narrow, horizontal ventilation holes placed just below the roof along the closed cattle byres.

Building work continued through the nineteenth century on the Sutherland estates, with more impressive and ornate buildings being erected at Tongue in 1843 and Clynelish in 1865. At Clynelish three wide cattle sheds with central feeding passages and large roof ventilators allowed for intensive cattle feeding under cover rather than in open yards as were erected at Tongue.

The buildings on the English and Scottish estates were substantially built; of brick and tile in England, and stone and slate in Sutherland.

## THE ROLE OF LANDLORD INVESTMENT

It is during the period after 1750 that the landlord's role as the provider of buildings became firmly established, but it was only the wealthiest landlords on the largest estates who could afford to sweep all before them and totally reorganize both the land and the buildings. However, some of the areas that became well known for their improvements, such as East Lothian, were dominated by small landowners, often little more than gentlemen farmers but with a certain amount of money made in trade or the professions in Edinburgh. Much of their effort would be concentrated on the home farm, while their few tenanted farms would also be brought up to the high standard of the time, but with more alteration and less complete rebuilding, and little in the way of elaborate architectural detail.

If farming was to improve and the land be kept in good heart, it was the quality of the tenant that was all-important. The landlords recognized this, and the main purpose behind farm and particularly farmhouse building was to attract tenants with intelligence and capital to continue the work of improvement. However good the buildings, without good tenants the full potential of the estate and its agriculture could not be realized. Although rents were rising during this period, most of the buildings erected were functional and relatively unostentatious. This is in great contrast with some of the developments later in the century.

26 (*opposite*) Dayhouse Farm, Cherrington parish, was rebuilt between 1812 and 1813 on a rather different plan to the Stallington example. The fold yard is separated from the cattle tyings and stables by a paved way and the turnip house ran the length of the cow shed with feeding hatches from one to the other.

# 5

# The Buildings of 'High Farming', 1840-80

## A CHANGE IN EMPHASIS

The end of the Napoleonic Wars against France in 1815 was followed by agricultural depression. Wartime profits had been made in cereals; arable acreages had increased and new land had been enclosed. Corn prices fell with peace as imports were again available. As profits fell, so did rents. Those estates that were still heavily committed to major improvement schemes, such as Lord William Bentinck's in the Fens, were likely to be in financial difficulties. On his return from Madras in 1808 Bentinck had purchased fenland just across the Ouse from Kings Lynn, Norfolk, at a time when there was a speculative land boom in the area. He then had to borrow money to drain, build new sea banks and set up a mill for manufacturing cattle cake. Without family support he would undoubtedly have gone bankrupt, but even so, a period overseas in search of a fortune was necessary. From 1827 to 1835 he was governor of India and returned with enough money to repay his debts. The estate, however, never made a profit.[1]

Tenants too had their problems, particularly where the land was newly enclosed and they were responsible for the expensive tasks of marling, draining and hedging. John Hastings at Longham, Norfolk, was depressed by the work involved. He was described by the Holkham agent in 1816, as 'a zealous and industrious tenant, but heart-broken by his present undertaking'.[2] As a result, rents were renegotiated at the end of leases, frequently at a much lower level than during the war period.

By the late 1830s, however, conditions were improving again. There was an expansion of the home market, both for cereals, as a growing population had to be fed, and for meat, as standards of living gradually began to rise. With little prospect of large-scale cheap imports from elsewhere, the future for British farming looked secure, and interest in intensification increased.

By this date the beginnings of a change in the type of improvements can be seen. Grain prices never again reached anything like their wartime levels, but instead the price of livestock began to rise. Cattle began to be valued in their own right, rather than just as manure producers. One of the first collections of farm plans to be published after the Napoleonic Wars was that of Charles Waistell in 1827. His plans show the once open yards being divided up allowing for the specialized feeding of different groups of stock. Ideally, the U-shape became the E-shaped plan, but this could only be achieved in buildings that had originally been built to a 'model' design. Not all farmers could afford to start again; most had to be content with adaptations, and two of the plans in Waistell's book suggest how this might be done. They show a farm in Caterham, Surrey, before and after improvements. The earlier plan shows scattered buildings, partly enclosing a fold yard. These include four large barns, stables, cart sheds and a small cattle shed. The improvements involved the demolition of one barn and the building of new stables and cattle sheds. The gaps around the old fold yard were filled in and the now completely enclosed area divided into two fold yards, a stable court and a kitchen court adjacent to the house. This division of the yard allowed for the subdivision of cattle into groups of ten to twelve beasts. As C. S. Read explained in

27 This plan of a farm at Caterham, published in 1827, shows the farmstead before (left) and after improvement (right). A barn, deemed unnecessary, has been replaced by a stable. New feeding and cattle sheds have been built and a wagon lodge and granary added. The large open yard has been divided into two to provide better accommodation for cattle.

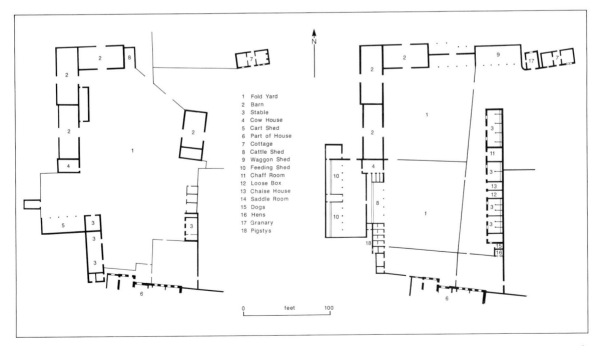

1 Fold Yard
2 Barn
3 Stable
4 Cow House
5 Cart Shed
6 Part of House
7 Cottage
8 Cattle Shed
9 Waggon Shed
10 Feeding Shed
11 Chaff Room
12 Loose Box
13 Chaise House
14 Saddle Room
15 Dogs
16 Hens
17 Granary
18 Pigstys

0   feet   100

1858, 'Cattle thrive in them, but in a community of a dozen, a few will be tyrants and the rest must be slaves'.[3]

Gradually, during the first half of the nineteenth century, there was a change of emphasis in farm building. The barn ceased to be the most important building of the farmstead. As mechanized threshing and winnowing replaced hand flailing the threshing floor with its draughts became obsolete. Instead of being the processing shop for the cash crop of the farm, it became merely a store and feed mixing area, often filled with belted gearing and machinery where the open threshing area had been. Now it was the cattle sheds that were important. In the yards and sheds, manure was well trodden with straw into an eminently usable form. Coke at Holkham was supposed to have told his tenants, 'If you will keep an extra yard of bullocks, I will build you a yard and shed free of expense'.[4]

As farming confidence returned, so did the level of expenditure of the progressive farmers. One of the attractions of the four-course system had been its self-sufficiency. The land was manured by the livestock, which were fed on the produce of the land. Very little had to be bought in. This began to change after 1830 with the increasing understanding of the science behind farming. This new attitude was epitomized in the motto of the Royal Agricultural Society, founded in 1838, 'Practice with Science'. The new scientific and highly capitalized farming became known as 'High Farming'. High Farming was not simply a method of farming; it was a state of mind. The Holkham tenant John Hastings said in 1841, when asked about the prospects for English farmers, 'Production itself will increase as knowledge, itself increases.'[5] Gone was his 'heart-break' and despair of 1816. Both the changing farming methods and the enormous confidence of landowner and farmer are reflected in the buildings of this new age.

The value of artificial fertilizers was the first subject to receive scientific attention. Large quantities of powdered animal bones were being imported from the 1830s, particularly for turnips. Imports rose from a value of £78,000 in 1832 to £254,000 in 1837.[6] From the late 1830s John Bennet Lawes at Rothamstead was experimenting with manures and the production of superphosphates, and was granted a patent for their production in 1842. From then on the profits of manufacture financed further experimentation and by 1850 'a fuller understanding of soil management was a necessity for the forward looking farmer'.[7] The increased use of fertilizer meant that farmers could break away from the four-course rotation, and on the Holkham estates many tenants asked for and gained permission to do so.

By 1844 H. & T. Proctor were manufacturing fertilizers from bone, guano and nitrate of soda at their works in Bristol. Their bill heading included the message, 'He who gives to the soil liberally will receive therefrom abundantly.' The firm was familiar with the research of the

German chemist Baron Von Liebeg into the value of artificial fertilizers. Indeed, his son spent some time working at the Bristol plant.

In the 1850s Thomas Proctor leased a farm near Bristol from the Duke of Beaufort and set out to prove that this poor holding, locally known as 'starve-all farm' could be more productive. Thousands of pounds were spent on drainage and manuring and a fine range of model buildings was erected. The E-shaped ranges of bullock sheds, 'an ecclesiastical-looking structure being lit by a three-light Gothic window', held 100 cattle and were connected by a railway to the food preparation rooms. The Proctors transformed Wallscourt farm into a model estate 'with rich herbage dotted with cattle' and even a school was provided for local children. However Proctor's interest was short-lived and he left the farm in 1860. Most of the farm buildings were demolished in 1984.[8]

## THE DEVELOPMENT OF CATTLE ACCOMMODATION

As cereal production was intensifying, so was livestock husbandry. Oil and cotton cake for feed was being imported by the most intensive farmers. For example, John Hudson at Castle Acre on the Holkham estate was spending £2000–£3000 a year to feed 150 steers and 2500 sheep, and £1000 for fertilizers on his one-thousand-acre farm. Cattle cake allowed for the efficient fattening of cattle, which could then be sent to market by train rather than losing weight walking. Their increased value was the incentive behind the improvement in cattle accommodation. Specialist buildings for efficient individual feeding of bullocks allowed for more intensive production.[9]

Interest in the arrangement of buildings reached a peak in 1850 when the *JRASE* ran a competition for farm building design. Six sets of plans were published, including one by John Hudson, who wrote, 'In this improving age, it would be unwise to recommend the building of large and expensive barns, the more especially as steam power is coming into general use.' It is clear from the introductory article to the competition, summarizing recent developments in layout and design, that interest was centred on livestock accommodation. 'In all plans now published, the old method of building around a rectangular area and using the enclosure as a stack yard has either been given up or very much modified.' Instead this area was filled with cattle yards.[10] The E-shaped farmstead, with the barn on the south and the shelter sheds abutting it at right angles, became the accepted plan.

An influential land agent, architect and agricultural engineer of this period of progress was G. A. Dean. He wrote several books on farm building design and worked for the prestigious Windsor and Holkham estates as well as for many smaller clients from Cheshire to Dorset. His buildings were usually plain and functional, only allowing architectural embellishment on home farms and estate workshops. His writings gave much helpful advice and many of his plans were printed. In *The Land Steward*, published in 1851, he wrote:

'We have been surprised by the great want of accommodation and arrangement in farm buildings: we have found them unsuited, almost without exception, to the improved system of farming now pursued... A compact and well arranged steading is of immense importance to the farmer; it is there his livestock are sheltered and fed a great portion of the year, it is there the produce of his farm is manufactured and consumed, and it is there he collected the means of enriching his lands and of increasing the quantity and improving the quality of his crops.'

He thought that buildings should not be crowded, but that there should be plenty of room to allow for future alterations and extensions. Animals should be well housed, as 'such an animal requires less food in winter than one exposed to the cold'. There should be adequate implement sheds, as more wear and tear was caused to implements by leaving them outside than by actual work. Finally 'there ought not to be the smallest convenience on a farm, down to a pigsty, that is not so precisely in the right spot that to place it anywhere else would be a loss of labour and manure.'[11]

### Egmere Farm

An impressive example of Dean's work, surviving almost unaltered from the 1850s and still in agricultural use, is on the 1222-acre Egmere Farm near Walsingham, Norfolk, built for the Holkham estate. The difference between this set and earlier farms is immediately obvious. The older barn still remains on the site, but the double doors across the threshing floors have been blocked up and the building subdivided to provide storage space and standing room for food preparation machines such as chaff cutters. The threshing would probably have been done by a portable engine working in the stack yard and the crop stored in the massive new granaries over the 14-bay cart shed. The straw would either have been ricked or kept in the barn until it was needed in the stables next door or in the six cattle yards and two rows of loose boxes opposite the barn to the west. These monumental shelter sheds and loose boxes, built in 1850 to house about 100 cattle, dwarf the barn and illustrate clearly the change in emphasis that had taken place over the previous 20 years. Yet unlike examples of Dean's work elsewhere, this set of buildings does not include such labour-saving devices as tramways, emphasizing the fact that even as late as 1850, labour was still cheap and readily available in Norfolk.

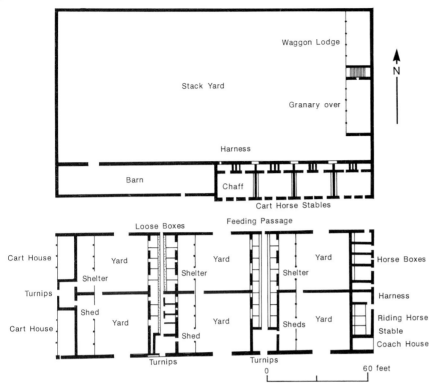

28 Egmere Farm was designed by G.A. Dean and built in 1853. It was the last farm on the Holkham estate to be totally rebuilt and is an example of the sort of intensive cattle production associated with 'High Farming'. Some 100 cattle were housed both in the yards and for final fattening in loose boxes. The buildings, serving 1222 acres, cost £5,500 to build between 1850 and 1856.

## 'HIGH FARMING' PERFECTED

This industrial approach to farm buildings was taken up by some of the agricultural writers of the period. In 1863 John Bailey Denton collected plans of farm premises built across England and published them with his own comments in a book called *The Farm Homesteads of England*. His position as engineer to the General Land Drainage and Improvement Company meant that he had travelled widely and was able to collect his examples from all over the country. He draws many analogies with industry, one frequently quoted:

'To farm successfully with defective and ill-arranged buildings is no more practical than to manufacture profitably in scattered, inconvenient workshops in place of one harmoniously contrived, completely fitted mill.'

Alongside the cattle yards, most of the improved designs had loose boxes. These rows of stalls for finishing cattle for market were usually built either side of a central passage with a turnip or cake house at one end. The floors of the boxes were frequently sunken, 'about three feet below the level of the feeding passage, and are formed of chalk well rammed down. The boxes are cleaned out twice in the season, once in January and once in July.'[12] By this time the level would be as high as that of the feeding passage and the animals would have been driven out for the walk to the railway and transport to market.

### The Duke of Bedford in the Fens

On the main A47 road between Wisbech and Peterborough, in the heart of the Fens, lies the village of Thorney, its ornate mock-Tudor architecture making a welcome break in the flat monotony of the landscape. This village, as the monograms on the cottages show, was at the centre of the Duke of Bedford's fenland estate, which in the mid-nineteenth century covered 20,000 acres of land, all of it between 2.7 and 3.6 metres (9 and 12 feet) below sea level. Drainage of the area began in the mid-seventeenth century with the work of Vermyden and by 1700 many religious refugees from the Continent had moved in and were working as labourers on the draining work, finally settling and introducing new farming methods in the former swamp, growing cereals and vegetables such as cabbages. However as the peat dried out the land sank and so the problems of drainage increased, with inundations more frequent. First, windpumps were installed to raise the water from the shrinking land into the drains and by the 1830s these were being replaced by steam-engines. Alongside improved drainage went both private and parliamentary enclosure and the building of new farms. Few of the original buildings survive as peat makes a poor foundation. By the late nineteenth century weatherboarding, a much lighter building material than brick, was being used in the hope that the problems of settlement would be less. Where possible they were erected on the gravel of old river beds, but even here they have often been rebuilt again and again.[13]

Between 1816 and 1895 the Duke of Bedford spent £1.5 million on his Thorney estate, a third of this being on 'new works and permanent improvement'.[14] The most impressive result of this expenditure is the estate workshop at Thorney with its castellated central tower, visible across much of the parish. It was surrounded by carpenters' shops and sawyers' yards as well as foundries and stores.

Two of the Duke's new farms were illustrated by Denton. They show ranges of stables, cattle sheds and yards with cast-iron window frames and sliding doors. Both plans show cattle being kept in open yards and in loose boxes, although in the larger example the latter have 'open courts' behind them. The barn often formed a subsidiary part of the farmstead, being no higher than the surrounding buildings. In one example an older barn with a threshing floor was included in a new range. A few long ranges, consisting of a large two-storey barn adjoining granaries above cart sheds, still survive in a mutilated form. One plan shows a steam-engine working machinery in a mill room and corn dressing room. They were built of local bricks, made by the estate to a size different from the usual standard, with slate roofs, boarded inside. Horse gearing was used on several farms and the shuttered opening for belting sometimes survives, along with the original shafting and dressing mill.

## The Knight family on Exmoor

Nothing as elaborate was built by Frederick Knight whose father, John, bought the 20,000 acres of Exmoor forest from the Crown in 1820. Although this area of open heath and moor was all over 240 metres (800 feet) above sea level he hoped to enclose and cultivate much of it. Until 1841 John planned to farm this huge area himself, bringing as much land into cultivation as possible and buying lowland sheep for summer grazing on the rest. However in 1841 he handed over control of the estate to Frederick, who decided to create tenant farms. His neighbour, Mr T. D. Acland, wrote of Frederick in 1850, 'He wants neither the energy nor the will to do his duty in it, and to bring the forest into a condition which an English gentleman may look upon with well-grounded satisfaction.'

During the winter of 1844 work started on farmhouses and buildings for six new farms with four more being equipped by 1847. All building work was complete by 1852 and 11 farmsteads still stand in a recognizable form. Frederick Knight was his own architect and local labour and materials were used. Unlike the Bedfords, the Knight family suffered from a lack of capital and frequently farms were not complete when the first tenant arrived.

29 White Hart Farm, Thorney. No engine house survives, although a main shaft runs down the length of these buildings at right angles to the barn.

The result was the simple squat groups of buildings so typical of the area around Simonsbath today. The two-storey, double-fronted whitewashed houses with their hipped roofs stand out on the dark hillsides, flanked by grey stone farm buildings. Usually sited below the top of the hills for shelter and on the south sides of the valleys, the farmsteads were surrounded to the north by a horseshoe of beech to keep some of the winds off houses and yards. The farm buildings usually abutted the house on either side, and surrounded a yard, often divided into two, behind. Typically, as at Warren farm, they included a small barn, in this instance originally provided with a water-wheel, now long since gone, a cow byre, shelter sheds, and stables with hay lofts above. Only the agent's farm at Emmet's Grange rose to the dignity of a separate trap house and riding horse stable. Here an open-sided shed near the house was used for a peat store, whilst the house was given the added status of a fine pillared porch and the garden protected from the sheep on the hillside by a small ha-ha.

Knight's agent explained in an article that an outlay of two guineas per acre on buildings should be sufficient and to prove this he published a plan of a farmstead for a 200-acre Exmoor farm which could be built for £600. An important asset was the window in the corner of the sitting room and the bedroom above from which the farmer could see

30 View of the farmyard at Warren Farm, Simonsbath, Somerset, from the north looking towards the house and the calf house, with hay loft above, adjoining. To the right is the barn.

into his yards.[15] The details of expenditure on one farm include a barn, stable and cart sheds costing half the price of the house as well as calves' houses, piggeries, open cattle sheds, turnip house, cow sheds, corn, gig and coalhouses.

Denied a family inheritance that Frederick had been led to expect, the estate ran into financial difficulties and farms proved difficult to let. In spite of deep ploughing using first oxen and later steam power, and massive doses of lime coupled with the determined efforts of Knight and some of his tenants, little headway was made; it was impossible to grow wheat and barley on Exmoor. By the 1860s a cattle and sheep rearing system based on pasture, alternating with crops of turnips and meadow grasses, had been established. The farms managed on this livestock-based system weathered the depression of the late nineteenth century better than many of their lowland counterparts.

This group of farms illustrate the real problems of hill farming, even in the heady days of 'High Farming'. Many tenants did not stay long

31 Plan of one of the Knight farms, probably Warren Farm, published in the *JRASE*, 1856. It was designed to serve a farm of 300 acres in hill country, half of which was arable.

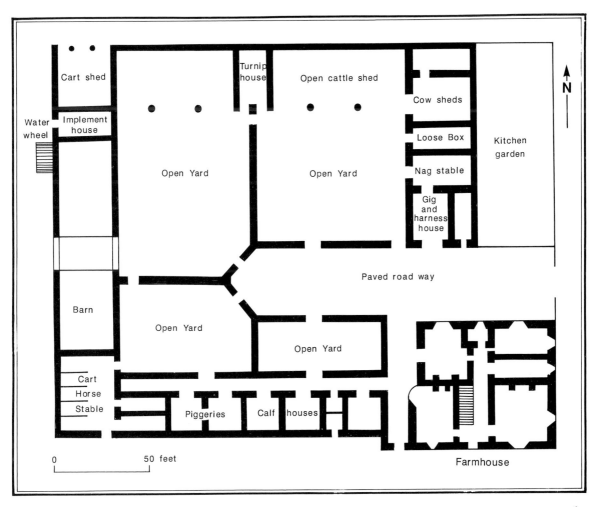

and were frequently in arrears with their rents. The estate was always in financial difficulties and the buildings represent the minimum needed to run a livestock-based (mainly sheep) hill farm in the mid-nineteenth century.[16]

Many permanent benefits of the Knight legacy remain. Roads were built across the moor, up to 3000 acres were enclosed into large fields by beech hedges on stone, turf-covered walls and a new parish, the parish of Exmoor, with a church at Simonsbath, was created in 1856.

## TWO INDUSTRIAL FARMS

As well as the hereditary landowners, newcomers to the ranks were often interested in farm improvements and were sometimes even more prepared than their long-established neighbours to spend enormous sums on extravagant schemes.

### Buscot and Leighton

In 1859 the three-and-a-half-thousand acre Buscot park estate in Berkshire was bought by Robert Campbell on his return from Australia with a fortune made in gold prospecting. Semi-derelict, it was to become the most highly industrialized farm in nineteenth-century England. First the land was drained and an irrigation scheme fed from a 20-acre lake that reputedly cost £80–90,000 to install. Next, following the example of similar establishments in France, Campbell set up a factory to distil alcohol from sugar beet, and in 1869 his distillery, costing £100,000, was opened. A narrow-gauge railway wound its way around the estate on which ran steam-engines with trucks to collect the beet. As well as this there was an oil cake mill, a gasworks and fertilizer and vitriol works using the by-products of gas production. A large corn mill was driven by water turbine, which was also used for threshing and other farm machinery. The sugar beet residue was used for fattening cattle in very intensive conditions.[17]

In 1870 Campbell, one of the first farmers who experimented with concrete as a building material for farm buildings, erected a spacious barn.[18]

Whether Campbell's enterprise ever made any profits is doubtful, but by 1879 it was certainly making a loss and he decided to sell. He died, a disappointed man, in 1885.

Another highly industrialized farming venture was that of the Liverpool banker John Naylor who was given the 4,000-acre Leighton estate near Welshpool in 1846 as a wedding present from his uncle. Nearby were five other estates, all competing to outdo each other in the grandeur of their farmsteads. He immediately erected a huge brick home farm. Two of its most monumental buildings were a pair of circular piggeries of cathedral-like proportions. A complex irrigation system was installed and a turbine pump drove water to a tank on the hill from which pipes ran to the fields supplying either water or liquid manure. The manure from the farm buildings was channelled into tunnels to be pumped up the bank. Again, the amount of investment involved was never justified by the level of returns. Many of the schemes were quickly abandoned and the estate was sold by Naylor's grandson to the county council in 1931. Since then the land and the buildings have been divided amongst several farming tenants and some buildings have become redundant. Alternative industrial uses have been found for some and the ornate poultry house is being restored for letting as a highly individual holiday home.

One change that was being advocated by improvers, but for which there is little evidence away from the home farms of estates, was the covered yard. Although the complete roofing over of the yard might protect and improve the manure, it created problems of ventilation and very few were built in Norfolk, although one very elaborate example was found in the survey area (illustration 87).

Secondly, many of the improved plans contained ideas from industrial plants, such as tramways to take chaff and animal feeds to the cattle sheds and manure away, sometimes even powered by steam-engines, but again very few were built and none have been found in Norfolk. They were hardly a justifiable expense except on the showpiece farms on the largest of the English and Scottish estates.

The English countryside by 1870 was as highly capitalized as at any time over the next 100 years. On the great estates buildings were in good order, hedges were well cut, and land weed-free and productive. On many farms, particularly in the industrialized regions, the throb of a steam-engine or the steady muted beat of wooden cogs turned by a water-wheel would have been part of the background farmyard hum.

There were of course many smaller farms, either owner-occupied or tenanted on less progressive estates, which remained unaffected by High Farming, and many of these farms were visited on the Norfolk survey. Even here, however, some new buildings were likely to have been added to the old. It was these generally high levels of maintenance that meant that most of the buildings survived the sixty years of neglect after 1880 that lasted until the modern era.

# 6

# The Period of Depression, 1880-1914

## THE END OF 'HIGH FARMING'

It was not until the mid-1870s that the collapse of British grain prices, feared at the time of the repeal of the Corn Laws in 1846, actually took place. The price of wheat at Norwich market fell from about 65 shillings in 1872 to below 55 shillings for the rest of the century. For many years it was little more than half this level; the lowest price of 25 shillings was recorded in 1894.

The slump had been foreseen by some, even in the general euphoria of the period of 'High Farming'. Clare Sewell Read farmed 800 acres at Honingham Thorpe, near Norwich, and in 1865 became the first tenant-farmer MP. As such he was the farmers' advocate in the House of Commons and was already worried about the dangers of foreign competition. He had visited Canada and seen the huge prairies of potentially productive virgin land that only awaited the arrival of the railways to be opened up. Unlike his contemporaries, he saw science as a 'two-edged sword'. New techniques and machinery saved time and labour, but not money. Artificial fertilizers were easily swept away by the rain and did not restore soil structure as did farmyard manure.

The situation was made worse by a run of bad harvests. Read told the Royal Commission on Agriculture in 1894 that there had not been an 'all-round good crop of farm produce since 1874'. A particularly disastrous year was 1879, while 1891–2 was cold and miserably wet. In contrast, 1893 was a year of drought.[1]

As prices went down, so did the acreage of wheat grown. The change was a slow one as many farmers felt that to give up cereals was an admission that the art of farming had failed. They also were not sure what they should change to, and as the search for alternatives increased much advice was available, mostly based on the theme, 'It no longer pays to plough, it pays to graze.'[2] The decline in cereals was greatest in the traditional pastoral areas where improvements in transport meant it was no longer necessary to be self-sufficient, and even feed grain could now be bought at a low price from nearby arable areas. In Northumberland the area of arable cropping dropped by 40 per cent between 1870 and 1890, continuing a trend that had begun in the 1850s.[3]

While the wheat price dropped by 50 per cent between 1871–5 and 1894–8, a change to grass could be difficult in the drier east and so a shift to other cereals such as barley and oats, where the decline in price had only been just below 40 per cent, was sometimes possible. The amount of oats grown in East Anglia doubled between 1875 and 1890, much of it for the London hackney horse market. Good malting barley could find a market with the Burton-on-Trent brewers. Other alternative crops included potatoes in the Fens, which covered almost a quarter of the arable by 1900, and fruit and vegetables, particularly near large towns.[4]

Where it was practical to change to permanent grass was the most favoured solution, with the acreage up by 25 per cent in the last quarter of the nineteenth century. Although fewer sheep were kept in 1900 than in 1870, the number of cattle had increased by 15 per cent. They were mostly kept on the new pastures, but they needed housing during the winter. They were usually kept for a shorter period than previously, being sold during the second year, while their meat was of a higher quality and therefore fetched more whilst at the same time allowing for a quicker turnover of cash.

The most important growth sector was dairying, particularly for liquid milk, the one product still free from foreign competition. The area of permanent pasture in Essex went up by 67 per cent between 1875 and 1900 and much of this was for milk production aimed at the London market.[5]

This fall in agricultural prosperity led, inevitably, to a fall in rent and a lowering level of estate income to be reinvested in farm improvements. Owner-occupiers who could not be cushioned from the depression by rent rebates were often worse off than tenants and so would have even less spare capital to plough back into the farm. As a result, interest in new farm building design declined. After 1880 there were far fewer new building projects on the Holkham estates and those there were, were small scale, rarely costing more than a few hundred pounds.[6]

Surprisingly, initial survey work in Hampshire has suggested that building work there can frequently be dated to the 1880s and 1890s. This may well be associated with the increasing pull not only of the London market but of the developing towns of Southampton, Bournemouth, Aldershot, Eastleigh and Portsmouth and particularly their increasing demand for milk, livestock and market gardening produce; all enterprises that could still prove profitable.[7] There were also several landowners in this area whose wealth had been made in London and who were prepared to invest in what might prove to be a loss-making enterprise, purely for show.

In spite of the lack of capital available there was a farm building competition in the *JRASE* in 1879 and one entry by John Bailey Denton was published. It shows the developing interest in livestock accommodation with even less emphasis on the barn, which was now little more than a food store. A steam-engine operated both barn machinery and a saw pit. The cattle yards were, however, covered and this was a development increasingly advocated during the last years of the century. W.J. Moscrop, writing in the *JRASE* explained how, gradually, covered yards were becoming accepted by landlord and tenant alike: 'I had much difficulty in carrying the tenant with me in the first yard I roofed over, but now, in letting farms, almost the first thing asked is, Will you cover the yards?'[8]

The decline in the availability of both estate and owner-occupier

32 (*below*) Plan and (*right*) drawing of 'Experimentia', designed by J.B. Denton and published in the *JRASE*, 1879. The yards are completely covered and the farm fully mechanized.

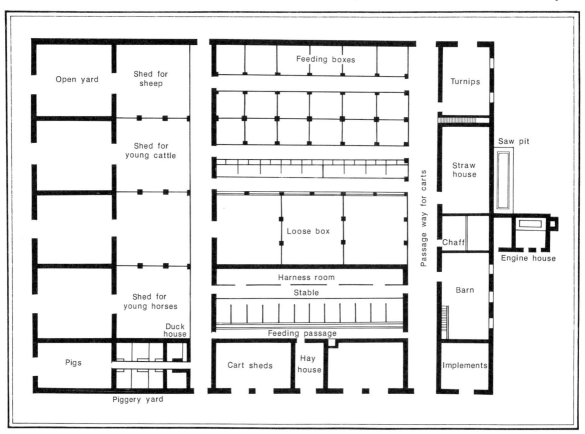

capital meant that repairs to buildings were liable to be neglected, but where buildings had previously been kept up to a high standard the result was not too immediately serious as they could withstand a few years with little spent on maintenance.

There was one important circumstance in which landlords would still find it necessary to erect new buildings, and that was either to attract new tenants or keep old ones. As it was chiefly in livestock that profits were made after 1880, it was increased cattle accommodation that most tenants requested. The last thing the agents of estates wanted was for land to be vacant, and so they were prepared to go to great lengths to keep land occupied.

A typical example is the Hastings' farm at Longham, Norfolk. It was occupied until his death in 1884 by a son of the John Hastings already mentioned. The son was faced with the difficult problem of trying to make the farm pay in the depth of the recession and threatened to leave. His rent was halved and, with the help of a loan from the Holkham estate, he agreed to stay on. After a third notice of intention to quit in 1891, the estate agreed to build a new cattle shed and yard and the tenant continued his occupancy. Finally, however, in 1907, the tenancy was given up and a family that had been on the estate for 200 years, left. At the final dispersion auction breeding hackney ponies were sold, showing that on this farm at least attempts had been made to diversify away from the traditional produce.[9]

Building work that was carried out was likely to be in a much simpler and cheaper style than had previously been the case. 'Where landlords now build, they often do so less substantially and permanently than

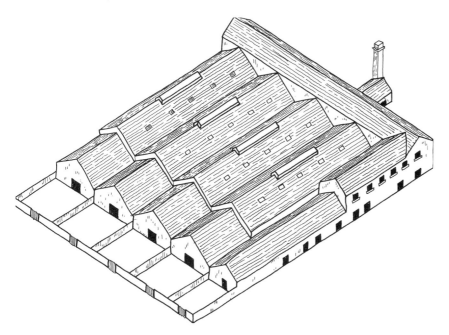

before.'[10] The use of weatherboarding and corrugated iron began to increase. A new type of building, the iron Dutch barn, began to appear on many farms and a few late nineteenth-century examples survive. The extension of the railway network allowed for the easy transport of building materials and the breakdown of local building characteristics, so long a feature of the regions of the United Kingdom.

## MECHANIZATION AND THE BREAKDOWN OF REGIONALISM

One of the chief complaints of the farmers at the time was the increase in farm labourers' wages coupled with a scarcity of workers to choose from. After 1851 the population in the countryside began to decline, and for the first time labour was at a premium. Wages rose by between 10 and 17 per cent between 1870 and 1876, and only in the east were farmers able to force them down in the 1880s. The cost of labour could account for between a third and a fifth of farm expenditure.[11] This encouraged mechanization, particularly in the harvest field. The reaper could cut nearly nine times as much corn in a day as a man could cut with a scythe. The self-binder came into general use in the 1890s and speeded up the process even more. By 1900 80 per cent of the crop was cut by machine; in 1871 it had been 25 per cent. Similar progress was being made in the hay field.

This meant that implement sheds, sometimes with smithies, were needed, especially on the larger farms. They were built, characteristically, in a separate block opening onto the roadway leading to the fields and not too far from the stables.

The coming of the railways into the remoter parts of the countryside allowed areas distant from towns to benefit from the urban market, and this was particularly true for dairy farms. Previously much of their produce had been made into butter and cheese, which were now increasingly threatened by foreign imports. By the end of the century a farm within reasonable reach of a station in Derbyshire, Gloucestershire or Hampshire was quite likely to be sending daily supplies of milk to London by rail.[12]

Although many farm dairy units were erected in the period of 'High Farming', the most prestigious of which must surely be the royal dairy farm built at Windsor in 1855, the growth of the dairy industry ensured that they would continue to be built. Unfortunately, few survive. The changes in milk production introduced after 1886 by a series of government regulations to control standards of hygiene have ensured that dairies have been altered more than any other nineteenth-century farm buildings. Cobbled and brick floors have been cemented over, wooden stall divisions replaced with concrete and tubular metal, interior walls have been rendered and evidence of original openings obliterated. The Milk and Dairy Order of 1926 finally established the familiar dairy with its corrugated cooler, washing trough and steam sterilizing chest as a necessary part of the cow house.[13]

In some cases, especially when newcomers to farming were bringing in capital from outside and expertise from the industrial world, changes were already evident by 1914. 'There was a time...when (farmsteads) lent a charm to rural scenery...Now that the industry has become more serious, more exacting and more precise, the picturesque side...has given way to lines of formality and stiffness. The older order was coupled with waste...the new order accepts thrift and watchfulness as essential to success.'[14] Examples of such cost-effective well-designed establishments were, however, few and far between in the early years of the twentieth century.

The 1914–18 War had a stimulating effect on agriculture as overseas supplies were disrupted. For the first time the government became directly involved and prices were guaranteed. For several years after the war foreign competition was slight and prices remained high. It was in these years from 1918 to the early 1920s that the pattern of landownership that had dominated farming and investment in farm buildings for the previous 400 years was drastically altered. Many landowners saw this temporary recovery of farming confidence as the ideal moment to sell, and between 1918 and 1922 a quarter of England changed hands. Many farms were bought by their tenants and, as prices began to decline again after 1921, there was no spare money for farm building maintenance. The important new crop of this period was sugar beet, providing the farmer with a much-needed cash crop. The first sugar beet factory was opened at Cantley, near Norwich, in 1921, but sugar beet growing did not require any new specialist buildings on the farm.

The needs of the farming community have always been changing, and, as this section has shown, new buildings have been built or older ones adapted to suit these needs. The pace of change has greatly accelerated over the last 40 years. Horses have been superseded by tractors and stables left redundant. Farm machinery has grown in size to a degree unimaginable 30 years ago. Specialist intensive buildings are needed for livestock and farm amalgamations have resulted in the centralization of farming activities on selected sites. The farming landscape has indeed been changing, but enough has survived to make the following study of Norfolk's farming past through its buildings a possibility, and to yield the wealth of information described and analysed in the following chapters of this book.

# 7

# The Dating of Farm Buildings

One of the most difficult problems faced by the Norfolk survey was that of dating the buildings studied. Datable features of buildings tend to be the non-functional extras; such as mouldings and decorative additions – which are noticeably absent from farm buildings. Most farmsteads are, first and foremost, functional with little room for architectural detail. There are, however, exceptions to this rule. The facades of home farms may well pick up details from the house, and farm buildings could be seen as an indication of the wealth of the farmer and regarded as status symbols. Whereas the medieval farmer may have given money for rebuilding the church, his Georgian descendant embellished the barn.

33 Datestone in the gable of the barn at Red Brick Farm, Thompson. This datestone probably reflects accurately the date of the barn, which is also the date of the enclosure of Thompson Common when this farm gained new land.

## DATESTONES AND MAPS

Usually the only method of dating a building is by comparing it to another with similar features in the same locality whose date is known. It was possible to date some buildings accurately and from these to generalize about others. Firstly some had datestones or scratched dates on the beams or walls. Although datestones have to be treated with caution, it is usually possible to establish whether they are original and to draw parallels with other undated buildings. Maps are also useful for the later period. Some seventeenth-century maps survive, but most of those consulted by the survey were from 1720 onwards. Buildings shown on maps can, of course, be replaced at a later date, but again this evidence can be used as a guideline for dating some examples. From these fixed points, it is possible to build up a series of features

that are typical of different dates. However, many building techniques continued to be used for a very long time, and as the diagram overleaf shows, there are long periods of overlap.

34 Dated beam in a barn at Morningthorpe.

Farm buildings tended to be completely rebuilt more often than houses and so not surprisingly the survey was not dealing with medieval buildings, although a few of the barns may date from the late-medieval period. It was the building techniques from the sixteenth century onwards with which we were mostly concerned.

## ROOF TYPES

Usually the best guide to the date of a building is its roof. This is also unfortunately the most vulnerable part of a building, particularly after a wet harvesting season when damp sheaves could heat up and catch fire. Many barns have had to be reroofed some time in the last 150 years.

Little has been published on post-medieval roof types, but gradually local typologies are being built up. This description is based on observations in Norfolk with comparisons from other regions where possible. The post-medieval roof types found in farm buildings fall into three distinctive types, but the periods of construction inevitably

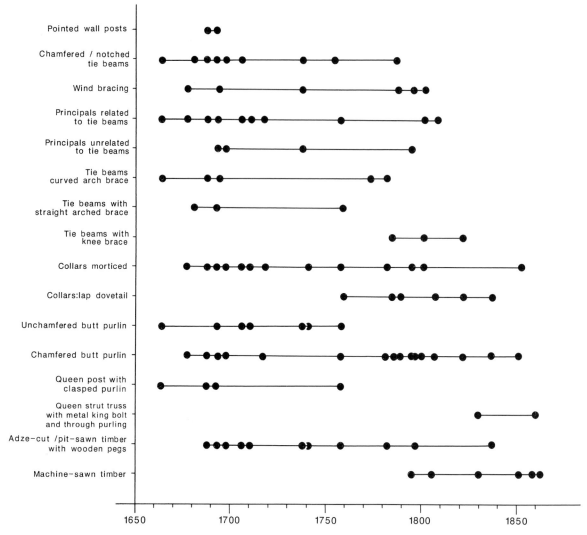

35 Dateable features from the roofs of dated farm buildings. Although the sequence that emerges from this diagram is helpful, it is obvious that there were long periods of overlap between different building techniques.

overlap. Features that were generally taken to indicate a pre-1700 date were mortised collars supported by queen posts resting on the tie beams, curved arch braces rising either from wall posts in brick buildings, or jowled principal posts when the building was timber-framed. The queen post construction was replacing the earlier crown post design during the sixteenth century and is found in Norfolk up to about 1700, although in Staffordshire its use carried on into the nineteenth century. Other seventeenth-century features include chamfered tie beams, often decorated with stops at both ends. The roof itself was strengthened with arched wind bracing and the purlins were mortised directly, without any wedging, into the principal rafter. An early characteristic is the reduced principal where the principal rafter and the collar clasp the purlin, so the rafter is narrower above the collar. Clasped purlins, clasped only by the collar, continue in use into the nineteenth century. This allows the purlin to be a continuous piece of wood and therefore is likely to be stronger.

During the eighteenth century the vertical queen post as distinct from the angled and supporting queen strut had fallen into disuse. As timber became less plentiful, techniques improved and there was a general tendency to reduce the amount of timber, both small and large, used in a building. Instead, the roof is held only by a tie beam and mortised collar, fixed to the principal rafters by wooden pegs. As the century wore on, the purlins were more likely to be wedged-shaped where they enter the rafters and to be staggered, rather than forming a continuous line. After 1750, a lap-dovetail joint replaced the mortise as the usual method of fitting the collar to the rafter, and by the early 1800s the old method of mortising had been entirely superseded. Wall posts gradually ceased to be jowelled and arch braces became straight. By the early nineteenth century, right-angle or knee braces under the tie beams, which were found in some buildings back to the seventeenth century, had also gone out of use. Wind bracing in the roof ended and the roof became less steeply pitched.

Although there had been a certain amount of prefabrication and mass production of, for instance, purlins, from the late Middle Ages, it was during the nineteenth century that many building techniques became more commercialized. Imported softwoods were more generally available and replaced native hardwoods, machine sawing replaced pit-sawn timber and metal straps, bolts and nails replaced the need for jointing and wooden pegs. In Staffordshire, for instance, bolts first appeared in about 1820. Roof design also changed, and particularly in smaller buildings a prefabricated wooden king post or metal king bolt – queen strut truss, came into use. The king post truss was by far the

36 Roof of a barn at Grove Farm, Merton. The collars (1) are pegged and morticed (2) as would have been usual in the early eighteenth century but the mortised queen posts (3) supporting the purlins (4) suggest an earlier date. The barn probably dates from about 1700.

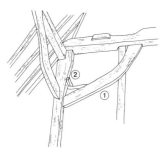

**37** The heavy curved arch braces (1) and jowelled wall posts (2) at Church Farm, Rollesby, indicate a medieval date.

**38** Interior of the barn at Corporation Farm, Hethel. The butted lower purlins (1), unwedged at entry, the curved windbracing (2) as well as the narrowing of the principal rafters (3) above the upper through purlin which it is clasping, indicate a pre-1600 date.

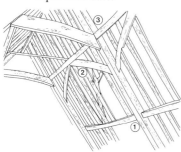

**39** Roof of the barn at White Lodge Farm, Antingham. This barn is dated 1694 on one of its tie beams. The roof differs from an eighteenth-century one as the purlins are not wedged on their entry to the rafter and are butted onto each other rather than staggered.

40 Early eighteenth-century carpenters' marks at Park Farm, Southburgh, indicating how the timber frame should be assembled and showing that timber-framed buildings were prefabricated for erection on site.

41 Detail of wedged purlins butted together and pegged into the principal rafter at High House Farm, Fleggburgh; an early eighteenth-century feature.

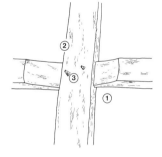

42 Detail of wedged purlins (1) staggered to allow for them to be pushed through the principal rafter (2) and pegged with a wooden peg (3) on the other side. These purlins at Bradmore Farm, North Walsham, are made of machine-sawn softwood and this is a nineteenth-century technique.

43 This wooden king post (1) queen strut truss (2) at Hall Farm, Bradfield, would probably have been bought ready to assemble and trusses of this type are frequently found in buildings erected after 1840. They could be used to span greater widths than those with a metal king post. The through purlin (3) is held in place by a wooden chuck (4) behind the truss and can clearly be seen here.

44 Roof of the covered yard at Park Farm, Bylaugh. This mid-nineteenth century wide-span roof is a king post (1)/queen strut (2) construction expanded and modified to span the covered yard. Metal tie beams and bolts have been widely used, but one of the most striking things about this roof is the amount of timber it contains.

45 Roof of covered yard, Hill Farm, Hethel. This scissor bracing spanning a covered yard is typical of the late nineteenth or early twentieth century.

most common roof type in Staffordshire, extending back to the mid-eighteenth century and occasionally earlier. In the pre-nineteenth-century examples it accounted for a third of those surviving, while for the period as a whole up to 1880, it accounted for half. The replacement of the wooden king post by an iron rod appears in Staffordshire from about 1865. Dean, writing in 1850, noted iron king posts as being a recent introduction.[1]

The arrangement of purlins changed again, some being clasped, while others were through purlins along the length of the building, carried on wooden chocks behind the principal rafters.

## WALLING MATERIALS

Where buildings have been reroofed or considerably altered, they are very difficult to date. The differential weathering of old brickwork can be very deceptive and generally reflects the quality rather than the age of brickwork. Very narrow bricks are usually pre-nineteenth century, although wide bricks were made back to Stuart times. The two most usual forms of brick bonding, English and Flemish, are found widely across the county, with English being the more common form before 1800, and gradually being replaced by Flemish thereafter.

Wattle and daub was the usual form of infill in half-timbered building until the end of the eighteenth century or somewhat later, but as supplies of local timber were exhausted, clay lump building took its place. (It might take up to 20 trees to build a three-bay timber-framed barn.) Old timber-framed buildings were repaired using imported weatherboard, brick and clay lump. No clay lump buildings could be dated before 1800. The earliest dated building of clay lump so far identified is a barn at Saham Hills, Norfolk, said to have been built by French prisoners-of-war and dated 1816 by a stone in the north gable. It appears to have been a typical nineteenth-century technique.[2] The most difficult to date were the stone buildings of flint, chalk and carstone, and no chronology for these building materials could be identified.

The late nineteenth century saw the introduction of several new building materials into farm buildings. Cast-iron was available for structural use from the late eighteenth century, with the famous iron bridge at Ironbridge being built in 1779 and cast-iron columns being used in churches from about the same date. However, it is not until the middle of the nineteenth century that we find it used frequently in farm buildings. Cast-iron was used for columns in open sheds and for often highly decorative ventilation grilles and windows. Many estate workshops had their own foundries producing distinctive castings for domestic and farm buildings.

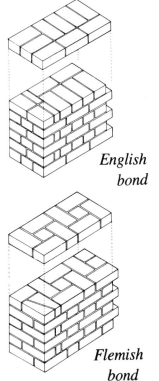

*English bond*

*Flemish bond*

**46** Drawing showing English and Flemish bonded-brickwork. English bond was more common in farm buildings before 1800, when it began to be replaced by Flemish bond.

Small details of ironmongery can also help date buildings. Nuts and bolts, for instance, were hand-forged up to the 1850s and their heads were usually square (illustration 41), this being the easiest shape to cut iron flats. After about 1850, mass-produced hexagonal nuts began to supersede the smith-produced square ones.[3]

Corrugated iron came into general use from the 1860s, and by the end of the nineteenth century was frequently used as a roofing material by crofters in north-west Scotland. It was not recommended for buildings where livestock were kept because of the problems of rust caused by condensation, but it was widely used, particularly for Dutch barns, by 1900.

Concrete was used for farm buildings from the 1870s, the earliest example being a barn at Buscot (Berkshire) in 1870. Articles appeared in the *JRASE* in the 1870s, and in 1873 the Earl of Leicester at Holkham paid £137 to Drake's Patent Concrete Co. for building apparatus and a few farm buildings were built on the Holkham estate.[4] Not many concrete farm buildings were ever erected, however. The walls were built up between shuttering and great care was needed in selecting the right materials to make a strong concrete.[5]

The use of imported timber for weatherboarding increased at the end of the nineteenth century in areas where it had not been traditionally used. In many cases, wattle and daub infilling of late medieval barns was replaced by weatherboarding during the last 100 years, and by 1900 some producers of pre-fabricated wooden buildings were advertising small farm buildings alongside their bungalows and cricket pavilions.

# 8

# The Farming Landscape of the Survey Areas

## THE NATURAL LANDSCAPE

It is a cliché of some 300 years' standing to emphasize the variety of Norfolk's farming landscape. Thomas Fuller was the first to draw attention in print to the great diversity within Norfolk's landscape. In 1676 he wrote, 'All England may be carved out of Norfolk, for here are fens and heaths, light and deep, sandy and clay grounds, meadow lands and pastures, arable and woodlands.'[1] William Marshall divided the county into distinct regions; his were the 'east', the 'west' and the 'south',[2] and in 1804 Arthur Young produced the first map dividing Norfolk into agricultural regions based on his observations of soil types.

The range of soils in the county is the result of its geological history. The underlying rocks of Norfolk are of a relatively recent date, laid down under the prehistoric seas that covered East Anglia. The area was then raised and tipped so that these chalk rocks only surface in the west. Here the soils are light and the landscape open and rolling, reminiscent of the chalk downs of southern England. To the east, the chalk plunges steeply to be 150 metres (500 feet) below the surface on the east coast. Most of Norfolk east of the chalk outcrops is covered with glacial deposits, laid down as the ice advanced and retreated over one-and-a-half million years. These materials vary from the good loam soils of the north-east through the heavy boulder clays of the middle and south of the county to the very light soils of Breckland in the south-west. Although regions dominated by any one of these types can be broadly identified, soils can vary enormously within one small area. It is not uncommon for a farmer to be draining one heavy clayey field

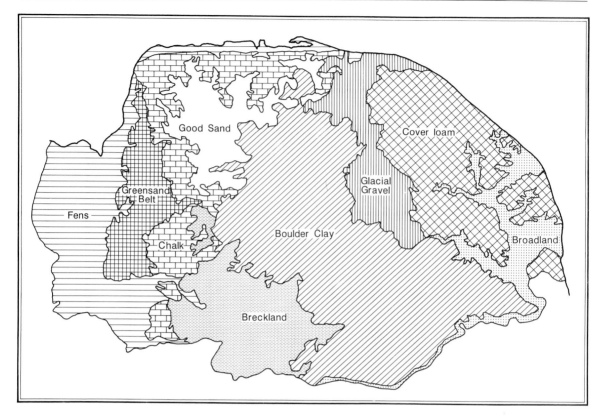

47 Map showing the distribution of soil types in Norfolk.

whilst irrigation is needed in a neighbouring sandy one.

Finally, the most recent of the county's soils are the river alluviums, silts and peats of the Broadlands in the east and the much more extensive Fens in the west.

## PATTERNS OF OWNERSHIP

Differences in the agricultural pattern of the county are not entirely the result of the soils, although they are certainly very significant. 'Farming systems are shaped by man',[3] and differences in land ownership and systems of tenure are also of great importance. By 1850 large areas of the county, particularly in the west and north, were dominated by great estates. The largest by far was the Holkham estate, consisting of 42,000 acres, divided between the area around Holkham and lands further south, between Dereham and Fakenham, around the original family seat at Tittleshall. The next two, by size, were the neighbouring Walpole and Townshend estates, owning huge tracts of farmland in the north-west of the county. In contrast, much of the south and east was held by owner-occupiers or small estates.

Patterns of land tenure are uniquely recorded in the tithe surveys of England and Wales, all compiled within a few years of the Tithe

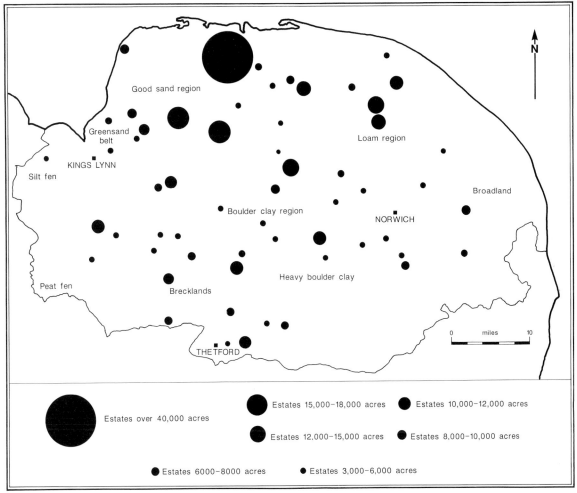

Commutation Act of 1836[4] and this evidence was made full use of in the survey. Not only is there a contrast in pattern of ownership across the county, but also in farm layout. The map of the farms in the Hunstanton area on the chalky soils of the LeStrange estate shows the landscape of parliamentary enclosure. The fields are large and of regular layout whilst the farmland is consolidated around the farmstead. In great contrast is the area of the southern heavy clayland parishes of Ashwellthorpe, Wrenningham and Hethel. Here we have a landscape of much earlier enclosure dominated by small landowners and owner-occupiers. The farms are much smaller, and scattered holdings still existed in the late 1840s.

48 Map showing the size of landed estates in Norfolk in 1873. The three largest estates, all in the north-west of the county, were those owned by the eighteenth-century political giants and agricultural improvers, Thomas William Coke of Holkham, Robert Walpole of Houghton and Charles (Turnip) Townshend of Raynham. The majority of large estates are in the north and west of the county, while there are very few in the heavy boulder clays of the south or the good loams of Broadland.

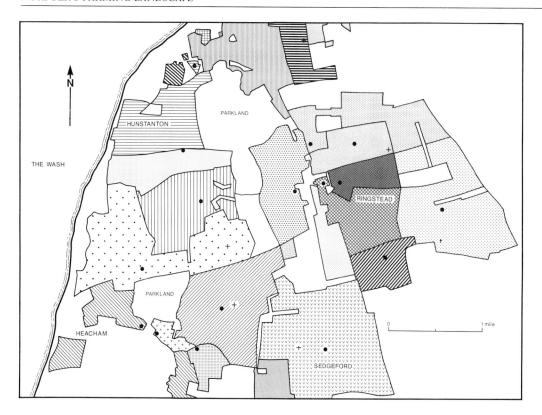

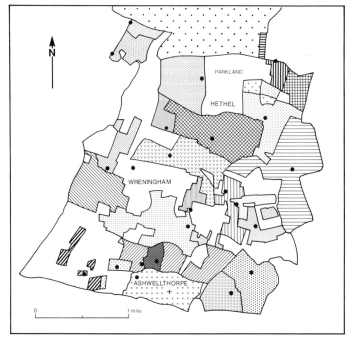

**49** (*above*) Farm layout in the Hunstanton area at the time of the tithe survey. The farms in this light-land area of late enclosure are large and compact and were all owned by the LeStrange estate. The dots represent the position of the farm buildings and it can be seen that many of them are centrally placed within their farms. The crosses represent field barns, which provided a second depot out in the fields on the largest holdings.

(*right*) Farm layout in the parishes of Ashwellthorpe, Wrenningham and Hethel at the time of the tithe survey. Here, on this heavy boulder clay of south Norfolk, the farms are far smaller and irregular in layout.

## THE SURVEY AREAS

Both the soil types and differences in systems of tenure have influenced the development of distinctive agricultural regions within the county. Arthur Young's regions are perhaps the simplest. When discussing farm size, he wrote, 'we must divide the county generally into two parts, the dry soils and the wet ones. Upon the former the farms are large and upon the latter, much smaller.'[5] Certainly his dry areas to the west and north contained most of the large estates, but there were large farms in the south, as on the Duke of Norfolk's estates and in parts of the Broads.

With rather more precision, C. S. Read, in 1858, divided the county into five regions.[6] Firstly, there was West Norfolk, Arthur Young's 'good sand' region, which 'by good husbandry, has been made to produce abundant crops.' By 1858 it was distinguished from the other regions by the large number of sheep kept, in some parts over 90 per 100 acres of cultivated land, whilst cattle were less important. It was the feeding of large numbers of sheep in the fields of turnips and on improved grasses that was supposed to have made this area into good corn growing land.

To the south was 'a large tract of blowing sand', still, in 1858, mostly rabbit warren and sheep walk, 'which, though much improved must ever remain poor and comparatively barren.' Again, 'sheep were the sheet anchor of the occupiers of these lands.'

In the centre of the county were Arthur Young's 'various loams' where much of the soil was heavy and needed underdraining before there could be much improvement. Here were 'the smallest farms in the county, not occupied by men of great capital...the farms are very circumscribed and the rents high, the fields small and badly shaped, the fences crooked and crowded with useless timber and the pasture lands cold and backward.' Read goes on to qualify this depressing statement by saying that this is true of only the worst parts of this very mixed area. Some parts presented 'a pleasanter aspect and are much better farmed' and the best barley in the county was grown here. As we move away from the western parts of the county, cattle, both beef and dairy, become more important at the expense of sheep.

In the north-east of the county are the areas described by Arthur Young as 'rich loams'. These were the best soils, 'well farmed for generations', according to Read. Here, the greatest number of cattle in the county were wintered in the 1850s and it was the 'country for splendid stall-fed cattle and good beef'.

Finally, in the extreme west and east were the wetlands of the Fens and marshes, both of which were being drained and improved by 1850, the Fens for arable crops and the eastern marshes for grazing.

One of the main aims of this survey of farm buildings has been to

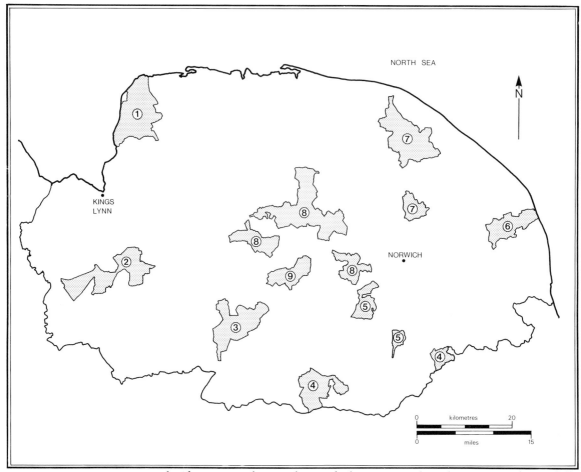

NORTH SEA

N

KINGS LYNN

NORWICH

0   kilometres   20

0   miles   15

50 Map showing the location of the survey areas.
1 The LeStrange estate (Hunstanton)
2 The Hare estate (Stow Bardolph)
3 The Walsingham estate (Merton)
4 The Duke of Norfolk Estate (Kenninghall)
5 Two areas in South Norfolk, held by various owners
6 An area of Broadland held by various owners
7 The Suffield estate (Gunton)
8 The Evans-Lombe estate (Great Melton and Bylaugh)
9 The Brampton-Gurdon estate (Letton)

clarify our understanding of these agricultural regions of Norfolk through the study of the farming landscape and the buildings within it, and to see what new light is thrown on the accepted interpretation by the examination of this long neglected source of evidence (see Chapter 18).

Areas were chosen for intensive study to reflect this variety as far as possible. The sandy soils of Breckland, the reclaimed peats of the Fens, the areas bordering on the marshes of Broadland, the rich loams of the north-east as well as the heavy soils of the south and the chalky ones of the north-west were all represented. Areas in the south of the county and also in the Broads were chosen because they were mostly farmed by owner-occupiers, while a cross section of estates, from the large and well managed lands of the Evans-Lombe to the small and neglected properties of the Dukes of Norfolk, were all included.

# THE AGRICULTURAL BACKGROUND

Until recently, our main source of information about eighteenth-century farm improvements in Norfolk has been the county reports of William Marshall, Nathaniel Kent and Arthur Young, alongside the material emerging from the great estates such as Holkham and Raynham. These very limited sources of information give a view of farming biased towards the improving landlords and ignoring the majority of Norfolk farmers. William Marshall, however, would have us believe that early experimentation with improved methods was carried out on the good loam soils of the owner-occupiers of the north-east rather than the great estates. 'In east Norfolk alone we are to look for that regular and long-established system of practice which has raised, deservedly, the name of Norfolk husbandmen. ... where, farms being comparatively small, have been enclosed, marled and ploughed since time immemorial.'[7] Before writing his report, William Marshall had worked as an agent on the Gunton estate in this region of the county, and so must have had first-hand knowledge of the area.

The cultivation of roots is seen as fundamental to agricultural improvement. The majority of early references to turnip cultivation refer to the south central area between Wymondham and Norwich as well as the Yare and Waveney valleys in the south; all regions outside the landowner-dominated parts of the county.[8] By the 1760s, however, it is clear that the ideas of the innovators were being taken up by the landowners seeking to improve the incomes from their estates. The estates on the chalk lands had the capital to enclose extensive sheep walks and tracts of heath, and to equip their new model farms with fine sets of buildings; certainly the standard of their buildings sets these areas apart from the owner-occupier ones. While it is far easier to build up a picture of farming on estate farms because there is so much more archive material than for the non-estate areas, it is hoped that the detailed study of the farms of the smaller farmers may well help to redress the balance and show that innovation was not confined to a few well-documented estates as has been the impression given in the past.

More written evidence is available for the period after 1815. Not only are there county reports, most notably that of R. N. Bacon, published in 1844, along with the original questionnaires from which he compiled his report (now in the Norfolk Record Office), but also there is the evidence given to numerous Royal Commissions and articles in national journals such as the *JRASE*. As in the earlier period, more information on individual estates is coming to light. Still, however, the evidence is very limited in scope and reflects the conditions on the farms of articulate farmers. In the case of the evidence given to Royal Commissions, the intention was to create an impression of the extreme distress of agriculture at the time.

The middle years of the century were ones of optimism and rising landlord incomes, while after 1870 the price of grain declined and rents soon fell. The agricultural depression brought not a total collapse in fixed capital investment, but a selective increase in a desperate rearguard action to keep tenants.[9] This survey will show the extent of this post-1870 investment and the conditions in which it was most important.

## THE AGRICULTURAL LANDSCAPE

Often older than the surviving buildings, and an indication of the type of agriculture practised, is the farming landscape. In an ever-increasing proportion of the county this is being altered beyond recognition, but where early maps survive the succession of early field systems and commons, followed by the reorganization of holdings and the enclosure of the open wastes, can be traced. The great variety of field types and the spasmodic survival of commons into the eighteenth century needs to be understood alongside the history of the buildings.

The oldest map surviving for any of the survey areas is one of Swanton Morley dated 1690. It shows the fields still mainly in strips and large areas of heath and common. All the farms and their buildings were shown. Barns could be distinguished by their large double doors and often small sheds are also marked. Unfortunately none of these seventeenth-century farm buildings survived in Swanton Morley.

The earliest period for which we can reconstruct the farming landscape over a larger area within the survey is the 1720s, using estate maps from two of the southern estates. In 1720 John Miller surveyed the south Norfolk estates of the Duke of Norfolk in the Lophams, Fersfield, Shelfanger, Kenninghall and Earsham. In 1723 John Buckenham surveyed the estates of Thomas de Grey in Merton, Thompson, Watton and Ellingham.

John Miller's maps show a landscape that has changed surprisingly little in the last 270 years. Except for the inevitable removal of some hedges, the fields around Hall Farm, South Lopham are essentially those surveyed in 1720. Field names such as 'horse croft' and 'coney hill' suggest the uses to which they had traditionally been put. A small area of detached strip fields farmed by Hall Farm was also surveyed, but has since disappeared. In Shelfanger there have been more boundary changes, but the area of low-lying Lammas meadows, in which several farmers held strips for hay and then put stock onto the land after Lammastide, still survives as traditional meadow. The substantial areas of common that survived in Kenninghall, Shelfanger and Lopham until the end of the eighteenth century were not included by Miller.

The survival of a pre-eighteenth-century field pattern is due to two

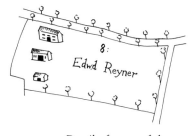

51 Detail of some of the buildings shown on the Swanton Morley map.

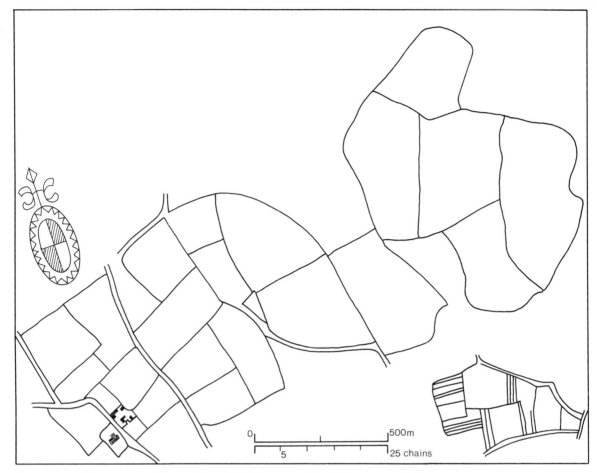

0  500m

5  25 chains

52 John Miller's map of South Lopham, drawn in 1720, showing irregular enclosed fields and farm buildings.

factors. In this region, the medieval field system had disappeared by 1650 and farms were already compact units, surrounded by small manageable fields in which crops were grown and stock kept (one field at Shelfanger Hall, near to the house, was called the milking yard). When the commons in Lopham and Kenninghall and the far smaller one at Fersfield were enclosed some time after 1790, new farms, such as Allotment Farm, South Lopham, were created involving the minimum of reorganization to existing farms. Secondly, the landlord (the absentee Duke of Norfolk) took very little interest in his estate until 1860 when a report revealed years of neglect. There followed a certain amount of improvement, although this involved repair and replacement of the buildings rather than reorganization of the fields. These maps of John Miller are also of particular interest because they show the farm buildings very clearly (illustration 59). Unlike the landscape, the buildings have mostly been swept away or incorporated in the post-1860 improvements.

The John Buckenham maps show a rather different situation in the area south of Watton. Many small hedged fields, strips and closes survived on the De Grey estate in the 1720s. Farms of between 15 and 30 acres were typical, but unlike the Lopham area most of these field boundaries have been altered beyond recognition. Only in the north-east of Merton parish do some of the boundaries of the large fields remain, although the internal strip and multiple strip boundaries have gone. Only to the west of Merton Hall, in an area since emparked, were there large rectangular fields, forming a 236-acre tenanted farm in 1720.

Although the landowner, Lord Walsingham, was an absentee landlord between 1780 and 1830 there was some interest in improvement, and by 1794 the area to the south of Merton Common had been reorganized. The enclosure of Watton in 1801 and Thompson in 1817 presumably resulted in the reorganization of these areas. Merton Common was still unenclosed in 1821, when it was thought that the breaking up of the common would be 'too great a speculation', but as agricultural prospects improved it was decided in 1824 that it would be worth undertaking. As a result, there is little in the Thompson and Merton areas that can still be recognized from the 1723 maps.

A rare early survival from a non-estate area is a 1736 map, redrawn in 1833, of part of the broadland parishes of Ormsby, Hemsby and Filby, showing the estates of Barry Love, Esq., and probably typical of the landholdings of many small proprietors who must often have owned land scattered across several parishes. It shows a haphazard arrangement of small fields and closes, all of which have been swept away.[10]

After these early maps we have a gap of 50 years before any survive for the survey areas. One of the largest eighteenth-century estates was that of Lord Suffield, centred on Gunton in the north-east of the county, and this was surveyed in detail twice, first by H. A. Beiderman in 1784 and again by James Wright in 1835. It is particularly fortunate to have these two sets of plans because they show the estate farms at the beginning and end of a period of improvement. The Biederman survey is neither as complete nor on such a large scale as that of Wright, but between them they show a situation very different to that in the areas already considered. Biederman's maps of Antingham, Roughton, Bradfield and Felmingham show the parish before the enclosure of the commons, while by 1835 the commons have gone; so also have the small, irregular fields and scattered farms that were no doubt rational-ized during the improving years of the Napoleonic Wars.

Several of the estates surveyed possessed books of farm plans, drawn in the second decade of the nineteenth century. Those of the LeStrange and Hare estates date from 1819, while those for the Evans-Lombe farms were drawn in 1811. The farms in the parish of Thompson were surveyed in detail a little later, in 1827. All of these plans show the well-laid-out farms with regular fields aimed at by all improving landlords in the early nineteenth century and a far cry from the situation

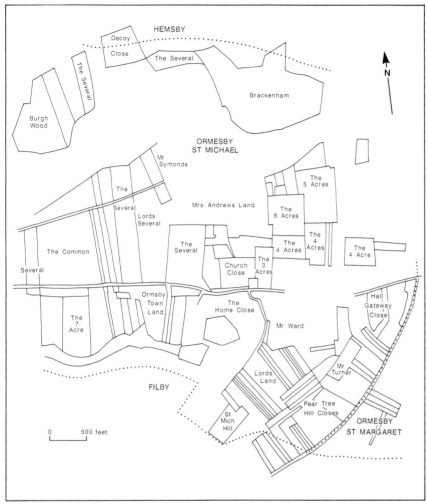

HEMSBY

Decoy
Close

The Several

Brackenham

The Several

The Several

Burgh
Wood

ORMESBY
ST MICHAEL

Mr
Symonds

The
5 Acres

The

Several

Lords
Several

Mrs Andrews Land

The
8 Acres

The
Several

The
4 Acres

The
4
Acres

The
4
Acres

The
4 Acre

The Common

The
3
Acres

Church
Close

Several

Ormsby
Town
Land

Hall
Gateway
Close

The
Home Close

The
7
Acre

Mr Ward

FILBY

Lords
Land

Mr
Turner

St
Mich
Hill

Pear Tree
Hill Closes

ORMESBY
ST MARGARET

0      500 feet

53 Map showing the
scattered estate of B. Love,
Esq., in 1736. Small fields
are spread across the
parishes of Ormsby,
Hemsby and Filby, and this
situation must have been
typical of many other small
estates of the period.

on many of their estates 100 years previously.

Maps were drawn of parishes when they were enclosed by parliamentary act, but were rarely used in this survey. They did not show the individual buildings of the farm and were often of a smaller scale than other maps available of a similar date.

A very important map source available for all parishes, estate and non-estate alike, was the tithe map, marking not only all the fields but also the buildings, and this provided the earliest evidence for farm building layout for many of the farms visited. Using the accompanying tithe apportionment, it was possible to calculate the acreage of farms in the 1840s and this was used as the base for comparing farm acreages across the county. The contrasts between the various survey areas was very clear and these field patterns and farm acreages reflect the farming practice at the time and both the landscape and tenurial history of the area.

The largest farms, some over 1000 acres, were to be found in the

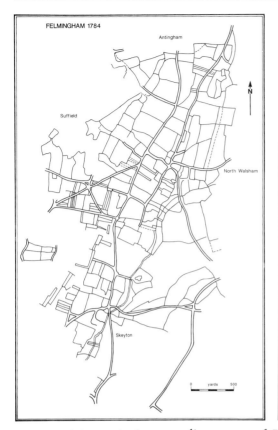

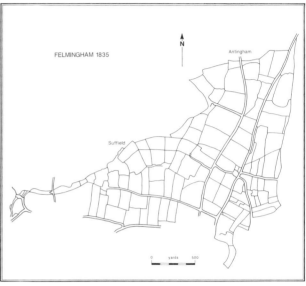

**54** Maps of the parish of Felmingham in (*left*) 1785 and (*right*) 1835. The later maps show the results of enclosure and the rationalization of fields (see also Antingham, illus. 79)

sandiest parts of Breckland, in Stanford and Tottington, enclosed in the late eighteenth century. The LeStrange estate on the light chalky soils around Hunstanton was mainly open sheep walk until the enclosures, when a pattern of huge rectangular fields and farm acreages well above 400 acres was created.

On the Fenland Hare estates the contrast between the earlier enclosed fields and the more regular fen enclosures of 1810 is very apparent. Some new farms were created in the Fens and, elsewhere, land was added to already existing farms.

To the east and south of the county farm and field layout is less regular. By 1840 most of the scattered holdings of a century before had disappeared or been rationalized, but the old field boundaries survived with few modifications alongside the enclosure of the few remaining small areas of common. In the heavier soils of the south and centre of the county far smaller fields survive, suitable for the dairy herds and cultivation of forage crops associated with mixed farming, and the fields around Letton and Marlingford are very clear evidence of the different types of farming found there.

From the maps alone the variety of field patterns and farm layout in Norfolk is already obvious. The huge, regular Napoleonic-period enclosure fields of the chalklands of north-west Norfolk have needed

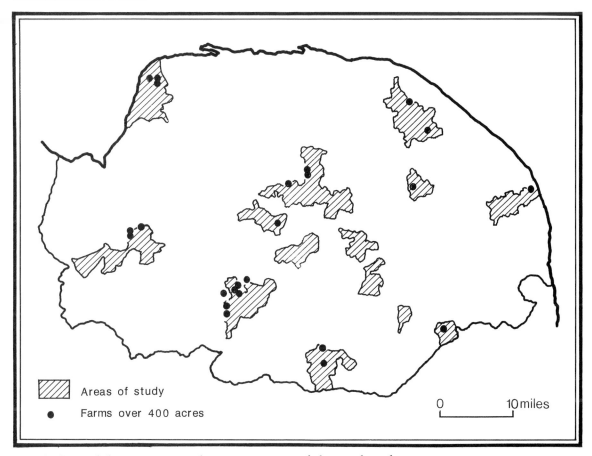

very little modification to suit the requirements of the modern farmer, while the small, irregular and often far older fields of the south have suffered far more destruction in recent times.

Changes in field boundaries have not been confined to the last 40 years and in some areas, such as the Suffield estates, the process of alteration can be seen between the two surveys of 1784 and 1835. It is possible, combining mapwork with fieldwork, to see whether periods of reorganization of the land coincided with the rebuilding of farms. It is against this background of fields and farm layout, some newly created in the nineteenth century, some dating back possibly to Roman times or to the Iron Age, that the agriculture of the various regions can be reconstructed.

55 Map showing the distribution of farms over 400 acres within the survey areas. Very few large farms were found in the Broads or south Norfolk while several of the Fenland, Breckland and chalkland farms were well over 400 acres.

# 9

# South Norfolk

'The southern hundreds partake of the Suffolk practice, and though well cultivated, do not exhibit, in its purity, the Norfolk system of husbandry'[1]

Of the eight sample areas surveyed, six were individual estates and two were made up mainly of owner-occupier farms. The six estates showed a great variety of estate management, which directly affected the buildings and farming types to be found, while the situation in the owner-occupier areas was different again.

In the south of the county, three groups of parishes were studied. The mainly owner-occupier parishes were those around Morningthorpe and Hethel, while estate farms were represented by the two small estates of the Duke of Norfolk and the Brampton-Gurdons. The Duke of Norfolk's extended along the River Waveney in the Lophams, Shelfanger, Fersfield, Earsham, and Kenninghall, while the Brampton-Gurdon estate was in Letton, Cranworth, Reymerston and Southburgh. With acreages of between 4000 and 5000, these two were the smallest estates studied in the county. Both were on heavy land, but here the resemblance ends.

The twelve farms of the Duke of Norfolk were much larger than the Brampton-Gurdon ones, with two over 400 acres as early as 1720. Only a new farm, created out of the common when South Lopham was enclosed in 1815, was less than 50 acres. Around Letton Hall, however, nine of the 28 farms were under 50 acres, with none over 300 and only three over 200 acres.

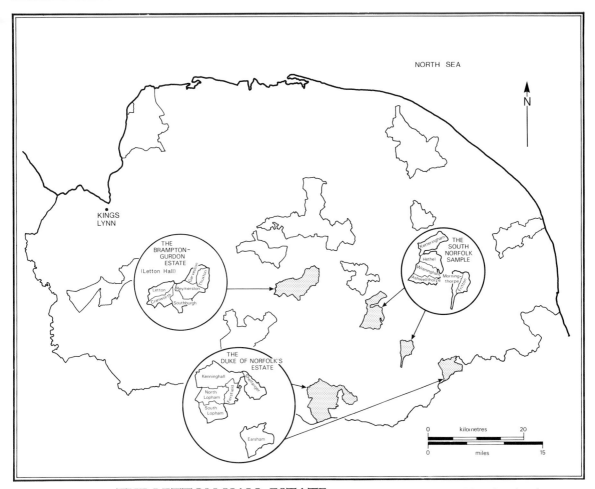

## THE LETTON HALL ESTATE

The Brampton-Gurdons were, on the whole, better landlords than the Dukes of Norfolk. Without the financial backing of great estates elsewhere, they relied on their Norfolk lands for their income and lived at Letton Hall, built 1785–8 when the park was laid out, commons enclosed and fields rearranged. They were relative newcomers to the Norfolk landed community, buying up land from the early eighteenth century. By the 1780s the estate consisted of 11 farms and 1286 acres while by 1838 there were 27 farms and 4498 acres. From 1783 to 1913, when the estate was sold, the family were resident at Letton and much involved in estate improvements. It was almost the only estate to receive a favourable report in the 1861 *Norfolk News* survey of 'The Cottage Homes of England', when the condition of the cottages (about 50) and the estate school were much better than found elsewhere.

### Farm management; steady consolidation

Some early nineteenth-century leases for farms survive; a few, such as

**56** Map showing the sample parishes in south Norfolk.

that granted to Samuel Todd in 1820, were only for a year 'on the same terms as he has held for several years passed'. More typical was the twelve-year lease granted to John Johnson in 1812 for his 286-acre farm in Cranworth. The lease only stipulated the simplest of husbandry restrictions. Grain crops were not to be grown in succession, but must be separated by a break crop. Red clover was not to be grown more than once in eight years. The rent for this large farm was £300 in 1812. Although obviously a substantial farmer, Mr Johnson could not sign the lease, but instead made his mark. On other farms a similar standard crop rotation was stipulated. The first year should be wheat, followed by summer tilth and turnips, then barley or oats and then finally grass. Old meadow land was not to be ploughed up.[2]

Rents of over £1 an acre were set on many of the estate farms during the high prices of the Napoleonic Wars, but proved too high for farmers to pay in the years of low prices that followed the end of hostilities. William Filby's assets were sold up for his creditors in 1819. No doubt the stock on the farm had been run down for some time before the final sale when, on his 231-acre farm, there were seven horses, one calf, 21 cows, three sows, and 20 store pigs. The relatively high number of cows and pigs is an indication of the importance of dairying on these heavy-land farms. The long-standing association of dairying with this area is suggested by the unsubstantiated statement in White's *Norfolk Directory* for 1884 in its entry for Letton, 'famous for its milk and butter as early as the reign of Elizabeth.'

All the surviving leases of the period 1810–1815 show rents of about £1 an acre; these would have risen mid-century and then declined after 1870 to about 25 per cent above their 1815 level. The income from rents, leaving out the park and Home Farm, would therefore have been between £4000 and £5000 a year in the last quarter of the nineteenth century. Figures for estate expenditure only survive for the periods 1821–35, 1851–55 and after 1873,[3] but there is every reason to believe, given the good reputation of the estate, that farms were generally kept in good repair. Up to 1887 the estate only paid half the labour costs of repair bills and supplied the materials, but after that the estate met the full cost of repairs. Other expenses were the maintaining of cottages and the estate school, which was entirely financed until 1873. The amount spent on estate repairs in the 1820s was between £175 and £225 (5–6 per cent of rents received).[4] Expenditure reached a peak of just over £2000 in 1881 and 1884, but was over £1000 p.a. from 1880 to 1886. It was always over £500 p.a. in the last quarter of the nineteenth century. Cottage expenditure was always over £400 at this time and total estate outgoings reached £3089 in 1883 at this time and were always over £2000 between 1880 and 1888. As no figures for rent survive we do not know what percentage of estate income the figures represent, but probably it was over a third and perhaps it is not surprising that the estate had to be sold in 1913.

The picture gained from the archives is of a small, well-run estate commanding good rents throughout the nineteenth century. Estate expenditure was high in the 1880s, presumably in an effort to keep old tenants and attract new ones in the years of depression, and this is reflected in farm layout. While nearly all the farmsteads were of an irregular, unplanned layout in 1840, by 1906 sixteen had been rationalized by the building of yards and livestock sheds in E and U shapes. The only unplanned arrangements remaining were on the smaller farms.

Farms on this estate are mostly medium-sized, with only three over 200 acres and the majority between 50 and 200. The land is heavy, with 17 out of 28 farms on clayey soils. Not surprisingly, crop yields were generally slightly lower than in the other areas studied in the south of the county, with up to 40 per cent of the acreage shown as permanent pasture on the tithe maps.[5]

## The buildings

The most obvious feature of these farms is the dominance of clay lump and the general absence of brick. The barns are usually the oldest buildings and those built before the late eighteenth century were timber-framed, while the later buildings are mainly clay lump. The use of clay lump rather than brick in the nineteenth century suggests that farm improvements were being carried out in the cheapest way possible and point to the problems of underfunding suffered by estates with no income from outside agriculture.

Bearing in mind the size of the farms and the importance of pastoral farming, and the very large areas of common surviving until the 1790s, it is not surprising that the barns are relatively small. Only one has a volume of more than 600 cu. m (21,200 cu. ft) and this late eighteenth-century brick building is on one of the largest farms on the estate (Church Farm, Cranworth). Only three other barns were over 400 cu. m. (14,125 cu. ft.), and, significantly, no barn had more than one threshing floor.

Although there are two barns that can be dated before 1700, by far the majority (eleven out of eighteen) were built between 1700 and 1800. Two-thirds of the barns contain a substantial amount of timber-framing and this type of construction seems to have continued in use until the 1760s. All except two of the pre-1750 barns are timber-framed and only three barns were built entirely of brick. As timber became scarce during the eighteenth century this method of construction was gradually replaced by clay lump, which was widely used for barns after 1800.

The low grain yields and importance of pasture is also reflected in the lack of granaries. Only four were found on the estate, two built before 1800, and all on farms of over 40 acres.

57 Granary, Church Farm, Reymerstone. Granaries are rare in this area. This timber-framed example dates from the eighteenth century.

Virtually all the farms had stables, and a seventeenth-century one with a hay loft or granary above survives at Old Hall Farm, Reymerston, while at Park Farm, Southborough, an eighteenth-century brick stable abuts a slightly later barn. There is very little to indicate the number of horses kept, but sales catalogues suggest eight to ten horses on the farms of about 200 acres.

As this area was predominantly a cattle grazing region we might expect to find greater emphasis on cattle accommodation. The cattle sheds surviving on fourteen of the farms were built between 1840 and 1906, transforming these farmsteads from irregular to U- and E-shaped groups of buildings. Loose boxes were found on four of the largest farms, but this is no more than one would expect in the mainly arable parts of the county. Dairying played an important part in the farm economy, but no evidence for this survives in the farmyards. The dairy was usually within the farmhouse, and milking parlours are not found before 1900.

The exception to this rather unimpressive group of farmsteads is, predictably, the estate Home Farm in Letton. Here there is a complete mid-nineteenth-century group of buildings with a small barn and cart lodges alongside, two cattle and one horse yard with shelter sheds, enclosed boxes and turnip houses. Unlike elsewhere on the estate, the buildings are entirely faced in brick, although, even here, the internal

walls are clay lump. Only on this farm does a gig house and riding horse stable remain.

From the documentary evidence, the estate appears to have been well run. No doubt the farm buildings were adequate, but built of the cheapest building materials to totally functional specifications.

58 Seventeenth-century stables with a hay loft above at Old Hall Farm, Reymerstone.

## THE DUKE OF NORFOLK'S ESTATE

The story of the Duke of Norfolk's estate is very different. While Kenninghall Palace was an important seat of the family until the Act of Attainder in 1536 it was abandoned after the restoration of the Duke's estates under Queen Mary, and from then on the family took little interest in its Norfolk possessions. By the 1850s these consisted of 4350 acres divided into twelve farms and let at an annual rent of £4827.

### Farm management; neglect and improvement

In 1720 John Miller was commissioned to survey seven of the Duke of Norfolk's farm (see illustration 52). All of them were, by the standards of the day, extremely large, being over 300 acres with two over 400 acres.

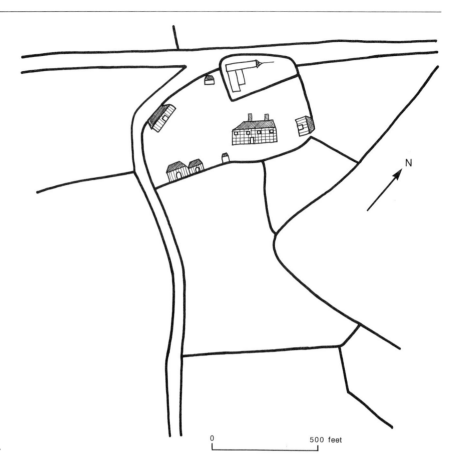

**59** Farm buildings at
Fersfield Hall, redrawn
from the John Miller map.

0                500 feet

The plans show the farm buildings as sketches in flattened perspective.
The houses are distinguished from the farm buildings not only by
having chimneys, but also by a different shading. None of the farmsteads
have a regular layout and on several there appears to have been more
than one barn. A smaller building, possibly a stable, is shown on several
of the plans. The only building shown on Miller's map to survive is a
typical early eighteenth-century long barn at Fersfield Hall. By the time
of the drawing of the tithe maps in the late 1830s and early 1840s many
new buildings had been added, although most of those from the 1720s
were still there. In 1861 the 17th Duke of Norfolk commissioned a
survey of his Norfolk estates to be undertaken by the well-known
Holkham agent William Keary. His report, now in the Norfolk Record
Office, was very critical. The main problem was that the land was
heavy and needed urgent draining, but there was nothing more
permanent or efficient than bush drains to be found anywhere on the
estate. These drains, always put in at the tenant's expense, only lasted
ten or twelve years. The buildings were also in a poor state and 'not
adapted to the present mode of farming'. They were mostly of wood
or clay lump with thatched roofs, and Keary reckoned they needed

entirely replacing. Clay lump was not suitable for housing cattle because they damaged it with their horns. There were more barns than necessary, but a lack of bullock sheds and yards, which meant there was no way of making the straw into good manure.

The two main recommendations Keary made were, firstly, that proper pipe drainage for the land should be installed. He suggested the system developed at Holkham whereby the landlord was responsible for laying the pipes and kept a team of men regularly employed for this. He then charged the tenant 50 per cent of the cost. Secondly, new buildings should be erected entirely at the landlord's expense and he should also be responsible for repairs.

The fact that the estate needed good tenants if it was to be made more productive was stressed over and over again by Keary; and the provision of new buildings and well-drained land would encourage such men. The example of 'improving tenants' was much needed on the estate. The policy of simply taking the rent and doing nothing, which had been followed by the previous dukes, may have meant they kept most of the rent collected, but Keary pointed out that it was very short-sighted because rents could not rise. The farms had mostly been let on yearly tenancies, but Keary thought that longer leases, which encouraged the tenant to make improvements, were far better. 'Under a lease (good tenants having been selected), with fair and liberal covenants, the land is generally improved in value by the combined skills and capital of such men; and at its termination, a legitimate opportunity, not considered grievous by the tenant, arises to the landlord, to relet, under a fresh lease, at an increased rent due to the improved condition of the farm.'

Keary concluded his damning report by saying, 'The time has come when a considerable outlay must be made if this property is to be raised to a condition worthy of its hereditary owner.'

The buildings that remain and the plans surviving at Arundel show that the result of this report was an intense campaign of rebuilding, and the result is a group of farms looking entirely different from those around Cranworth.

## The buildings

The Duke of Norfolk's farms are remarkable for their size. Acreages were surprisingly constant from 1720 to 1840 when half the estate farms were over 300 acres and only two were under 50 acres. We might therefore expect extensive ranges of buildings and large barns, yet this is not usually the case. One barn, the only one to survive that is shown on the 1720 map, at Fersfield Hall, has two threshing floors and a volume of 600 cu. m. (21,200 cu. ft). The rest were considerably smaller (between 200 and 500 cu. m), and this must surely be an indication of the difficulty of growing cereals prior to the introduction of tile drainage.

Unlike the two other areas studied in the south, none of the surviving buildings can be dated before 1700. The three earliest are timber-framed, while another timber-framed one is dated 1794, a late example of this technique. One early nineteenth-century barn is of clay lump while two of the three brick barns are on farms completely rebuilt after 1860. The only explanation for the lack of early barns here, while they are found on neighbouring owner-occupier farms, is that they had been so neglected that they needed completely replacing by the mid-nineteenth century. The Dukes of Norfolk, with increasing urban rentals from their Sheffield estates, had the capital to contemplate such a project. It is unusual to find barns being built in the second half of the nineteenth century, yet a third of the surviving barns here are of that period.

Keary was very critical of the use of clay lump as a building material, especially for cattle sheds, yet a few do survive. 'A new clay lump and slate cart lodge' described by Keary at Lodge Farm, Fersfield, still remains. At Boyland New Farm, the buildings were described as being of clay lump and thatch and in 'fair repair'. Clay lump cart sheds, shelter sheds and a barn remain, although the stables have been rebuilt in brick, presumably after 1860. There are no brick buildings at Lopham New Farm, a completely new farm built when the parish was enclosed in 1815. Keary wrote that the carthorse stable and cow house needed replacing and, if this work was done, clay lump was used. At Shelfanger Hall, the buildings were all clay lump 'erected by the tenant to no plan at all'. The buildings remain somewhat scattered: some new brick yards were built although the clay lump and weatherboard cart shed with a granary over survives.

The policy of the Duke of Norfolk seems to have varied from farm to farm after 1861. In some a few new buildings, particularly stables, were erected, but with no effort to integrate them into the plan. On others complete E-shaped ranges were built. At Fersfield Hall nothing but the early barn remains, although the 1906 map shows extensive ranges, which must have replaced the 'old sheds for cattle of thorn faggotts and thatch erected by the tenant' there in 1860.

Of great interest is the plan of the proposed rebuilding at Hall Farm, South Lopham, where Keary reported that 'the buildings, except for the barn, were not worth repairing and should be pulled down and rebuilt'. In fact everything, including the barn, was pulled down and we have the finest 'model' farm in the south Norfolk area. As we would expect, the barn is small, but there are three yards for stock (two for bullocks and a third for young stock) and one for cows. There is both a cake and turnip house for intensive feeding of stock, but no loose boxes or covered yards. There are three separate horse yards with stables, each housing probably six horses with an adjacent cutting

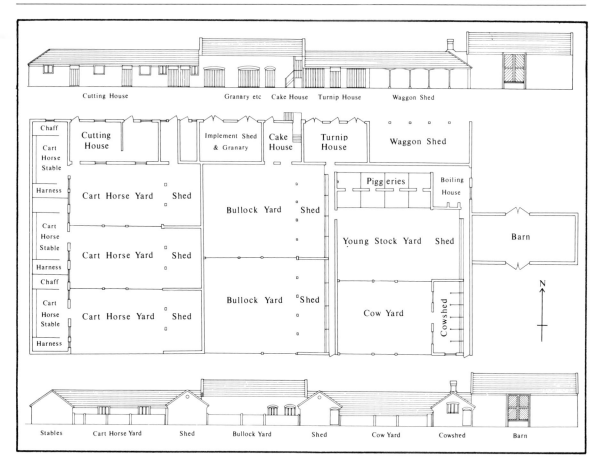

Cutting House  Granary etc  Cake House  Turnip House  Waggon Shed

| Chaff | Cutting House | | Implement Shed & Granary | Cake House | Turnip House | Waggon Shed | |
| Cart Horse Stable | | | | | | | |
| Harness | Cart Horse Yard | Shed | | | Piggeries | Boiling House | Barn |
| Cart Horse Stable | Cart Horse Yard | Shed | Bullock Yard | Shed | Young Stock Yard | Shed | |
| Harness | | | | | | | |
| Chaff | | | Bullock Yard | Shed | | Cowshed | |
| Cart Horse Stable | Cart Horse Yard | Shed | | | Cow Yard | | |
| Harness | | | | | | | |

N

Stables  Cart Horse Yard  Shed  Bullock Yard  Shed  Cow Yard  Cowshed  Barn

house for chopping straw into chaff. Piggeries with a boiling house and a wagon lodge and implement shed with a granary above complete this well-planned complex designed to serve a farm of 320 acres.

When we turn to consider the features of individual buildings elsewhere, we find that no stables survive from before 1800 and none have haylofts; an indication in itself that the stables are of a later date. There are more granaries in this part of south Norfolk than in the others studied. They were found on two thirds of the farms and four of the six were over cart lodges. It may seem strange that they were so important, while barns were relatively unimpressive, but in a mainly livestock area and on farms of large acreages it was important to have a good dry store for stock feed for the winter.

At Letton there was a resident and paternalistic landlord taking an interest in his estate, but relying on agricultural rent for his income. This meant that with the decline in rent after 1870 he had not the reserves of money made outside agriculture to modernize and replace older buildings with the more durable brick and tiled livestock sheds to be seen, for instance, on the Duke of Norfolk's estates. The Duke

60 Plan with elevations of Hall Farm, South Lopham, drawn when the farm was rebuilt in 1862. Typical of a mid-century farmstead, the yards and livestock sheds are of far greater importance than the barn.

**61** The granary over a cart lodge at Place Farm, Kenninghall.
(*top*) Exterior view
(*bottom*) The wide external staircase leads into the loft, which is divided into bins.

of Norfolk, on the other hand, was an absentee landlord who relied on agents for information, but was not short of money for the improvements necessary to keep tenants on the estate. These findings support the view that, whilst the income from agricultural rents could not support substantial building schemes after 1870, landowners with income generated elsewhere continued to invest in their farms. This 'uneconomic investment was therefore one of the costs of owning the land'.[6] Here we have two estates on similar soils and broadly within the same agricultural region, but managed very differently; a fact supported by both the documentary and building evidence.

# THE HETHEL AND MORNINGTHORPE REGION

The third region studied in south Norfolk had yet another set of characteristics. It consisted of two blocks, one covering the parishes of Ashwellthorpe, Wrenningham, Hethel and Ketteringham, and the other a few miles to the south-east included Fritton and Morningthorpe. A group of nineteen farms was visited, although the documentary background for a further 23 was assembled. The area contained a mixture of tenants of small estates (of mostly between 1000 and 1200 acres) and owner-occupiers. Lord Bernes owned land in Ashwellthorpe while much of Hethel was owned by a branch of the Gurney family. In contrast, half of the farmers in Fritton were owner-occupiers but the Irbys of Boyland Hall and the Revd Howe also owned land there. Both families also owned land in Morningthorpe. Ketteringham was the only parish that was part of a larger estate. The Boileau family of Ketteringham Hall owned about 4000 acres.

## Farm management; individual owners and a farming diary

We know little about the type of management practised on any of these estates because the documentary evidence is scrappy. Estates of just over 1000 acres would produce a large enough income to allow the owner to live modestly in the style of a gentleman. Mr Wilson, with lands in Ashwellthorpe, Wrenningham and Fundenhall, had a rent roll of £1,265 in 1809, but people like him would have accumulated little capital for estate repairs and so we would not expect to find any grand schemes for improvement to be undertaken here.

No estate surveys for the area exist, and so the tithe maps were the only nineteenth-century maps consulted. In the 1840s only two of the farms in these parishes were over 300 acres, both on the Boileau estate in Ketteringham. The majority (27 out of 40) were under 100 acres. Most of the farms were compact with only a few outlying fields, although a few remnants of intermingled strips survived on the west side of Fritton Common. We would expect the small size of farms and the lack of money for investment to be reflected in the buildings.

The most interesting document surviving from this area is a diary kept by a member of the Howe family at Morningthorpe from 1803 to 1810.[7] The Revd Thomas Howe owned a small estate in Morningthorpe of about 150 acres and farmed about 40 acres of it from the manor house. The rest was let to Mr Claxton at Church Farm. The two men seem to have worked very much together, sharing men and even each others' barn space. Thomas Howe's diary describes a mixed farm with Chinese pigs, cows and sheep being kept. Turnips and vetches were grown as break crops while barley, wheat and oats were all produced on the farm.

The diary begins in January 1803, when winter work on the farm consisted mainly of muck spreading and the last of the wheat was threshed and sold. Two acres 'off part of Fritton little close' yielded 19½ coombes. By 1840 the average yield in Morningthorpe was between six and eight coombes per acre,[8] so Howe was doing well that year.

By March, muck spreading was finished and trees were being trimmed and leaves raked up. A few new trees were planted. The last of the oats were threshed for seed. Lambing began on March 16th. April began with the sowing of the oats and the selling of spare seed. The first of the calves was born and the cows were put on 'the Grove to pick about' as the hay was nearly finished. The last of the wheat and oats was threshed at the end of April. Seven days were spent threshing and two days dressing to produce six coombes, two bushels of wheat and two coombes, three bushels of oats. This low figure was blamed on the amount of mildew in the crop.

By May, all the hay was finished and there was still little grass growth because the weather was cold, so Howe was forced to feed his horses wheat chaff. June tasks included emptying the yards of muck, cutting vetches, and furrowing and harrowing the summerley for turnips. In July the hay was cut and the horses could be turned out on the grass at night. It took seven men seven days to mow two pieces 'hardly an acre a day per man, but this year, it cut particularly badly.' By 16th July the hay was all stacked and by the 22nd all the vetches had been cut for the horses. The wheat was harvested between 13th and 18th August. The dates of the barley harvest are not mentioned, but 22 coombes were threshed in eight days in September. By October the winter tasks were well under way with muck spreading and ploughing. Ten coombes of wheat were threshed off the 'near two acres'; not a high yield for the area. In December the cows' feed was changed to turnips and the farming year began again.

There were few changes in the pattern over the years. By 1810 a threshing machine was used to thresh the wheat and a total of 32 coombes was produced for sale. The general picture is of small-scale mixed farming. Although the crops and rotations were those of progressive farming the fields were still small and scattered. In contrast, by 1840 most of the fields were held in a block except for two small ones to the south-west of the main area.

Nothing of the Revd Howe's farmstead survives but a record in the diary illustrates the chequered history that the timber-framed buildings traditionally associated with this area frequently experienced. An entry for the end of January 1803 reads, 'Carpenters making a cart shed out of the old carpenter's shop and lime house by taking away one floor, and taking out one side of the building (note: this building was brought by my great grandfather from Carlton Rode which could not be less than 100 years ago, and set up where it is).'

## The buildings

The most striking feature of this group of farms was the very high survival rate of early timber-framed barns. Nine out of the 22 barns visited in this area were built before 1700 and all except one of these was timber-framed. Early cart lodges and stables also survived on many farms. The use of bricks in this area is mainly confined to the period after 1700. Some of the early barns were very large (four had a volume of over 500 cu. m; 17,660 cu. ft), but none had more than one threshing floor. Generally, the size of the barn does not seem to be related to its age or the size of the farm it served.

There is a concentration of fine early barns in Hethel with three neighbouring farms in the south-east of the parish all containing at least one seventeenth-century barn as well as seventeenth or early eighteenth-century cart lodges. The 156-acre Church Farm at Hethel was unusual in that not only was there a timber-framed seventeenth-century barn (a second 'very old' thatched barn was said to have been demolished within living memory) with an early stable and cart lodge, but it was the only farm in the area to have achieved an E-shape layout by 1840. The farm was occupied by John Claxton, who was perhaps related to the Claxton farming in Morningthorpe and Fritton. Next door at Hill Farm (296 acres) are two barns, one of which is seventeenth

**62** Seventeenth-century timber-framed stables with hay lofts above, Church Farm, Hethel.

century, as well as an early eighteenth-century cart lodge and stable with loft over. Both Church Farm and Hill Farm were owned by Hudson Gurney, a member of the banking family and therefore not short of money for investment in his farms. Certainly both Church and Hill Farms were well endowed with buildings.

In the eighteenth century the Beevor family had considerable estates in Hethel and lived at Hethel Hall, where Thomas Beevor ran the Home Farm. He was visited by Arthur Young who was impressed by the lengths he went to to conserve manure, even collecting the fallen leaves from the parkland around the house to augment the straw in the yards. Arthur Young mentioned specifically the existence of yards in which 20 cows, 14 young calves and 11 horses were kept. There were also 40 pigs on the farm and all together they produced 14,000 large loads of dung. These are the earliest yards mentioned in Norfolk and it is a pity the site has now disappeared under the Lotus car works.[9]

A much more impressive group of buildings survived at the neighbouring Corporation Farm, so called because it was owned by the Great Hospital from the thirteenth century, and after 1835 by Norwich Corporation who took over the administration of the city charities. The farm was therefore unlikely to have received much personal attention from the owner. On this 200-acre farm there were two substantial seventeenth-century barns as well as stables of a similar date on the end of one of the barns. That these large early barns were not confined to extensive farms is shown by the fact that on three farms in Fritton, one of 67, one of 47 and one of 46 acres, there were barns with capacities of 515 and 642 cu. m (18,190 and 22,700 cu. ft) and two with a combined capacity of over 500 cu. m (17,660 cu. ft).

Substantial early buildings are found on all sizes of farm in the region and in the hands of various owners and owner-occupiers. There is no common denominator linking them to any size, landlord or type of tenure. Generally, the barns are slightly larger than those in the richest grain-growing area of Wales (Breconshire), which we would expect to be somewhat less productive than East Anglia.[10]

The eighteenth century saw a shift from timber-frame to brick building. A very large (687 cu. m; 24,260 cu. ft) eighteenth-century barn remains at Ashwellthorpe. It is the only barn with two threshing floors in this area and was built to serve a well-laid-out owner-occupier farm of only 136 acres. The earliest dated building in this area was a brick barn at Morningthorpe, dated, both inside and outside, 1806.

Only on a few farms were buildings constructed entirely of clay lump, although it was often used for patching and repairing older buildings. Church Farm, Morningthorpe is the only farm with a clay lump barn. It has a brick front, but the rest of the building and outshuts are clay lump and dated 1830. This is the largest clay lump building in this area and is a good-sized barn (513 cu. m; 18,100 cu. ft). Most of the

buildings on this farm, including the stable, cart lodges and shelter sheds, are also of clay lump and possibly all of one build.

On several other farms the typical nineteenth-century additions, such as shelter sheds and cart lodges as well as a few stables, are of clay lump in spite of the damage livestock, particularly horned cattle, could do. Surprisingly, two farms in Fritton are built entirely of brick, but they are exceptional. No flint is used in this area, except as a plinth for clay lump and timber-framed buildings.

A wide variety of stables survive on these farms, with three dating from before 1700. One of these is in the end of a barn, which seems to be the most usual position for early stables, but two are free-standing. Only one has a hay loft. Most of the stables remaining are brick eighteenth- or clay lump nineteenth-century buildings. The majority (eleven) face east and in nearly all the horses faced the rear wall rather than the gable when they were stalled. The floor area varied from 42 to 168 sq. m (450 to 1800 sq. ft), but with only two being more than 140 sq. m (1500 sq. ft). At Church Farm, Ashwellthorpe, the stable measured 150 sq. m (1600 sq. ft) and ten horses were kept, while at Ivy House, Ketteringham, twelve horses were kept on 144 sq. m (1550 sq. ft). Most of the stables were under 100 sq. m (1075 sq. ft). Church Farm, Ashwellthorpe, was 142 acres, which gives a figure of about one horse for every 15 acres; a very reasonable one on this heavy land. Ivy House

63 Seventeenth-century timber-framed barn, Corporation Farm, Hethel. The steep pitch of this roof suggests that inside there is evidence of a seventeenth-century date. This is one of two early barns on this 200-acre farm and is part of a group of remarkably high quality seventeenth- and early eighteenth-century buildings (for the barn interior, see illustration 38).

Farm was 381 acres, but only had twelve horses, which seems very low. About half of the stables have hay lofts and most opened onto yards.

Perhaps a surprising feature of these south Norfolk farms is the lack of granaries. Only five farms had granaries on them, three of which were over cart lodges. Two were over stables, which cannot have been an ideal arrangement as the damp rising from the hot horses coming in from work would have tainted the grain; but perhaps they were in fact converted hay lofts.

Nearly all the farms had one cattle yard and several had two, dating from the nineteenth century. Documentary evidence indicates that livestock were an important element in the economy of the area. The Revd Howe's diary suggests that cattle were being kept in yards by 1800 and some of the surviving shelter sheds may be of that date. Those at Church Farm, Hethel, are probably late eighteenth century.

The tithe map shows that by 1840 only one farm had an E-shaped layout, allowing for the keeping of cattle in yards between shelter sheds on the south side of a barn, and thirteen plans were very irregular with small yards in inconvenient corners. By 1906 the situation had changed, with six farms having a regular E-shaped arrangement and only seven still being irregular. At Hill Farm, Hethel, a nineteenth-century covered yard survives. Very few of these were built, although they were recommended by the agricultural improvers. Other known Norfolk examples are on the home farms of large estates. It is therefore all the more surprising to find this tenanted farm on the small Hudson-Gurney estate with such an expensive and progressive building.

Most of the cart lodges in this area were clay lump and nineteenth century, but one appeared to be seventeenth century. We do not usually expect to find cart lodges surviving from such an early date although we know they existed in the Middle Ages. Remembering the words of Revd Howe's diary, perhaps, like his, this one started its life serving a different function.

Buildings specifically designed to house riding horses and a gig are found on only six of the farms and only two of these were under 100 acres. They were mostly late eighteenth or nineteenth century, although one was in a building possibly dating from the seventeenth century but much altered. The existence of these buildings suggests something about the social standing of the farmer, but the lack of them does not mean that the farmer did not possess a riding horse or trap. Most farmers must have had at least one such horse, but it could well have been kept in the partitioned-off section of the carthorse stable.

## CONCLUSIONS

We should now look at these farms of south Norfolk as a whole and decide whether they suffered from undercapitalization as a result of being either owner-occupied or on small estates. In fact, there is no obvious·distinction to be made between the buildings on the various small estates themselves, or between them and the owner-occupier farms. There was no shortage of capital on the Duke of Norfolk's estates, but until the 1860s he chose to neglect them. The relatively high survival rate of very substantial barns from the period before 1720 is an indication that there was no lack of finance for building in that period, and that good-sized barns were required (four of the nine are over 500 cu. m, or 17,660 cu. ft, in volume) in what has traditionally been regarded as a heavy soil livestock area. Again, during the eighteenth century, adequate brick barns were built and a very large one (687 cu. m; 24,260 cu. ft) with two threshing floors is dated as late as 1833. However, the later (post-1850) additions, mainly for livestock, are not of such a high standard. They are mostly of clay lump. The only exception to this is the late nineteenth-century covered yard in Hethel: a development usually only associated with the most progressive of estates.

Having looked at these three sample groups in the south, is there anything that unites them as a region and delineates the area from other parts of the county?

One important uniting factor is the use of timber-framing, replaced by clay lump in the nineteenth century; the use of which is a reflection not only of the geology of the area but also of the general lack of landlord capital.

When we move on to consider the improvements made at the end of the century there is a very clear division between those landlords with income from outside agriculture, such as the Hudson-Gurneys and the Dukes of Norfolk, and those without support, such as the Brampton-Gurdons.

There is little except the geology to link this area into a distinct region. Generally the differences are more obvious than the similarities.

64 Clay lump stable, Malthouse Farm, Fritton. This unusual little building with one original lunette-style stable window surviving would have been large enough to house the two horses needed on this 33-acre farm.

# 10

# West Norfolk

'The western division is either marshy, lowland, applied chiefly to the dairy, after the manner of Cambridgeshire, or open sheep walks, extensive heaths whose flocks are sheep and rabbits; or newly enclosed country, in which no general plan of management has yet taken place'[1]

As William Marshall found, the western side of the county is a far less homogeneous region than the predominantly boulder clay south, but it is dominated by great estates, three of which were studied as part of this sample area. The Hare, the LeStrange and the Walsingham estates are all on different soils, which partly explains the different farming systems found.

The soils of the region vary from the sandy Breckland farms of Lord Walsingham around the family seat at Merton in the south, to the light chalky soils of the LeStrange estates, centred on Hunstanton in the north. In the extreme west of the county near Downham Market are the loams and fen soils of the Hares. The result, not surprisingly, is a great variety of agricultural practice.

The early histories of these estates are remarkably similar. All three families were well established by 1600 and the family seat of each was a fine Elizabethan house, either improved or completely rebuilt in Elizabethan style in the nineteenth century. The LeStranges are the oldest family, being established at Hunstanton by 1200. Sir Thomas De Grey became the owner of the manor of Merton in 1306, beginning the family connection with the Breckland area. His descendant William De Grey was made Baron Walsingham in 1780. The third estate was founded by Sir Nicholas Hare, a lawyer and politician. He was a privy councillor and Keeper of the Great Seal for Mary Tudor, buying Stow

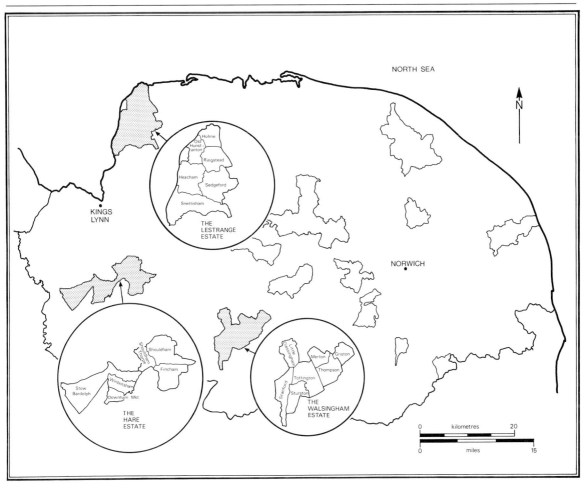

65 Map showing sample parishes in west Norfolk.

Bardolph in 1553; his family too have been there ever since. By the 1870s all these three family estates had grown to cover over 8000 acres each.

## THE WALSINGHAM ESTATE

By far the most difficult land to farm was that on much of the Walsingham estate. Of the 26 farms, only two were on good loam soil. Five were on sandy peats, ten on sandy loams and nine on very poor acid sands; and the largest farms (over 700 acres), were to be found on this last type of soil. The better land was in the parishes of Thompson and Merton while the worst were on the sandy heaths or brecks of Stanford and Tottington.

### Farm management; sheep, silage and ambitious improvements

One of the things that distinguishes these western regions from the others studied is the importance of sheep within the farming system.

Traditionally it was the leggy and agile Norfolk Horn that were kept in the brecks. It was difficult to curb their wandering habits so they were ideal for open heathland grazing but quite unsuited to enclosed pastures. A bad lambing for Breckland sheep farmers could affect the supply of store lambs throughout the region. In 1780, 'The heat and drought of the latter part of the summer has in many places been disastrous to the aftergrass and the turnips; this has introduced a stagnation of purchasing lambs at Ipswich fair where 100,000 are usually sent by the farmers of the open country.'[2] Similarly, tenants were frequently unable to pay rent until after the lambs, sheep or wool had been sold. Together, Thompson farmers grazed 1000 sheep on the open sheep walk in 1789 but this had increased to 1300 by 1812. By the 1840s the Norfolk Horn had declined greatly in popularity as more of the open heath was enclosed and was being replaced by more favoured commercial varieties. Lord Walsingham kept a flock of prize South Down ewes and tups at Merton and was selling to Germany by the 1860s at a time when his one-month-old lambs were said to be worth £50 a piece.[3] The flock was finally sold in the 1880s to pay debts. The story of agriculture in the Breckland area is unique in Norfolk, being based upon the disastrous combination of sheep and rabbits in the Middle Ages, which led to soil erosion and sand storms, a frequent hazard in dry, windy seasons.

Perhaps it was his interest in livestock that led to Lord Walsingham's enthusiasm for the development of silage. He promoted the use of silos in Norfolk and by 1886 there were 77, the third largest figure per county in England. He was chairman of a Royal Commission looking at the potential of silage. However there were many problems in its production and attempts were dropped until the early twentieth century.[4] None of these early silos have been identified on this survey.

Sheep grazing did not produce as high an income as arable, and so the estate was anxious to break up the heaths, wherever possible, for cropping. This frequently led to conflict between the tenants and their landlord. Traditionally, a type of infield-outfield farming had been practised in shifts of varying duration and intensity. At Merton in 1775 recently reclaimed land was regarded as outfield and grew grain only one in five years, while on the old arable it was one in four. This resulted in different rents for land managed under different systems; three shillings for infield, two shillings to two and six pence for outfield and two shillings for open heath.[5]

At Starston in 1780 100 acres of warren were ploughed each year, but it is not clear how long it remained under cultivation. Warrens were still important as 1400 dozen rabbits were to remain on the land. The rent was four shillings an acre for this 1800-acre farm.[6]

Parliamentary enclosure was not important before 1800 in this area. There had only been nineteen acts affecting Breckland before 1801, but there were 26 between 1801 and 1817.[7] Once the land had been enclosed it had to be improved, and to bring this very light land into permanent cultivation large quantities of marl had to be spread on the land. Leases from the early nineteenth century required that 75 loads per acre should be applied each year for the first four years, 50 loads for the next four years and 25 loads for the rest of the lease, which might run for 12 or 18 years. The problem was that the farmers claimed these very high marling levels made the land unhealthy for sheep. Mr Lincoln of Tottington claimed in 1836 that he had lost 200 lambs 'being warped in consequence of claying land'.[8] Warping is a sheep disease frequently mentioned by farmers, probably caused by mineral deficiency resulting in this case from extensive claying and is most likely to have been a disease known nowadays as staggers. When another tenant, Mr Taylor, went bankrupt in 1878, his solicitor claimed that the land was 'unhealthy for sheep and stock, and crops were eaten by game'. His sheep had died by scores and he had lost £300 'by sheep and stock and the 100s of hares on the farm'.

In spite of the landlord's efforts, conversion to arable made slow progress. By the 1840s only 20 per cent of Stanford was arable. No wheat was grown and although a quarter of the arable was used for barley, the yields were low (16–24 bushels per acre). Similarly the turnip crops were poor when compared with the rest of the county.[9] The Walsingham estate documents suggest that the tithe evidence used by Kain may be giving too pessimistic a picture. Wheat barns as well as barley barns are mentioned on most of the estate farms in the 1860s and wheat is shown in the field books of the 1820s.

The survival of documentary evidence for farming practices on the Walsingham estate is patchy. The earliest documents consulted were the maps of Thompson and Merton drawn in 1723 by John Buckenham and described earlier. Most of the landscape of small irregular fields shown on them disappeared over the next 100 years. In Thompson this is likely to have taken place at the time of enclosure in 1824.

The parishes of Stanford and Sturston were added to the estate in 1769 and the documents show that at this date schemes for tree planting and the creation of tree nurseries were the most popular activities. In spite of the fact that William De Grey only visited his estates rarely, plans for improvements were proposed; local expert opinion was, however, sceptical. Ralph Cauldwell, the Holkham agent, travelled through the area in 1780 and wrote to Lord Walsingham, 'When I rode about your estates, I observed the best soils towards the extreme parts of your land, and could it be considered to enclose and cultivate with corn and cattle some of those parts and leave the worst for rabbits, it might suit every purpose.' Not to be deterred, plans for the enclosure of Stanford went ahead; two new farms were created there in 1780, to be let at a rent of four shillings per acre, and negotiations for tenants began. William Smith wrote to William Black the agent stating the buildings he required if he were to take on Lodge Farm. If 100 acres of warren were to be brought into cultivation every year, a barn 24.4 by 6.1 metres (80 by 20 feet) was needed. After negotiation with the agent he was prepared to accept a barn 18.3 by 5.5 metres (60 by 18 feet) 'with proper lean-tos for the support of it, which small barn will be absolutely necessary for the corn grown on the land. I shall not have enough stable room to contain my horses without an additional one to hold 10 horses at least.'[10] The dove house was to be converted into a carpenters' shop with a granary above. Pigeons were no longer the highly prized winter meat they had been; instead they were regarded as vermin on the new cereal farms. The agent was still not prepared to accept these terms. 'I continue of the opinion that a barn 3 bays near Sturston Lodge will be sufficient while a warren is permitted upon the estate, for a barn of the same size upon the Stanford farm will in my opinion be necessary which is an addition of six bays to what Mr Smith now has, who is to be the occupier of the whole.'[11] Later, as negotiations with the tenant dragged on the agent wrote to Lord Walsingham, 'The Norfolk farmers have long since ceased to be humble dependents; we must therefore bear with their language which is to be treated on equal terms. If you wish to be master of your estate, you must reject Mr Smith; if you wish for ease and less profit, you must accept him on the best terms that can be made.' He pointed out, 'The landlords and tenants now feel the inconvenience of great farms because of the difficulty of finding those who have capital for such an undertaking. This alone is the hazard of refusing Mr Smith.'[12] Mr Mathews for instance had resigned the tenancy of a farm at Stanford 'due to lack of capital'.[13]

Nothing remains of Mr Smith's farm, which is now in the 'battle' area, but compared with other barns found nearby Mr Smith's requirements seem very modest.

After the boom years of the Napoleonic Wars, when even Mr Smith growing grain in ploughed-up rabbit warrens would have made a profit, there were years of uncertainty. In 1821 the agent wrote to Lord Walsingham that the breaking up of Thompson Common would be too great a speculation, but by 1824 he felt that the prospects looked better and it would be 'a very great improvement'. Gradually many of the estate's farms were improved. In 1827 Rowland Andrew's farm in Merton had a newly erected farmhouse and outbuildings, while Nathaniel Weston's farm in Great Ellingham and Deopham had been improved to such an extent by the enclosure of Great Ellingham Common in 1800, that an increase of rent seemed justified. In contrast, the rent of another farm in Merton was reduced. 'The soil of this farm is of a poor, light, sandy quality and very uncertain as to produce in hot seasons.'[14]

Plans of the six farms in Thompson were drawn in 1827 and cropping in the fields was recorded 1826–8. The best husbandry techniques of the period were adopted, in that cereal crops of barley, wheat, oats and rye were alternated with either turnips or grass. Nowhere were two crops of cereal grown in succession.

From 1840 the 5th Lord Walsingham was resident at Merton and by his own account taking a great interest in estate improvement. 'Though much was done between 1830 and 40, very much remained to be done, when about that time the present owner came into possession...the farm houses were insufficient, large tracts of land paying little rent were

**66** Griston Hall Farm, early eighteenth-century brick barn
(*top*) Exterior
(*bottom*) Interior

occupied principally by rabbit warrens. Since that date churches have been restored, a school built, residences suitable for clergymen erected . . . Five new and large farmhouses with necessary buildings have been erected and others much enlarged and improved. The land is generally in a much better state of cultivation.'[15]

## Clay lump to palatial barns

A few valuations and descriptions of premises in the 1850s and 60s survive. Of those on the better soils, Griston Hall is the only one remaining. This 311-acre farm was described in 1858 as having a wagon lodge, a gig house with granary over, a range of piggeries, two loose boxes, a cow house, a riding stable with a two-horse yard and shed, a barn with lean-tos, cart horse stables, chaff house and hay loft, a second brick barn with lean-to turnip house, bullock lodge and yard, a four-bay wagon lodge and implement shed as well as a field barn.[16] Not all the buildings of this substantial complex survive. Of the two barns, the older is timber-framed and probably seventeenth century, while the brick barn is early eighteenth. Most of the other buildings are clay lump. The clay lump shelter shed, attached to the now crumbling field barn and dating from the early nineteenth century has a very primitive

**67** Remains of a large two-threshing-floor barn at Westmere Farm, Tottington.

68 Unusual lozenge-shaped ventilation holes at Mortimer's Farm, Tottington.

and unusual roof. There are no timber roof supports; instead there is simply a pile of small branches supported by tie beams and then thatched over with reed to form a pitched roof.

In contrast, Westmere Farm was one of the late eighteenth-century creations on the very sandy soils of Tottingham and only the huge, much-altered barn survives. In 1869 there was a second barn with a lean-to chaff and straw house, a bullock shed, a cart-horse stable for ten horses, a cow house for ten cows, a riding-horse stable, a gig house, granary, stack yard, carpenter's shop, wagon lodge, bullock shed, chaff cutting house, blacksmith's shop and turnip shed. Unlike the older farms, the barn, built of dressed flint on a brick plinth, was a fine building with two threshing floors and we can assume that the second barn was similar. The other barn surviving in Tottingham, at Mortimer's farm, is of a similar design. The rent for this 593-acre farm, some of which was sheep walk, was £365, to be raised to £400 in 1869.[17] Like Griston Hall, this newly created farm had a very substantial set of buildings, but of a very different design and apparently, from what little remains, of a very high standard.

Only two other estate farms survive in anything like a complete form. College Farm, Thompson, is an extensive range of brick buildings comprising a porched barn, lofted stable, shelter sheds and gig house dating from the late eighteenth century. The regular layout of the farm, still apparent today, was established by the time of the 1827 estate survey.

Another impressive, well-arranged, brick-built farmstead is Redbrick Farm, Thompson, where the large two-threshing-floor barn is dated 1824, coinciding with the enclosure of Thompson Common, which increased the acreage of this farm from 214 acres to 390. It looks as if

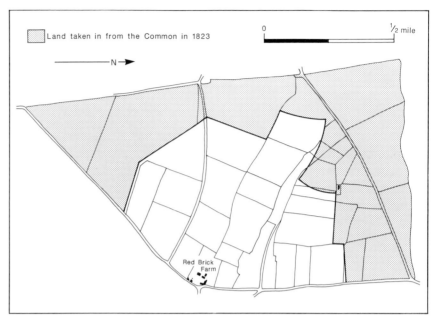

Land taken in from the Common in 1823

0        ½ mile

N →

Red Brick Farm

**69** Plan of Redbrick, or Red Barn Farm, Thompson, redrawn from the 1827 survey, showing the fields added to the farm when the commons were enclosed in 1823.

the entire farm was rebuilt at this time and the bricks were probably made on the farm, in a kiln in the north-west corner of its lands.

The documentary evidence, coupled with the substantial well-planned layouts shown on the tithe maps for most of the estate farms, makes the fact that so few farms survive particularly frustrating. The seven within the present battle area have been reduced to rubble, while one at nearby Great Ellingham is now under an airfield. In Merton, barns survive on only three of the five farms and two of these are no longer used for agriculture. One has been converted for residential and the other for commercial use. In Thompson there has been much conversion and demolition and only three farms still have a good range of old buildings. The reason for this low survival rate outside the battle area must be that all those still owned by the Walsingham estate are farmed directly by it and elsewhere there have been a great many amalgamations resulting in redundant buildings.

Only twelve barns were recorded and some of these are now little more than foundations. Curiously, what was obvious from even this small sample was that the barns were very large indeed. Four had two threshing floors and the largest barn, with a volume of 1239 cu. m (43,750 cu. ft) was on the poorest soil on the estate, at Tottington. Although the farm covered 593 acres the grain output can never have been great. As little wheat was grown in this area these huge barns must have been mainly barley barns.

Most of the early barns (pre-1750) were timber-framed, while only one was brick. One late eighteenth-century barn was timber-framed while another porched barn at Top Farm, Thompson, has clay lump side walls and brick and weatherboard gables. Perhaps the clay lump and weatherboard is replacing earlier timber-framed walling. Another barn within the battle area appears to have been originally clay lump on a brick and flint plinth. As well as their size, these barns are characterized by their porches, providing extra standing room for loaded wagons.

Not enough examples of any other individual buildings survive for any meaningful conclusions to be drawn, but it would seem from the small remaining sample and the map and documentary evidence that, in spite of the poorness of the land, these very large farms were well provided with buildings by the mid-nineteenth century. No records survive that indicate the cost of these building schemes and whether the investment involved paid off is difficult to say. The rents from the 12,000-acre estate, just before they began to fall with the agricultural depression in 1876, was nearly £10,000. A rent of over £1 an acre would have been more usual on the better soils of Norfolk.

In contrast to the early nineteenth-century investments stimulated by agricultural boom, there are no buildings that can definitely be dated to the late nineteenth century. As prices slumped it became clear that much of the land was unsuited to cultivation. The estate was in debt and shooting was becoming an ever more important activity. In the 1890s the Prince of Wales took the shooting at Merton, involving Lord Walsingham in some very expensive entertaining. Finally, in 1912, he was forced to sell property in Yorkshire and London, but kept his Norfolk estates intact until they too were much reduced with the takeover of land for the battle area during the Second World War.

## THE HARE ESTATE

Like Lord Walsingham on Breckland, the Hare family on the fen edge at Stow Bardolph faced unique problems created by their soils. About 8,500 acres of the estate were on good loams over either sand or clay, most of which was enclosed and improved by 1809, but 2000 acres were fen, regarded until the 1840s as very poor land, and let with the 'upland farms' as it was 'incapable from its poverty of separate occupation'.[18]

### Farm management; fen drainage and farm improvements

The estate went through two well-documented periods of improvement, one between 1811 and 1821 when the 'upland' parts were fenced, clayed, drained and supplied with improved buildings. Bricks from a new brick kiln were used to replace the former 'ill-constructed timber buildings'.[19] The second was between 1846 and 1849 when six new fen farms were created. The same agent, John Wiggins, was in charge of the estate from 1815 and directed both sets of improvements, details of which were meticulously recorded by him.

Some of the farms were very large. Marham Abbey Farm covered 1270 acres in the 1840s, although some of this was unimproved fen. Eleven of the seventeen farms were over 300 acres. All were in large rectangular fields by this date, presumably as a result of the early nineteenth-century improvements. The enclosure of the area was complete by 1801. It is surprising that although a high proportion of the land was arable by 1840 only a small part of it was recorded at the time of the tithe survey as being under cereal or roots (under 20 per cent in each crop); yet yields were amongst the highest in the county.[20] Potatoes and vegetables were already becoming an important fenland crop, accounting for much of the rest of the arable land. John Wiggins was very scathing about the management of the estate before 1811. There were 'many bad farmers', buildings were neglected and land needed improving. Gradually these necessary improvements were implemented and two visits were made each year by the agent to check the tenant was keeping everything in repair.[21] The yearly tenancies were replaced in 1811 by 21-year leases that included clauses requiring the tenant to plant and maintain hedges, put in new drains, clay the fields, and maintain and repair ditches and buildings. A new brick kiln was providing bricks and tiles for building and draining. Rent in 1809 had amounted to above £7000, but by 1821 it had risen to £11,131. Much of the expense of the improvement was borne by the tenant and was estimated at about £10 an acre, with the estate providing the bricks and tiles. John Wiggins admitted that building improvements were secondary to land improvements up to 1832, but he commented favourably on the improved cattle sheds that kept stock warm and helped conserve manure. When the farms were relet in that year on 14-year leases the total rent for the estate was increased by £3000, as a result, so John Wiggins claimed, of the estate improvements. 'More particular attention was paid to buildings, which the expense of other objects prevented being more than partially done during the former lease.' This helps to explain why very few surviving buildings can be dated to the early period.

What building was undertaken between 1832 and the end of the 14-year leases in 1846 is unclear. John Wiggin's report at this time describes a field barn and yard at Marham Hall as 'recently built', although the need for field barns is frequently noted and two farms required barns. Certainly most of the farmstead layouts shown on the tithe maps were substantial and well planned. That the estate was generally in good order is demonstrated, according to John Wiggins, by the fact that, in spite of the uncertainty caused in 1846 by the final repeal of the Corn Laws, leases were renewed for a further 14 years at the same rent as in 1832. 'It is an incontrovertible fact that, had nothing been done to increase produce, the rent of 1832 having been calculated at 60 shillings a quarter of wheat, could not have stood under free trade and a prospective price of 45 shillings a quarter.'

## The fenland farms

The main effort of these years was concentrated in the creation of six new farms in the Fens. Instead of letting the fen with the 'upland' farms, the area was ploughed and marled, 'which vastly increased the value and produce of these lands', so that they could be let as separate farms. £10,000 was spent on claying, and building roads and premises. Plans of the buildings are to be found in John Wiggins' report, although unfortunately none survive on the ground. Settlement of foundations was always a problem in these peat soils and many collapsed and had to be rebuilt early in this century.

The plans are all very similar and form a distinctive group. All the farms have piggeries with a steaming house for food preparation next door. All except one have a cow house next to the pigsties. Pigsties and steaming houses were also found on other Hare estate farms and point to the importance of vegetables, particularly potatoes, in the farming system of this area. The report on West Nordelph Farm in 1849 states that 'full advantage has been taken of the superior locality of this land, next to a high road and on a navigable canal with the privilege of selling potatoes.' The provision of barns, granaries and turnip houses shows that a cereal rotation was being practised. The terms of the lease show oats being grown instead of barley, and then followed by a wheat crop, thus following a five- rather than a four-course rotation with, unusually, two grain crops, oats then wheat in succession. All the farms also have two cattle yards, and except for one farm with a bullock lodge, there is no enclosed provision for cattle, such as loose boxes or covered yards. The granaries are often next to the hay house, on the ground floor rather than raised above other sheds. All except one farmstead had a wagon lodge and all had a nag stable. The barns on the less extensive (under 200 acres) Nordelph farms were smaller (15 m by 5.5 m; 50 ft by 18 ft), but only slightly, than those on the larger 300–500 acre farms of Stow Bardolph which were 18 by 6 m (60 by 20 ft). Two other farms were also rebuilt at this date and plans included in John Wiggins' report, but again no buildings survive.

Also included in John Wiggin's report are plans of several new farmhouses built at this date which indicate the social aspirations of the type of people sought as tenants for these large fenland farms. The estate was looking for farmers with substantial capital and so a six-bedroom house with a servant's room above the dairy, two kitchens, a parlour and a keeping (dining) room was thought appropriate.

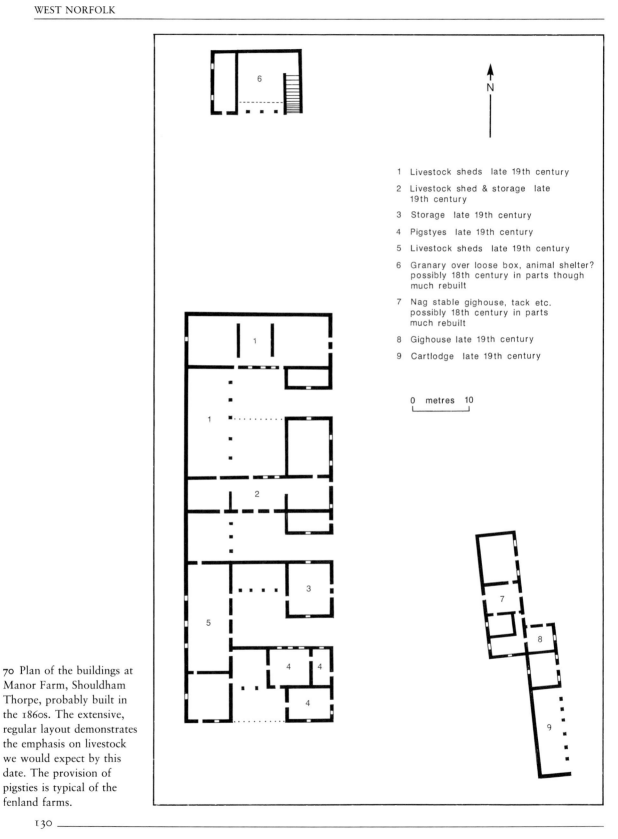

1 Livestock sheds late 19th century

2 Livestock shed & storage late 19th century

3 Storage late 19th century

4 Pigstyes late 19th century

5 Livestock sheds late 19th century

6 Granary over loose box, animal shelter? possibly 18th century in parts though much rebuilt

7 Nag stable gighouse, tack etc. possibly 18th century in parts much rebuilt

8 Gighouse late 19th century

9 Cartlodge late 19th century

0 metres 10

70 Plan of the buildings at Manor Farm, Shouldham Thorpe, probably built in the 1860s. The extensive, regular layout demonstrates the emphasis on livestock we would expect by this date. The provision of pigsties is typical of the fenland farms.

## Farms built after 1860

After 1850 the documentary evidence becomes more scrappy, but it is from this period that most of the buildings survive. Two farms in Stow Bardolph have date stones of 1860 and Park Farm is dated 1878. Several others in Shouldham Thorpe appear to have been built about the same time. All these farmsteads are very substantial indeed with large rectangular layouts and built of an attractive mixture of carstone and brick. The farmhouses in these 'upland' parishes indicate farmers a cut above their fenland counterparts with one or two gig houses and ample riding-horse accommodation, often including a groom's room. As well as cattle and horse yards the farms have piggeries with rooms for steaming food beside them. A very distinctive feature of all these farms is the design of doors and windows. The bottom two-thirds of many of the windows in livestock sheds were made of sliding slats, while the upper third was glazed, 'by which wind is excluded without excluding light'. Sliding rather than hinged doors, which could be left open without the danger of being blown closed, were also typical of this new phase of building in the 1860s. One specification states 'Doors to be of foreign fir framed and braced and hung on the jambs with hooks and bands, except for the barn and turnip house doors (presumably the largest ones) which are to slide on pulleys on the bottom.'[22]

Westhead Farm, Stow Bardolph, was rebuilt in 1860 and a description written in 1862 starts, 'The buildings are said to be nearly a perfect arrangement in plan for a farm of £500 rent (297 acres) a year and as such have been visited by many persons from a distance,' and carries on, 'the site is chosen for its southern aspect and its convenience with respect to its gravelled road, the foundations are on concrete under all the walls, there is a course of asphalt instead of mortar in the walls to stop the damp rising, the floors of the chaff house, barn, harness room and gig house are of asphalt, the bullock houses are particularly well arranged as the mangers are of brick.'[23] Both concrete and asphalt were new building materials at this date.

One of the most striking features of these farms was that they were all of one build. There were few additions or attempts to incorporate earlier buildings. The farms created in the 1860s were adequate until the post-cart horse era and some of the more substantial ones have been successfully converted to modern use. The contrast between the 'upland' and fenland farms where no nineteenth-century buildings survive, is obvious.

71 Pigsties at Manor Farm, Shouldham Thorpe. The chimney is over the feed preparation room and originally there was a small yard alongside the building.

72 Sliding doors and ventilation windows at Manor Farm, Shouldham Thorpe, a feature of estate building in the 1860s.

## THE LESTRANGE ESTATE

The LeStrange estate, centred on Hunstanton Hall, covered nearly 8000 acres and consisted of 35 farms in the parishes of Hunstanton, Holme-next-the-Sea, Heacham, Snettisham, Sedgeford, Ringstead and Barrett Ringstead.

### Farm management

All this area is light chalky soils: twelve of the farms are almost entirely on chalkland, another thirteen are on light loams. Only three are on loamy clays. It is not surprising that on this mainly light land the farms are large, with two over 500 acres and a further twelve over 200. It is an area of large rectangular and enclosure fields, mostly enclosed shortly before Faden's map was published in 1797.

The survival of farm buildings here was rather patchy. Although most of those in Ringstead, Barrett Ringstead, and Sedgeford still remain, much less was left in Heacham, Hunstanton and Holme. Some had been converted into houses, while on several farms in this popular tourist area conversion for holiday accommodation had taken place.

## The buildings

The local availability of good building material is unusual in Norfolk and has resulted in particularly substantial buildings that once built did not need replacing. The only building stone found in Norfolk is still quarried at Snettisham, but may have been worked more widely in the past. It is a reddish, iron-rich sandstone known as carstone. As well as this, chalk blocks, flint and an ironstone conglomerate were used. Although the chalk blocks were considered too soft for outside work by the nineteenth century many eighteenth-century houses and barns of chalk seem to have stood the test of time quite well. No timber-framed or clay lump buildings are found. Because of this durability most farmsteads were added to and adapted many times over the centuries. Buildings were substantial and large, but it was not until the second half of the nineteenth century that they were rationalized into E- or U-shaped plans. There were no classical E-shaped yards in 1840 and only three U-shaped ones. By far the majority (23) were

73 Rear wall of the stables (probably a barn) at Hall Farm, Ringstead, showing the variety of building materials, brick, chalk and carstone, found in so many of these buildings.

irregular. By 1906 the situation had reversed, with 23 E- and U-shaped layouts and only two irregular ones remaining.

This picture of continual expansion and modification of buildings rather than a single phase of modernization is borne out in the figures for investment by the estate in the period after 1851.[24] This is over £1200 per annum nearly every year until the 1890s, and this was equal to anything between 8 per cent and 15 per cent of estate income from rents.[25]

This very light land was predominantly open sheep country in the Middle Ages and early modern period, and so perhaps it is not surprising that, in spite of the durability of the local building materials, no pre-seventeenth-century buildings survive. A very large two-threshing-floor barn with a capacity of 972 cu. m (34,300 cu. ft) remains on a 258 acre farm in Ringstead. It is dated 1630, but there are no datable features in the building to confirm this. Two other barns associated with date-stones may also be late seventeenth century, but have been altered to such an extent that they are impossible to date with any confidence.

With late eighteenth-century enclosure, the situation changed dramatically, and by 1840 there was virtually no permanent pasture except on the coastal marshes. Over 80 per cent of the area was arable at the time of the tithe survey.[26] A classic four-course rotation appears to have been practised with about a quarter of the land in wheat, barley, turnips and clover or seed grass at any one time. The majority of barns probably date from the time of the enclosures, 16 of the total of 28 being late eighteenth-century. Many of them are very large. Four had two threshing floors and a volume of over 900 cu. m (31,800 cu. ft). All of the large barns were found on farms of over 270 acres. A further

**74** Large barn at Gedding's Farm, Ringstead, dated 1630. The roof has been replaced and the walls of mixed chalk, flint, carstone and brick are impossible to date.

eleven were over 400 cu. m (14,100 cu. ft) and again found on larger farms (over 150 acres). However, as in the other regions studied there are very wide differences in the relationship between the size of barns and the acreage of farms.

A very high percentage of granaries survive: they were found on a third of the farms and five were eighteenth century. The reason for their survival may be the building materials used here, more durable than elsewhere. All are above cart lodges, and the nineteenth-century examples are built of carstone with stone steps on the gable end up to the second floor, often with what is traditionally called a 'dog kennel'

75 (*top*) Granary at Neats Lyng Farm, Ringstead. The exterior stone staircase with dog kennel is typical of this area. The weatherboarded front helps provide ventilation for the grain stored upstairs.
(*bottom*) The building is dated 1862, but the mortised arch braces in the cart shed look older; however, there is much reused timber in the building, which adds to the confusion.

**76** This fine eight-bay eighteenth-century cart lodge with granary above at Downs Farm, Barrett Ringstead, is of two builds and must have provided ample accommodation for the produce of this 220-acre farm.

alcove under the steps. Many of the cart lodges were impressively long; five of those on the larger farms being more than five bays.

By the mid-nineteenth century, cattle were widely kept and yard-fed in the winter, as the survival of extensive cattle yards on most of the farms demonstrates. However, cattle were always secondary to cereals in importance, probably being valued mainly for their manure, and so no attempts to intensify production by building rows of loose boxes were made at the end of the century.

Most stables were arranged around yards and some dated from the eighteenth century. Three of the eighteenth-century yards had hay lofts, whilst one was found over a nineteenth-century stable. In spite of the lightness of the soil, many farms, particularly the larger ones, kept several horse teams. Stables for as many as 24 horses were not uncommon.

These well-arranged spacious farm layouts in a countryside of large carefully-farmed arable fields are amongst the most attractive in Norfolk. Many are well maintained, and the variety of building materials and the care with which they were built is obvious. Great efforts were lavished on the decorative use of the combination of brick, chalk, flint and carstone to its best advantage. Although the use of small brick or stone chips set in the mortar around the stone blocks, known as galleting, may have been to strengthen the mortar against, for instance, pecking by birds, the result is very attractive. The overriding impression gained is of an area of solid agricultural prosperity throughout the eighteenth and nineteenth centuries with an emphasis on cereals. Both the tithe survey and the size of the barns confirm that heavy crops were produced. The farms were subjected to a continuous repair and updating programme, with no total nineteenth-century rebuilds. The picture is of a gradual accumulation of substantial, durable and attractive farm buildings.

## CONCLUSIONS

These three west Norfolk estates each have their own very distinctive features, but they also have much in common that helps classify the region as a whole.

Firstly, the farms are generally much larger than those of the south of the county: of the 58 farms visited in the south only one was over 500 acres in 1840, while of the 71 in the west, 11 were over this size. This helps to explain the fact that the buildings too are larger. Fourteen barns in the west had a volume of more than 500 cu. m (17,660 cu. ft) and seven had two threshing floors, while in the south the comparable figures are only nine and two.

Secondly, the building materials available in the west are better. Only four barns in the west contained any clay lump or timber-framing and they were all on the breck-edge farms, while over half in the south were of this construction. Only 19 of the 46 south-Norfolk barns contained substantial amounts of brickwork while in the west brick combined with chalk, carstone or flint was by far the most common building material.

Thirdly, in spite of the lack of good building materials, more older buildings survived in the less progressive south. A quarter of the barns in the south were dated before 1750, while only a tenth in the west were that old, which suggests that grain farming was a relatively late development in this area. It was known as an area of open sheep walk for which no buildings and little feed was required and it was not until enclosure in the late eighteenth century that large-scale barns, cattle accommodation and granaries were built.

The result is an entirely different landscape in the west, with wide open views of large rectangular fields with substantial brick and stone-built buildings providing, by the 1850s, roomy, sound accommodation for the often well-to-do men of capital who rented these large, predominantly cereal-producing farms.

# 11

# Central and East Norfolk

'In East Norfolk, alone, we are to look for that regular and long established system of practice which has raised, deservedly, the name of Norfolk husbandmen, and which in a principal part of this district, remains unadulterated to the present time.'[1]

This final region to be studied covers a very diverse area in the good loams and clays in the centre and east of Norfolk. It also contains just over half of the farms surveyed and two of the ten largest Norfolk estates. The Evans-Lombe estate, centred originally on the family seat at Marlingford and latterly on Bylaugh Hall, to the north-east of East Dereham, covered 14,000 acres. The Gunton estate, based at Gunton Hall, covered a similar area near North Walsham. A third area in Broadland consisted mainly of owner-occupier farms in south Flegg and provided a contrast to the great estates.

## THE GUNTON ESTATE

The Gunton estate covered a dozen parishes and over 80 farms mainly situated in the good loams of north-east Norfolk. The farms varied greatly in size, with two over 500 acres, the majority between 200 and 400 and a good scattering of much smaller holdings. Yields were good, but not amongst the highest in Norfolk, and a four-course system was universally practised by 1840. Over 80 per cent of the land was arable with none either in commons or left fallow.

### Farm management; progress and stagnation

Not only is Gunton one of the largest Norfolk estates to be studied;

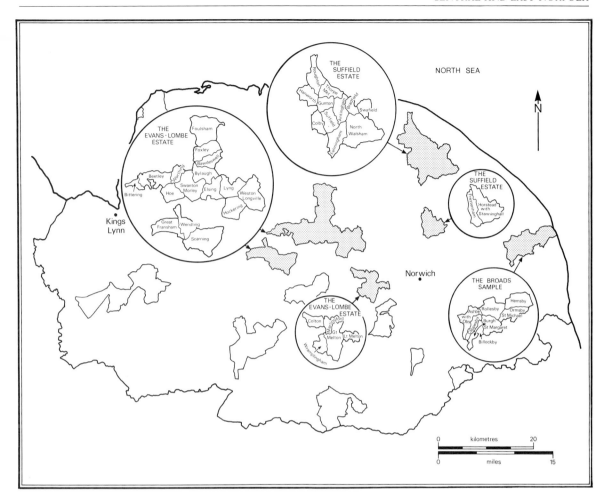

77 Map showing the sample parishes in central and east Norfolk.

but it is also the best documented. The accumulation of the estate was begun by Charles Harbord in the first half of the seventeenth century when he bought land at Stanninghall and then, in 1647, at Gunton. He was Surveyor General to Charles I and later to Charles II. When he died in 1679 one of his sons took over Stanninghall and the other Gunton. Gradually land was added, and in 1742 Gunton Hall was rebuilt and the park altered.

By the 1780s the estate was well known for its progressive management, and the agricultural writer William Marshall worked there as a land agent for a year before writing his report on Norfolk. He described the Gunton estate as 'one of the first in the county'. In 1786 Sir Harbord Harbord was created first Baron Suffield, and the tradition of good management continued until the death of the third Baron in 1835.

The third Baron Suffield, who ran the estate from 1821 until his death in 1835, had 'put all the farms and cottages in thorough repair, made roads, built a wharf on the (North Walsham and Dilham) canal at Antingham, and erected a bone-crushing mill that proved most profitable to the farmers'. He also reduced the emphasis placed on game preservation by removing the spring guns designed to catch poachers and having the hares shot. As a result, 'the estate was almost unique as regards the housing of the tenants and the perfect order it was in generally.'[2]

From 1835 to 1849 the estate was owned by the fourth Baron, Edward Vernon, who was an absentee landlord, showing no concern for the property and the fact that it was falling into disrepair. In 1849 the fifth Baron inherited and, to begin with, took a great interest in putting the estate in order again.

However, this enthusiasm did not last long, as the fifth Baron became more involved at court with the Prince of Wales, who was frequently entertained at Gunton. This proved to be a great drain on the estate, and although it remained one of the finest game reserves in the county, management was neglected and money was always in short supply. When there was a fire in the hall in the 1880s, it was many years before the money for repairs could be found.

78 Topps Hill Farm was laid out at the north end of Gunton Park between 1789 and 1830. Its fields are regular, but it is within the game park and surrounded by trees providing cover for the pheasants. These factors made it difficult to let.

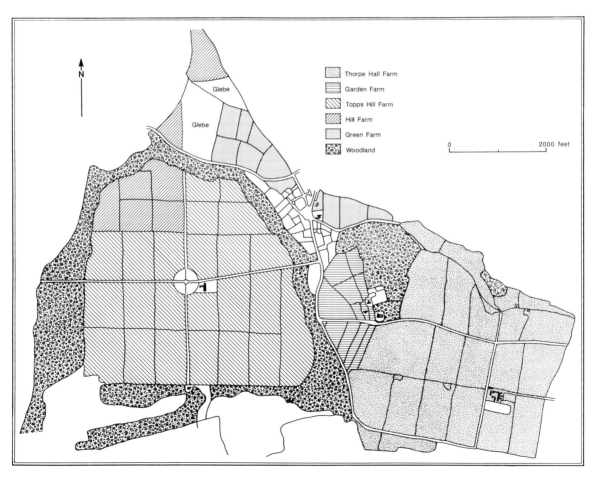

## Map evidence

It is likely that this fire also destroyed a large number of documents, but even without them a good selection of sources is available. Firstly, there is a volume of estate plans drawn by H.A. Biederman in 1784. These parish maps showed field and farm boundaries as well as the position of farm buildings, but on a very small scale. A second and more detailed survey was undertaken by James Wright in 1835. The estate had increased in size between the two surveys; 49 farms covering 4000 acres were surveyed by Biederman, 87 farms on 14,000 acres were covered by Wright. The two surveys show very clearly the great changes that had taken place in many parishes in the intervening years. Commons had been enclosed and fields rationalized and rearranged in Felmingham, Antingham, Bradfield and Suffield (illustration 54). The number of farm buildings had also increased and the layout of buildings changed; an indication of the major improvements that had been undertaken by the third Baron.

## Estate surveys

Other estate records include a repairs book in which repairs carried out are described in detail. Unfortunately, the farms are only identified by the names of their tenants. The book is undated and it is unclear how long a period it covered, but it was probably compiled in the 1820s. A total of £11,750 was recorded as being spent on repairs. The details given show how often farm buildings were altered rather than replaced. Entries such as 'West gable of barn taken down and part of side wall to be rebuilt and 20 feet added to the barn', 'New roof to stable, raise the walls, rebuild gable and repair hay chamber floor' and 'New barn walls; roof, tiles and doors good', only serve to emphasize the problem of giving specific dates to buildings. A frequent repair was to the floors of the hay chambers above stables. Presumably the weight of the hay and the moisture rising from the stalled horses made these floors particularly vulnerable to rot. Although the building of a few new barns is mentioned in the repair book, the most usual new buildings were cart lodges, bullock sheds, turnip houses and cow or calf houses. One entirely new farm was built in Suffield. This cost the estate £572 and consisted of one barn, 21.9 × 6.7 m (72 ft × 22 ft), a stable for nine horses (seven cart horses, two riding horses), a cow house and shed, piggeries and a cart lodge for one wagon and four carts.

A further detailed source of information is an estate survey of 1894 compiled by a Mr T. Rose. He described the condition of all the farms and drew plans of 20 of them. The general dereliction of many of them is stressed, the result presumably of 30 or so years of neglect. Mr Rose regretted the fact that repairs had frequently been left to the tenant,

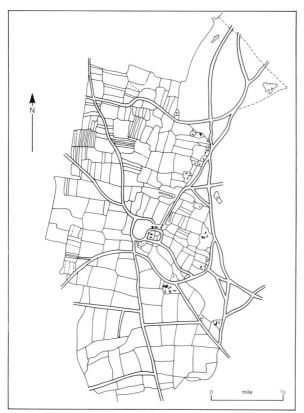

**79** Antingham in (*left*) 1784 and (*right*) 1835. The maps show the enclosing of the common and the rationalizing of the fields in the north of the parish. Those in the south had already been reorganized.

who could not take an overview of the estate. 'Buildings should not be built solely for an individual or sitting tenant, but built with a view to the general requirements of the estate as a whole.' Rose noted with disapproval that several farms were frequently let to a single tenant. Much of the parish of Bradfield, for instance, had been let to George Ives. At Shepherd's Farm the barn was being used as a cattle shed, 'consequently a most valuable building is being spoilt. I cannot understand why these small places should have been let to a big farm.' Neighbouring Howes' Farm was also becoming dilapidated, because, according to Rose, there was no resident tenant. An 180-acre farm at Roughton was also 'a sad example of ruin caused by a non-resident tenant.' Rose considered it to be 'of a lettable size and of an acreage more likely to be let than a large occupation... I believe the day of the large farm is over.' He estimated that it would cost up to £25,000 to put the estate in repair and his final comment was 'This is without doubt a magnificent estate, but now and for some time to come requiring outlay under judicious management.' Unfortunately for the estate this did not take place and finally in 1919 much was sold. The plans included in Rose's survey show extensive groups of buildings, with both horse and cattle yards, sometimes with loose boxes, but usually of an irregular plan, suggesting that the farmstead had been

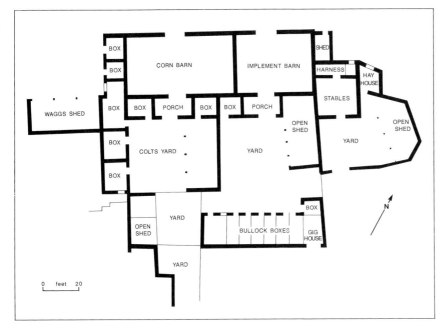

**80** Plan of farm buildings at Manor Farm, South Repps, drawn by Rose in his survey of the Gunton estate in 1894.

added to many times over the years. Very few appeared to have been built as a single unit.

A final source of information is the sales catalogues of 1919 when much of the estate was sold. More buildings than can now be identified are described and, as is usual in estate agents' particulars, there is no suggestion of the degree of dilapidation that must have existed at the time.

## The farming landscape of the Gunton estate

The size of the farms on the mid-nineteenth-century estate varied greatly from over 500 to just a few acres behind a village pub or blacksmith's shop, which proved impossible to identify in a modern village street. About 60 farms were, however, fully recorded. The parishes that showed greatest change between 1784 and 1835 were Antingham, Bradfield, Felmingham and Roughton. The common at Antingham was enclosed, while generally field boundaries were rationalized and farms consolidated. At Antingham there is a very clear division between the north and south. Hall Farm, Bayfield Farm and Old Pond Farm had already been consolidated in 1784, and remained with very few alterations, while in the north, Read's Farm, Heath Farm and Bushell's Farm were completely reorganized. The fields of these farms were very small and intermingled in 1784 (illustration 79). Although the acreage changed very little, by 1834 the boundaries had been altered to form well-laid-out compact holdings. One might expect that the buildings too would have been rebuilt in this effort at rationalization, but this, in fact, was not the case. At both Read and Heath Farms early barns remain (that at Heath Farm is dated 1694). Similarly the farms that had been rearranged by 1784 contain mostly early nineteenth-century buildings with nothing that dates from an earlier period of improvement. The reorganization of fields did not therefore go hand in hand with farm building renewal. No new farms were created here by the enclosure of the common. Instead it was included in farms bordering the old common in neighbouring parishes. The number of farms therefore remained fairly static between 1784 and 1835, although the purchase of small intermingled parcels of land allowed for the general increase in their size.

## The buildings

Although there was no connection between periods of estate building and reorganization of fields, there were certain characteristics of estate building as a whole. During much of the nineteenth century the typical Gunton building had a hipped roof. Although hipped roofs are common in Norfolk on smaller buildings such as cattle sheds, barns constructed in this way are not, and they help to give the estate farms a distinctive appearance. Even neighbouring farms that were visited in North Walsham had not copied this feature. Another oddity of the Gunton barns was that the great majority of barn porches were placed assymetrically to the barn door, giving a much wider bay to one side of the door than the other. No use for this wider area was obvious, but there was a noticeable lack of granaries on the estate and so it is possible that it was used for temporary grain storage after threshing and prior to sale or feeding to stock. Many of the barns are large. A third have two threshing floors and one at Thorpe Hall had three. Five have a capacity of over 1000 cu. m (35,300 cu. ft) and over half over 500 cu. m (17,660 cu. ft). In contrast to the areas to the south, there are no timber-framed or clay lump buildings. Most of the barns are brick, with a few flint and brick and some mainly flint.

Early barns were unusual on the estate: only four of the surviving 52 could be dated to a period before 1700, while a further eleven were built before 1784. The majority dated to the period between 1784 and 1835; the period when, as we have seen, many farm holdings took on their present size and layout. Stables appear to date from a similar period to the barns. Only one stable can be dated before 1784, while eighteen were built in the following 50 years. The position and arrangement of these stables is interesting. Hay lofts are very much a feature of the earlier stables, only one occurring in a stable built after 1835. The problems of maintaining hay loft floors noted in the repairs book may well have led to the gradual abandonment of this design in favour of a separate hay barn. All but two of the stables built before

1835 were on the end of barns, suggesting that it was only later that stables became the more typical free-standing buildings.

The lack of granaries is strange. Only a third of farms have them, and these were mostly small. Only three are above cart lodges, and even here they do not go the full length of the building. The rest are above single-cell units such as gig houses or workshops. Perhaps, as this is primarily an arable area, less feed grain was kept back for stock through the winter and so storage space was not needed. However, in all nineteenth-century farming systems yard-fed cattle played an important role, and they would have been fed cereals as well as turnips and cattle cake. The lack of granaries may in fact reflect the lack of late nineteenth-century expenditure on buildings. Granaries were not so important in a period when grain could be threshed a little at a time, as it was needed. Later, when threshing by contract machines and teams encouraged the threshing of most of the crop at once, the grain would have required storing. Whatever the reason, it seems that the storage of grain in granaries was not traditionally part of the system adopted in this area.

One mid-nineteenth-century feature that is found on several estate farms is the sunken loose box. When the cattle were first put in these boxes at the beginning of winter they walked down into them from the yard. Gradually the straw and manure built up and by the time they were fattened they could be driven out at or above the surrounding yard level and the boxes would then be mucked out. These boxes were to be found on many farms from about 1850 and survive on six of the Gunton farms. A further six farms have rows of loose boxes with a

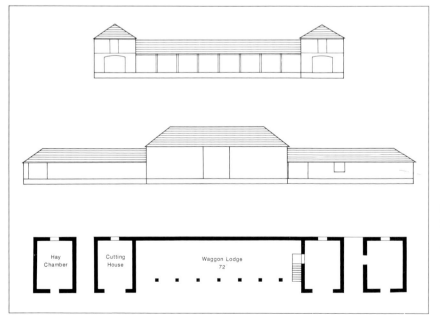

81 Cart lodge with second-floor granaries over workshops at Aylsham Road Farm, Felmingham. It is unusual for farm buildings on the Gunton estate to exhibit this degree of architectural symmetry.

feeding passage, but the floors are not sunken. Cattle yards survived on two-thirds of the farms visited, emphasizing the fact that yard- and stall-fed cattle had a very important part to play in every Victorian arable farming system.

An unusual building that survived, albeit in a very ruinous form, was a malt house. In the eighteenth century farm malt houses were common in Norfolk, but by the nineteenth century, and particularly after the opening of the railways, malting was becoming centralized in the towns. In 1894 Mr Rose thought there was no point in spending money on the repair of the malt house simply to please the eccentricities of a particular tenant. 'Would these malt houses be required by any other tenant in the case of Mrs Horsfield's retirement or death? I should say 'no' as country malt houses in the present day are of very little use or profit.'

An exceptional set of buildings stands in the southern parish of Stanninghall. This was the first parish to be bought by the Harbords in the seventeenth century and remained the home of a member of the family thereafter. This may explain its unusual treatment. The farm itself is by far the largest on the estate (625 acres). As it was nearly all arable, it would have needed a large barn and extensive buildings. With a volume of 1417 cu. m (50,050 cu. ft), the barn is the largest seen on the survey, but it is surprising that a barn 35.3 m (116 ft) long should only have one threshing floor. It is a huge cruciform structure with decorative brick arcading both inside and outside the building. Although it has been reroofed and is difficult to date, it is thought to be late seventeenth century and may date from the farm's purchase by the Harbords. The repair book of the 1820s mentions the building of a bullock shed and turnip house 18 m (60 ft) long and this building still stands, built at right angles to the east end of the barn. Originally a shelter shed with a turnip house at the end, it has now been enclosed to form a dairy. The building of the lean-to along the back of the existing stable block (illustration 100) is mentioned in the 1820s repair book as well as repairs to the riding-horse stable and gig house. Since 1840 a row of sunken loose boxes has been constructed, again on the south side of the barn, abutting the porch. Six doors open into double loose boxes, so twelve bullocks could have been fattened at once. There is a turnip house on the end.

As a group, the buildings of the Gunton estate are substantial but not impressive. It is perhaps surprising that on an estate of this size there are no farmsteads laid out with architectural pretensions. Nothing remains of the farms within Gunton Park, although Dairy Farm may well have originally been designed by the architect Samuel Wyatt. Only at Aylesham Road and Thorpe Hall Farm is there any sign of a planned layout. On both these farms there are symmetrical facades of granaries over workshops at either end of ranges of cart lodges. E- and U-shaped layouts developed with the addition and rationalization of scattered buildings. In 1840 there were 32 irregularly arranged farms and nine U-shaped ones, while by 1900 there were ten E-shaped and fourteen U-shaped farmsteads (illustrations 115 and 116).

The fact that there was this continuous development suggests that it is wrong to assume that there was no building after 1860. Some new work there certainly was, and some farmsteads, such as Thorpe Hall, were highly progressive units by 1890. By 1835 this 500-acre holding with the farm centrally placed within well-laid-out fields consisted of a long, three-threshing-floor barn, with a stable block and yard abutting at the north end and cattle yards and sheds along the eastern wall. By 1890 the accommodation was sufficient for 24 horses and 150 cattle. Twenty-eight of these could be fattened in a range of loose boxes, which also contains a two-storey turnip and cake house. Two small granaries at either end of a cart shed had also been added, making a very good set of premises.

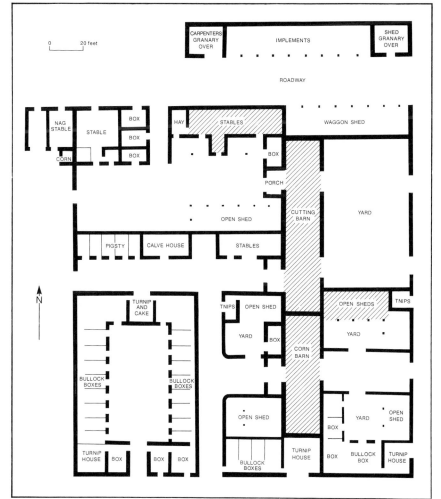

82 Plan of Thorpe Hall as drawn and captioned by Mr Rose in 1894, showing the pre-1830 core of barn, stable and single shelter shed and the post-1830 additions, mainly for livestock.

This pattern of pre-1835 barns and stables with later cattle yards and loose boxes is repeated on many farms. The existence of loose boxes, whether sunken or not, is an indication that improvement on the estate continued well after 1850. Rose in 1894 even noted a row at Roughton that had 'recently been erected'. It would be a mistake to dismiss the Gunton estate as one where nothing was happening in the second half of the nineteenth century. Some farms were well provided with buildings and capable of being progressively managed.

## THE EVANS-LOMBE ESTATE

The 12,000-acre Evans-Lombe estate was one of the largest in Norfolk; yet the family were relative newcomers. They were descended from Thomas Lombe, silk manufacturer of Derby, who built one of the town's earliest silk mills in 1722. By the middle of the eighteenth century they were established at Great Melton, and in 1783 John Lombe was made a baronet. A style of life commensurate with his new title resulted in the acquisition in 1796 of the 6000-acre Bylaugh estate in settlement of a gambling debt. The construction of the great Victorian mansion, described as a 'stone pile' in the 1917 sales catalogue and costing as much as £100,000, was undertaken to fulfil the will of Sir John Lombe who died in 1817. Construction did not begin until 1849 and this period of activity coincides with a time of estate improvement on the neighbouring farms. When the hall was completed in 1852 the owner, Sir Edward Lombe, was already very elderly and probably never lived there. His son, the Revd Henry Lombe, lived at Bylaugh Hall for much of his life and it became the focus of estate management with its own brick kilns and estate workshops at Elsing. Henry Lombe died in 1897 and his heirs preferred to live at the less pretentious Great Melton Hall. Bylaugh Hall and its 8000-acre estate were finally sold in 1917.

### The buildings; mid-Victorian opulence

A total of 64 farms were visited, almost equally divided between the Melton and the Bylaugh areas and nearly all of them on good loam soils. Farm sizes ranged from 800 to under 50 acres, with over half of the farms being under 100 acres. The estate management suggested by the very limited documentation and the remaining buildings went through a very different history to that at Gunton. Whilst at Gunton the main period of improvement was over by 1840, on the Evans-Lombe lands the greatest improvement took place later. On over half the farms where a considerable number of buildings survive, substantial rebuilding took place in the second half of the nineteenth century in a very characteristic style. Nearly all the farms in the Bylaugh area

were remodelled, retaining only their eighteenth-century brick barns,
sometimes with a stable and hay loft abutting. The surrounding shelter
sheds and yards were completely replaced on a totally regular layout.
Work was either in brick, or more often, in the more decorative flint
work with brick lacing. A distinctive circular ventilation grille was
usually placed in the apex of the gable walls of both shelter and enclosed
livestock sheds, and sometimes inserted in the barns. Rectangular
ventilation grilles are often found just below the roof along the length
of the stables. The slopes of the gables were topped with coping tiles,
presumably made in the estate kilns. Similar improvements were carried
out on the Great Melton part of the estate, but not on such a lavish
scale. As a result, by 1900 only four of the smaller farms still retained
an irregular layout.

No barns built before 1700 survive, although many are shown on a
map of Swanton Morley drawn in the 1690s (illustration 51). Only a
couple contain any timber-framing or clay lump. All the rest were
replaced by brick barns in the period after 1750. Many of the barns
were very large. Of the 39 visited, twelve had two threshing floors and
eight had a volume of over 600 cu. m (21,200 cu. ft).

Stables on the Evans-Lombe estate have a distinctive style in that
very few have semi-circular lunette windows. In the parish of Lyng,
where both estate and non-estate farms were visited, the non-estate
examples have the usual lunette-type windows, while the windows on
the Evans-Lombe farms are of a standard rectangular design. Only five
of the 37 surviving stables had hay lofts, a reflection of the fact that
they are mostly of a nineteenth-century build.

As on the Gunton estate, very few farms had granaries. Only three
survive, while in the 1917 sales catalogue they are listed in only six of

**84** Horse collars on hooks in the harness room, Green Farm, Elsing.

the 30 farms described. This does seem to be a feature of the good loam districts of the north-east of the county.

As is to be expected on farms subjected to so much improvement in the late nineteenth century, it is the cattle sheds and cart lodges that are most impressive. Many of the cart lodges are eight to ten bays in length, while of the 30 surviving, half contained more than five bays. Cattle yards remain on 40 of the farms, ten with rows of loose boxes. Fine ranges of cattle yards often flanked by enclosed boxes and always facing south were added to most farms. They were sound, solid buildings that have stood the test of time, and by the end of the nineteenth century the estate was well known for its consistent policy of improvement. At this date no landlord could expect his tenants to pay for repairs, and on this estate, unlike Gunton, the landlord undertook all repair work, providing both the materials and the labour, a situation that would have been unthinkable earlier in the century. F.H. Purchas, in an article in the *Estates Magazine* in December 1905 (Vol.5, no.12, 451), explained that as a result of this good management farms were always occupied and hardly ever changed hands. When the Bylaugh farms were sold in 1917, the sales catalogue described them as 'substantial and very complete model homesteads with yards open to the south'. They were in good repair, 'unequalled by any similar estates in the county', and the photographs in the catalogue seem to support this view.

The 30 farms described vary in size from 40 to nearly 900 acres. Details of the buildings and their capacity is given. All farms had cart horse stables and horse yards, housing between four and twenty horses.

By 1917 nearly all farms had a cow house, indicating the increase in the importance of dairying, particularly on farms near an urban centre

85 Eighteenth-century barn and the back wall of the nineteenth-century cattle sheds, Manor Farm, Hoe. The contrast between the style of the brick and flint work of the two periods is very clear.

such as Dereham, and also near a railway line. Farms in Hoe and Swanton Morley, within a few miles of North Elmham station, were keeping up to 40 cows. Piggeries are mentioned on thirteen of the 30 farms, probably linked to dairying activities.

Manor Farm, Hoe, is a fine example of a well-laid-out late nineteenth-century farm. Typically, only the barn is earlier. It is a brick building with two threshing floors and porches both to the east and west. In the mid-nineteenth century a large cattle yard divided into two was created south of the barn. A horse yard was built to the east with a six-bay cart lodge and implement shed beside it. By 1917 the loose box accommodation by the cattle yard was used for 30 dairy cows. All the newer buildings are of flint laced with brick and show all the decorative features typical of an Evans-Lombe estate farm. An interesting detail mentioned in the sale catalogue is a 'water wheel, fed by the overflow from a large pond, which drives the grinding and chaff cutting plant.' No sign of this can be seen today.

At Field House Farm, in nearby Swanton Morley, is the most extensive group of buildings on the estate, not surprisingly built on the largest farm, whose size varied between 1200 and 800 acres during the nineteenth century. The 1690 map shows that already, the farm had more farm buildings apparently arranged around a central yard than any other farm shown. Two barns and two other buildings as well as the house are plotted, but none of these early buildings survive. A 'large barn' is mentioned in the 1917 sales particulars, but none remains today. Instead there is a very fine set of south-facing shelter sheds and loose boxes arranged around six yards with a long low building and engine house nearby. They were all built at once and are typical of the Evans-Lombe designs of the mid- and late nineteenth century. These

86 Gable end of ranges of cattle sheds at Field House Farm, Swanton Morley.

very extensive cattle yards could be justified by the fact that the farm included between 100 and 200 acres of pasture for summer grazing and these animals would need to be overwintered. This large amount of pasture may help to explain why there was stabling for only 20 horses, which does seem rather low for this large farm. The progressive mid-nineteenth-century tenant Robert Freeman corresponded with R.N. Bacon and provided information for his survey of Norfolk agriculture, published in 1844. Freeman followed a four-course system, yet even here, on this large intensive farm, some of the crop was still hand-threshed. Wheat was usually machine threshed, but barley was flailed in the barn.[3]

The most impressive buildings on the estate are those at Park Farm, Bylaugh. Its proximity to the new and prestigious Bylaugh Hall may explain why this farm received such special treatment, for here are the only complete sets of covered yards to be found on the survey. C. S. Read, writing in 1858, said that covered yards were not numerous in Norfolk.[4] There was always the problem of providing adequate ventilation in a covered building. This was overcome at Bylaugh by using a complicated louvre system in a very high staggered-roof construction. The ventilation could be further controlled by shutters above the loose boxes surrounding the yard, and the yards were used until recently. As well as the two identical yards, stables, a horse yard and workshops were also built.

It is a great pity that there is no record of the date of the erection of these buildings. The barn, although much rebuilt appears to be older in origin and is shown on the early nineteenth-century estate plans. Although extensive buildings are shown on the 1842 tithe map, they

do not include the covered yards. It is most probable that they were built during the period when Revd Henry Lombe was resident at Bylaugh, in the third quarter of the nineteenth century, and they show him as a builder of substantial – in this case monumental – farm buildings. They are, however, merely the finest example of the wide-ranging estate improvement for which he was responsible and are an indication of the significance of this estate around 1825–75 in the encouragement of improved farming through the investment of very large sums of money.

87 Photograph of the interior of the covered yards, Hall Farm, Bylaugh, showing pens and ventilation shutters above.

## THE BROADLAND AREA

About 60 farms in the Broadland parishes of Hemsby, Rollesby, Ashby-with-Oby, Ormsby and Fleggburgh were studied. The area was chosen for two reasons. Firstly, it is a distinctive region of the county, containing much good land on the edge of the Broadland marshes. When Arthur Young travelled this way he expected to see a well-farmed region, as he had been told that the Hundred of Flegg was 'cultivated in a most complete manner'.[5]

Secondly, the area was chosen because it was dominated in the nineteenth century by small farms and owner-occupiers or owners of less than 1000 acres of land. Only three farms were over 300 acres while nearly half were under 50. Not all farms were owner-occupied; in Hemsby, for instance, there were only three owner-occupiers, one of whom, Mr Copeman, farmed 640 acres. All the other farms were rented from a variety of small landowners. Rollesby was dominated by the Ensor family, who owned nearly 1000 acres and farmed Rollesby Hall Farm, and let six farms in 1840. Only five farms were owner-occupied, two with under 20 acres. In Ashby-with-Oby, Ormsby and Fleggburgh there were very few owner-occupiers, but there were no dominant landowners either.

### The farming landscape

There were no distinctive architectural features to link these buildings, except very general ones associated with this region. Nearly all the buildings were brick. There were a few brick and flint shelter sheds and yards and one early timber-framed wattle and daub barn, but all the eighteenth-century buildings were brick, very often with the reed thatch roofs so typical of this region.

The earliest map available over much of the area was the tithe map, which showed the large number of small farms in existence in the mid-nineteenth century. Many of the smallest ones have now disappeared. On only about 60 per cent of the tithe map farms do any historic buildings remain.

The tithe map of Rollesby shows how irregular and scattered were the holdings of many of the farms. John Ensor owned half the farms in the 1850s and a cattle shed at Church Farm is dated 1870, with the name S. P. Ensor carved on a stone; yet he did not have enough control over the parish to attempt a rationalization of the field layout. Over half the sixteen farms in Rollesby were under 100 acres and many had fields scattered across the parish. A similar disorder is obvious in the farm buildings themselves. Although many of the Broadland farmsteads consisted of large complexes of buildings they were never all built at once. All were added to over the years and as a result more farmsteads were still of an irregular layout in 1906 than in the other areas studied (illustration 116).

### The buildings; early barns to substantial complexes

It was in this area, never subjected to the programme of improvement of a well-run estate, that some of the earliest barns were found. In the two neighbouring parishes of Rollesby and Hemsby were the only aisled barns located on the survey. Dating is difficult, as their construction is of a type that changed little from medieval times to the seventeenth century. Supporting the roof on aisle posts allowed for a wider area to be spanned, and one of the Hemsby barns serving, by 1840, a farm of 640 acres was particularly massive, having two threshing floors and a volume of 1329 cu. m (46,950 cu. ft). This, however, was not the only large barn in the Broadland sample. There were four other substantial

brick and thatched eighteenth-century barns with a volume of over 600 cu. m (21,200 cu. ft) each. This period of building coincides with the period of high grain exports between 1700 and 1750 and suggests that this region on the edge of the Broadland marshes and with easy river access to Yarmouth was one that prospered at this time. Very few barns had two threshing floors and as in other areas many of the barns dated from between 1750 and 1800; half of those visited were built before the nineteenth century. All but one were brick and originally had thatched roofs. Not only were the barns large, but also most of the farms over 150 acres had more than one. As well as the pre-eighteenth-century aisled barn, there were two eighteenth-century brick barns at the 184-acre Church Farm at Rollesby, one abutting the earlier one. At Sowell's Farm, Rollesby, there were two barns, one dated 1719 and one probably built a generation later. Similarly, the two abutting

88 Rollesby parish at the time of the tithe survey, showing the scattered nature of the farm holdings and the large number of small farms surviving.

barns at South House Farm, Fleggburgh, date from about 1720 and 30 years later. A similar pattern emerges at Ashby Hall Farm. This need for increased barn capacity during the eighteenth century is surely an indication of a higher grain output. The scale of building shows there was no shortage of capital amongst the owner-occupiers and small landowners alike and very substantial barns were being built here during the same period as on many estate farms. Instead of demolishing and replacing old barns with new, larger and impressive structures, they added to what was there already. The barns are an indication of the prosperity of the good loams of east Norfolk, an area of small farms and landowners, where, according to William Marshall 'That long-established system of practice which has raised, deservedly, the name of Norfolk husbandmen' began.[6]

Stables survived on two-thirds of the farms, with a fifth of them being pre-1800. Some abutted the barn, while others were at right-angles to it, forming an L-shape, to which cattle yards were later added. As elsewhere, most of the pre-nineteenth-century stables had hay lofts and most stables had a horse yard associated with them. In common with the rest of the region it was reckoned that six horses were needed to cultivate every 100 acres of arable.[7] As elsewhere in this region, granaries were not common and were found on only seven farms. At Hall Farm, Fleggburgh, a cart lodge and granary above abutted an eighteenth-century barn. It was unusual because the cart shed was open across the width of the gable with the weatherboarded granary above. Behind this building, between it and the barn, was a strange store room open to the roof and reached through brick arched openings from the back of the cart shed. The use of this room is a mystery and nothing similar was found elsewhere.

Cattle yards still remained on fifteen of the farms visited, but more had recently been cleared from many farms. By 1850 Church Farm, Rollesby, was one of seven owned by John Ensor, and in 1870, when his son built new stockyards for his tenant, he put a plaque with his name and the date in the gable. A six-bay cart lodge with implement sheds at either end, a riding-horse stable and gig house completed the accumulation over 300 years of a very adequate set of buildings for an 180-acre farm in the late nineteenth century.

Loose boxes were found on five farms and two ranges of sunken loose boxes survive. As early as 1771, cattle were fattened in sheds on turnips. 'They (the farmers of Flegg) reckon they fatten best in sheds; but one evil is, they won't drive so well in this method.'[8] None of the remaining cattle sheds can be dated before 1850. At Heath Farm, Ashby-with-Oby, a range of boxes, four on each side of a central passage with a feed store on the end, was built in the second half of the nineteenth century between and at right angles to the two porches of the large two-threshing-floor barn built in 1801. This group was unusual in that

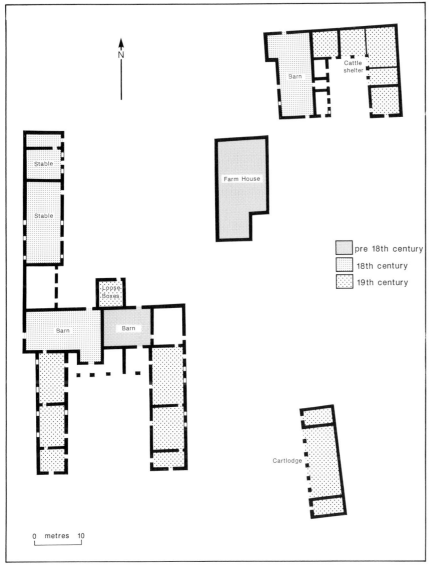

Legend (on plan):
- pre 18th century
- 18th century
- 19th century

Labels on plan: N, Cattle shelter, Barn, Farm House, Stable, Stable, Loose Boxes, Barn, Barn, Cartlodge

0  metres  10

89 Plan of Church Farm, Rollesby. This is an example of a large building complex gradually added to from the sixteenth century to 1870.

the shelter sheds forming a U with the barn appeared to date from 1801 as well. At Church Farm, Fleggburgh, a long range of 28 loose boxes arranged on either side of a central passage was said to have been built about 1912. In the Broads, as elsewhere, farming was adapting to the post-High Farming situation and more cattle were being fattened. All of these farms would have hired summer grazing on the nearby marshes and would have needed yards and buildings for the final fattening for market. On none of these larger farms was there any indication that there had been a shortage of capital for building. All were as well equipped, if in a less regimented way, as their neighbours on large estates.

Even the small farms had a barn, stable and yard, if on a more modest scale. Highfield Farm, Rollesby, owned and farmed by Ann Wright in 1840, consisted of 18 acres in six fields outside the village just west of the church. There was an L-shaped range abutting the house consisting of a barn and stable. Later a second range to the south of the barn was built as a shelter shed, the stable was converted into loose boxes and a new stable, now demolished, was built. All the buildings were brick with reed-thatched roofs, but all are now redundant and the house is derelict.

## CONCLUSIONS

All three areas covered in this region have different histories that are obvious from the buildings. At Gunton, the main period of landlord interest was the late eighteenth and early nineteenth centuries, while on the Evans-Lombe estate the main phase of building was much later when many farms were entirely rebuilt on a completely regular layout, including impressive ranges of cattle accommodation. In the Broads the farms were substantial, but mostly the result of the gradual accumulation of buildings. As in the other mostly owner-occupier area studied in the south of the county, several pre-eighteenth-century barns survived, the aisled barns possibly being late medieval; as more barn space was needed, further barns were erected. Although the buildings in this region are mostly larger than those in the south, they are not as massive as many of those in the west. This is particularly true of granaries and cart lodges, which are on a much smaller scale. Provision for cattle fattening, however, is often more sophisticated here than elsewhere. Sunken loose boxes were not only found on many estate farms, but also in the Broads; nothing comparable to the covered yards at Bylaugh was found elsewhere.

The main building material was brick, although flint was used on the Gunton and Evans-Lombe estates, particularly after 1850. Reed thatch was the distinctive roofing material of the Broads.

The main features that distinguish this region from those to the west and south are the generally smaller scale of building than to the west, particularly in the case of granaries and cart lodges, and the superior provision for cattle management. The lack of early barns, except in the owner-occupied Broads farms, is similar to the pattern in the south of the county where there is also a contrast between estate and owner-occupier barns.

# 12

# Barns

The individual studies that make up the second section of this book may be interesting, but the value of this type of survey can only be assessed by comparison and analysis of the evidence gathered. First we will consider the various buildings of the farmstead, and then what they can teach us about two very important themes of agricultural history: regionalism, and the part played by the landlord in agricultural improvement.

The barn is nearly always the oldest and largest surviving building on the farmstead, easily identified by the wide double doors through which the heavily-loaded wagons would have rumbled, bringing in the part of the crop to be stored and then threshed in the barn. Usually there was an opposing door that could be opened to create a draught for winnowing the chaff from the grain. This might be a double door lower than the other doors but high enough for the unloaded wagon to be driven out, thus avoiding the need to turn in the barn. Some of the earlier barns, built before wagons took over from the smaller two-wheeled carts, only have a single-width winnowing door.

One-fifth of those visited by the Norfolk survey were built before 1750, and 22 of the total of 252 were built before 1700. These early barns were widely distributed across the county, but none survive in the areas of late enclosure and reclamation in the extreme west and south-west. Three were found in the north-west, in the Hunstanton area, an indication of the slow, but steady investment levels of the LeStrange family, who added to existing buildings rather than rebuilding them. The durability of local building materials and the high standard of construction also helps to explain their survival.

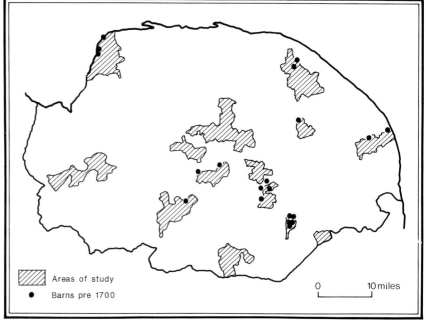

90 Distribution map of barns built before 1700 in the survey areas. Although widely scattered, none have survived in the extreme north or south while there are several in the areas of small landowners in the Broads and southern clays.

In contrast, on the Evans-Lombe estates, where the building evidence points to a massive investment in the mid-nineteenth century, there are no pre-1700 barns, and on the Duke of Norfolk's south Norfolk lands most of the buildings were rebuilt after 1860.

## BARNS BUILT BEFORE 1700

Nearly all the early barns are on farms of less than 150 acres and half are on non-estate farms; the large sums of money needed for a major project such as the rebuilding of a barn were not available here and the older barns were probably quite adequate anyway. It is mainly the larger pre-1700 barns that survive. None is less than 200 cu. m (7060 cu. ft) in capacity while two of the eleven barns of over 1000 cu. m (35,300 cu. ft) were built before 1700.

The majority of the early barns were timber-framed, originally infilled with wattle and daub, but most have been patched and repaired in recent centuries. Seven examples, scattered across the county, were of the more durable but more expensive brick, while three in the north-west were a mixture of stone and brick.

The aisled construction, which was found in three of the pre-1700 barns in Broadland, allowed for a much wider and therefore more capacious barn than in those limited by the breadth that could be roofed in a single span. The resulting huge barns point to a productive grain-growing area in the fertile loams of the Broadland edge by the late Middle Ages, while their survival has been secured by their non-

estate status. That aisled barns previously existed in other parts of the county is shown by the example on the Holkham estate in Castle Acre, demolished by Thomas William Coke in his enthusiasm for new improved farm buildings (illustration 8).

It is clear that, with a few notable exceptions, such as at Hales, Waxham and Paston, most of the largest late-medieval barns in the county were built by ecclesiastical rather than lay owners. The Broadland examples were part of the Norwich Cathedral estates and that at Castle Acre was owned by the priory there. The early barns at Corporation Farm, Hethel, were originally owned by the Great Hospital at Norwich, while other examples on several 'College' farms across the county were owned either by Cambridge colleges or small religious institutions.

## THE HEYDAY OF BARN BUILDING, 1700–1850

From 1700 to 1850 the number of barns surviving within the survey area from each 50-year period increases, until it reaches a peak in the early nineteenth century, with a third of the barns visited being built between 1800 and 1850. The increase in grain production in the late eighteenth century, stimulated after 1796 by the Napoleonic Wars, created a need for increased barn capacity resulting in either the rebuilding or enlarging of existing barns or the building of additional ones.

The capacity of barns varied greatly across the United Kingdom, and this contrast was obvious by the end of the seventeenth century. Roger North, in 1698, noted, 'In the west and north of England, the use of stacking (on stone staddles, or wooden posts with cross boards, called hovels) is so constant that people care not for barns, but only to thresh.' He suggested several reasons, the most likely being 'the thrift of landlords has not afforded barnes, so the people have found out ways of making up their stacks with tolerable security.' In contrast, in East Anglia, 'the farmes are great and croppes bulky and there they know nothing willingly, but clapping into the barne.' North said the farmers did not have the same skills at stacking and so 'they cease not to grumble 'till more barn-room be provided.'[1]

One hundred years later agricultural writers were still commenting that Norfolk barns were too large and involved too great an expense for the landowner. Norfolk farmers were against stacking their corn outside, even though, as Kent pointed out, 'wheat is preserved sweeter and better on staddles than in barns.' He should have known that the stone for staddles was not available in Norfolk, but he went on to say of Norfolk farmers, 'they are always crying out for barn space and they certainly are indulged in a greater proportion than farmers in any other county.'[2] His views had not changed since 1775, when he wrote, 'Barns, which are very expensive, may often be contracted and much necessary expense saved.'[3] Marshall too found Norfolk barns 'superior to those of every other county; numerous and spacious,'[4] and Arthur Young wrote in 1804 that 'The farmers are however advocates not only of barns, but of great barns...'[5] A survey of estate farms at Holkham undertaken by Kent in the 1790s shows that nearly all the farms he visited had at least two barns, and several four.[6] While yields had been

92 Barn at Hall Farm, Fleggburgh; a large eighteenth-century brick and thatched barn, typical of the Broads.

low all the crop had been housed, and many Norfolk farmers wanted to keep it that way as output rose. However, eventually, some of the crop had to be ricked. The large barn at Leicester Square Farm, South Creake, could only house 120 acres of the crop of an 800-acre farm, at least half of which would have been producing cereals in a given year. The rest must therefore have been stacked in a yard.

It is true that all these authors were most familiar with the conditions on the great estates, Young and Kent with Holkham and Marshall with Gunton. It is on the estates within the survey areas, such as Gunton and Merton, where the greatest period of improvement was stimulated by the high Napoleonic grain prices; well over half the barns were built or replaced in the years 1790–1830. Our findings suggest, however, that buildings elsewhere could be as substantial.

## BARN CAPACITY

Although Norfolk farmers wanted to store all their unthreshed crop in the barn, it is unlikely that this was possible by the eighteenth century. Fourteenth-century accounts for the Prior's Farm at North Elmham show that one of the largest barns there would house only five stacks, presumably after they were brought in for threshing. In 1820 the stacks of the tithe barley produced 95 quarters of grain.[7]

In the wetter, mainly pastoral areas of the country where farms were small, such as the Lake District, most of the crop could be housed. It is highly unlikely, however, that the increasing yields of the late eighteenth century could have been kept under cover in Norfolk even with the contemporary enlarging of barns for which there is so much evidence.

One of Joseph Hill's watercolours of the Houghton estate, sketched about 1800, shows a large stack on the end of a substantial barn. Two barns served this 873-acre farm in Great Bircham and this certainly would not have been enough to house all the crop in 1800.[8]

Randal Burroughs, farming near Wymondham in the 1790s, recorded in his diary exactly what he did with his crop as it came off the fields to await threshing. Certainly much of it was stacked and there seems to have been little logic or planning behind what was put in the barn. Most of the oats were, but barley and wheat was both stacked and then moved into the barn. 'We finished the two Spikes Lane Closes of barley, viz fifteen acres. Nine loads were stacked and the rest put in Browick barn...on Wednesday, eleven loads off the Black Close were stacked at Sutton and on the following day the remainder got into the barn – in all 24 loads.'[9]

Throughout the year the crop was threshed out, stack by stack. In November Randal wrote 'on the first day of the preceding week carted one of the wheat stacks at Browick into the barn and it employed nine men.' One man was kept employed threshing all winter at a field barn to keep up a continuous supply of straw for the bullocks there.[10]

In more recent times, just before the Second World War, a corn stack, 11 metres by 5.5 metres (12 yards by six yards) would thrash down to about 100 coombes (400 bushels, or nearly ten tons of grain). At this date a yield of half a tone to the acre could be expected from average land, a figure that is not very different from those given for Norfolk yields in the tithe surveys. This means that one large stack would represent the harvest from about 20 acres. Similarly, Peter Love, a farmer in Nottinghamshire, calculated in 1860 that over 600 sheaves could be expected from an acre and that twelve sheaves with long straw would take up a cubic yard in a barn.[11] Arthur Young, describing one of the largest barns on the Holkham estates, serving a farm of over 800 acres, calculated that if the crop was well trodden down the produce of 140 acres could be squeezed in.[12] From the pieces of evidence it is clear that in arable and productive Norfolk there would not have been enough room for an entire crop to be housed in the barn.

The size of the barn only bears a very loose relationship to the arable acreage of the farm. All the barns with a capacity of under 200 cu. m (7060 cu. ft) are on farms of under 200 acres and the three largest farms (over 600 acres) have at least one barn over 1000 cu. m (35,300 cu. ft), but this is as far as the correlation can be taken. Not surprisingly the size of the barn varies across the county from soil region to soil region. There are no large barns (over 800 cu. m; 28,250 cu. ft) in the south; instead the majority are between 200 and 400 cu. m (7060 and 14,100 cu. ft). In the west the majority are between 400 and 600 cu. m (14,100 and 21,200 cu. ft) and three are over 1000 cu. m (35,300 cu. ft).

## STACKYARDS

Stackyards are named near the barns on many of the farmsteads shown on the tithe maps. A favourite place for stacking was on the gable end of the barn, below the pitching hole. There was often a wall forming an enclosure for the stacks, and when the stack had been threshed out the enclosure could be used as an extra livestock yard in the winter. This arrangement is described by Marshall[13] and is shown on a mid-eighteenth-century plan of Hillington Hall, but no evidence of it was found on any of the farms visited.

Although there is no way that the whole grain crop could be stored in the barn, it is possible that the barley crop was. In Suffolk, barns were used for storing barley before threshing.[14] Barley is said to be difficult to stack because of the smooth nature of the straw.

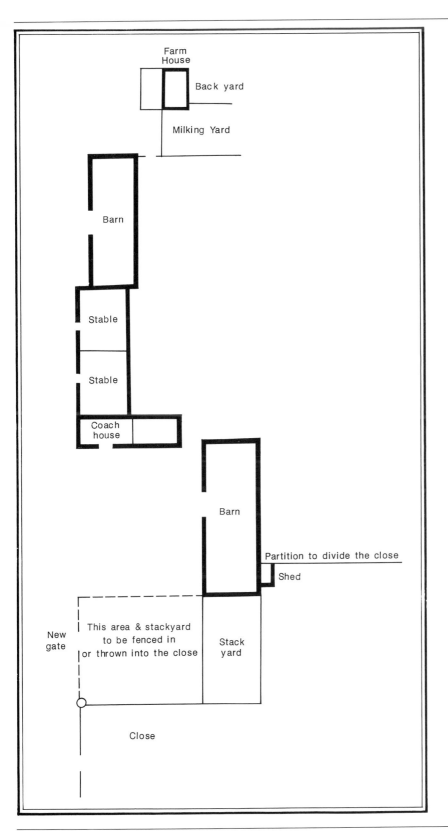

Farm
House

Back yard

Milking Yard

Barn

Stable

Stable

Coach
house

Barn

Partition to divide the close

Shed

New
gate

This area & stackyard
to be fenced in
or thrown into the close

Stack
yard

Close

93 Map of the farm
buildings at Hillingdon Hall
c.1760 showing a fenced
stack yard on the end of the
barn (redrawn from a map
in the Norfolk Record
Office).

# THE THRESHING PROCESS

The main purpose of the barn, other than storage, was to house the threshing floor. Before the days of threshing machines the crop would be threshed out a little at a time through the winter with a hand flail, and this hard and tedious work would be undertaken on the threshing floor where the sheaves would be broken open and the heads of the corn beaten with a heavy flail until the seeds were separated from the head. On larger farms two threshing floors could be worked at once. The remaining straw would be stored, either in part of the barn or, if that was full with the unthreshed crop, in the porch, until it was needed in the livestock sheds, yards or stables. The threshed seed had then to be 'winnowed', or cleaned ready for sale. In Norfolk, according to Marshall, this process involved throwing the grain in shovels from one end of the threshing floor to the other. The double doors at either end of the floor which were often kept tightly closed during threshing, would be opened, creating a good through draught and the chaff would be blown from the grain. A long distance was needed over which to throw the grain and so porches were often built. 'To obtain this necessary length of floor (24 feet), a porch on one or both sides of the barn is almost universal.'[15] Porches do not seem to have been a feature of barns before 1750. No seventeenth-century porches survive and the elevations, admittedly idealized, that appear on seventeenth- and eighteenth-century maps do not show them.

Usually the crop would be threshed as the grain was needed, either for animal feed or sale, and so there was little necessity for storage space on the farm. The wider part of the porch, so frequently found in the Gunton barns, may have provided a temporary storage area.

The construction of the threshing floor needed great care so that grain was not lost between the cracks. 'It was absolutely essential that there should be no leakage, no open joints between the planks through which the threshed corn would trickle. Also the planks had to be of tough hard wood to enable them to withstand the thumping of flails, wielded, day after day, by strong men threshing the kernel from the straw.'[16] Sycamore, wych-elm and ash were the favourite timbers for their compactness and their freedom from any tendency to shale, which would have hindered shovelling.

The late eighteenth century was a time of timber shortage and as the life of a wooden floor was thought to be between 15 and 20 years, there was a great deal of interest in improvements in design that might increase its longevity. In 1796, the Society of Arts offered a 30 guinea prize for such a design. This was won by John Upton of Petworth, for a movable floor. It was made of hollow oak sections that could be taken up and stored upright, so that it was protected from damp and traffic and could be moved from building to building. It had the added attraction that the hollow floor magnified the sound of threshing, so that the farmer could tell whether his men were idle or not wherever he was on the farm.[17]

Both brick and stone-flagged floors were also found on the survey and Marshall took a very cynical view of Norfolk farmers, writing that they preferred brick because a little brick dust in the grain would increase its volume. 'For the same dust which gives roughness to the handle in the sample, prevents the corn, thus soiled by the clay's beating up, from settling close in the bushel as that which has been thrashed on a clean wooden floor.'[18]

On many farms visited, great double barn doors remain, made up of several sections so that different parts could be opened to control the draught. The boards, or thresholds, that could be inserted at floor level across the door when threshing was in progress, both to stop the threshed crop spilling out and the farmyard fowl from coming in, are often still in place.

As a good draught was needed across the barn floor for winnowing, we might expect the barns to be orientated in such a way as to catch the prevailing wind, and certainly this is more usual amongst the barns built in the days of hand-threshing than in later years. Nearly half the barns built before 1700 have their double doors facing east and west, while by 1850 only a third are orientated this way. Recent work on fourteen barns at Wharfdale, Yorkshire, and 22 in West Cumberland has produced similar evidence. There is no distinction between the barns by date, but there is a marked tendency for east-west orientation to be avoided in favour of something near north-south.[19]

On either side of the porch there was often a range of lean-to sheds or loose boxes along the length of the barn. These served two purposes; providing shelter for animals in the yards, and adding strength to the barn walls, which would be under great strain when the barn was full. Mr Black of Sturston wanted a barn 'with proper lean-tos for the support of it', when he was negotiating for new buildings with Lord Walsingham's agent in 1780.[20]

The gradual introduction of the threshing machine from the late eighteenth century meant that the barn with its threshing floor became obsolete, but change was very slow and one of the surprising findings of this survey was the importance given to the barn in Norfolk long after the introduction of the threshing machine in other parts of the country. Well into the 1840s many farmers were still flail-threshing part of their crop, mainly because it was a way of finding work for their men through the winter. On the 12,000-acre Evans-Lombe Field House Farm, Swanton Morley, the wheat was machine threshed in 1840, but barley hand flailed.[21]

The introduction from the 1850s of the portable steam-engine, working threshing machines, heralded the end of the barn as a storage

94 Barn, Maytree Farm, Bawdeswell; a substantial brick and tile barn. The gable wall has been rebuilt in the mid-nineteenth century in a style typical of the Evans-Lombe estate.

place for unthreshed corn. The threshing machine had to be loaded from the top and it was far easier to cast down a stack into the machine in a yard, as is so graphically described by Thomas Hardy in *Tess of the D'Urbervilles*, than to load from a barn.

In areas where there was considerable rebuilding up to the mid-nineteenth century, such as the Evans-Lombe estate, large barns, some with more than one threshing floor, were still being erected. As the barn became obsolete for threshing and the importance of keeping cattle in warm sheds was becoming better understood in the early nineteenth century, the value of south-facing yards, sheltered from the north by the barn, meant that barns, with their lean-to sheds, were increasingly orientated with their doors facing north-south rather than east-west.

## THE BARN AFTER 1850

By 1850 the days of the barn were numbered. A Norfolk tenant farmer, John Hudson, wrote in a submission for the *JRASE* farm building competition of 1850, 'In this improving age, it will be unwise to recommend the building of large expensive barns.'[22] Gradually, the use and appearance of the barn changed. Some were reroofed, but no new ones were built in the owner-occupier areas of the survey after 1860. The only new ones were those that formed part of a complete rebuild on an estate farm, and even here the new barns were a very small element alongside much larger livestock sheds. They did still have the traditional double doors, presumably to allow a loaded wagon, perhaps with threshed-out straw, to come in, unload and continue out through the opposite opening. Several of these late barns did not form part of the livestock complex, but were built separately, typically as part of a cart lodge and granary block.

95 A great variety of building materials were used on the Walsingham estate, whose soils varied from light sands to heavy clays. Half-timbered barn at Broom Hill Farm, Merton.

96 A simple eighteenth-century brick barn at College Farm, Thompson.

Barn machinery was often powered by either a steam-engine or horse gin placed outside the barn, and several examples of small hatches being cut in barn walls to take belting into the building were found on the survey. These square hatches are unlike the tall slit-like ones found by Peters in his Staffordshire survey, but it is difficult to suggest any other reason why they might have been cut. No surviving horse-gear was found, although a water-wheel for driving barn machinery is mentioned in the sales particulars of one farm on the Evans-Lombe estate. Steam-engines were sometimes housed in small lean-tos built on the gable end of the barn, and several belting holes survive linking

97 Barn, Home Farm, Holme; this attractive brick and chalk barn is typical of the north-west of the county.

98 Belting holes in barn wall, Old Hall Farm, Griston.

these lean-tos with the barn interiors.

As hand-flailing was given up on all but the smallest farms the uses to which the barn was put changed. Instead of the barn housing the threshing floor, dressing and winnowing machines were installed and the building was often used as a feed store. Internal dividing walls were erected and floors inserted to provide more storage space. A barn on the Gunton estate in 1894 was described as excellent, 'very wisely, it has been turned into a chaff cutting house, dressing house and turnip house.' Sometimes, particularly in off-premises or field barns and where farms had been amalgamated, the barn doors were removed and the building opened up to provide extra cattle accommodation; a practice that usually resulted in the rapid deterioration of the building.

The barn, therefore, remained an important building on Norfolk farms even after it was technically obsolete; one was included in all the post-1850 farmsteads built on the Hare, Evans-Lombe and Duke of Norfolk estates. Large barns were by no means an innovation introduction by landlords, and they are found on owner-occupier farms well before 1700.

At no period were landlords leading the way, but rather they were satisfying the demands of their tenants in building the barns that they felt were needed for the working of the farm, often against the advice of the agricultural writers of the day.

99 Pitching and owl holes in barn at Home Farm, Holme. Some of the crop would be pitched in from the top of a laden wagon through an opening high up in the gable wall. Owls were encouraged to roost in barns in the days before other methods of vermin control.

# 13

# Stables

## THE VALUE OF HORSES

Horses were the farmer's most valuable possessions, both in money terms and because the efficient working of the farm depended upon their well-being. John Hudson of Castle Acre, a great advocate of progressive farming and a founder member of the Royal Agricultural Society of England, wrote in 1850. 'The keeping of cart horses is a very important item in the economy of the farm; they require at all times to be in good condition and always ready to do a good day's work.'[1] Because of this, farms had well-built stables from an early date and, after the barn, the stable is often the oldest surviving building. Rarely did improvers comment on poor stabling in the way that they criticized cattle accommodation.[2]

Few stables date from the seventeenth century while many predate the nineteenth-century improvement of farms. The amalgamation of farms during the eighteenth century meant that farmers needed more horses. Various estimates of the number of horses that were needed to work on farms were made in the early nineteenth century and a figure in the region of one per 20 arable acres seems a reasonable one. The larger the farm and the lighter the soil, the fewer were the horses needed and Arthur Young quotes one 1000-acre Holkham farm with only one horse for every 30 acres.[3] Smaller farms still needed a team of horses, so even a 50-acre farm would usually have four horses. The sales particulars surviving for just over 70 of the farms in the survey area which were sold up immediately after the First World War give a picture of the situation just before the end of the period of horse power.

On the Evans-Lombe estate 27 of the farms were sold in 1919 and

the amount of stabling on each farm is given. It is unlikely that the sales catalogue would underestimate the accommodation available, yet on five of the farms there was less than one horse for every 30 acres and this situation was not confined to the larger farms. Similarly, there is a great variation in size amongst the nine farms, with more than one horse for every 20 acres. The situation is the same on the Gunton estate where 26 farms were sold in 1919 and on the much heavier land of the Letton Hall estate where 20 farms were sold in 1913.

100 Lunette windows are traditionally associated with stables, as in this example at Hall Farm, Stanninghall.

## THE IMPORTANCE OF OXEN

The other reason for increased building in the eighteenth century was that horses were replacing oxen as the main draught animal. Oxen were hardy animals that did not need stabling; instead they were usually kept with the rest of the cattle. One possibly seventeenth-century building at Hall Farm, Reymerston, divided into two stalls, larger than are usually found in stables, has been tentatively interpreted as an ox stable. Coke worked twelve oxen at Holkham in the 1780s and 'found them a considerable saving',[4] but he had given them up by 1803 because of the problem of getting them shod, 'and the inveterate prejudices of the men against them'. Another enthusiast at that time was Mr Purdis at Egmere who worked 32 Devon oxen, four to a plough. 'I saw them at work and was much pleased to see them step out so nimbly, as to be fully equal to the horses ploughing in the same field.' The advantages of oxen were that they required 'nothing but food'.[5] While a horse lost value as it grew older, a bullock gained, and the initial outlay was less. However, oxen did not work as fast as horses. Four oxen ploughed only slightly more than two horses and by the 1840s they were only used on a few of the larger farms.[6] Some teams of oxen were kept throughout the nineteenth century, probably more as curiosities, and were a frequent subject for the early photographers.

There was no clearly defined Norfolk breed of horse. 'The pedigree of the Norfolk horse can be traced to no particular stock, but probably they might claim kindred with almost all the breeds in the kingdom.' The advantage of the Norfolk horse was that 'it did not tire easily, it was hardy, strong and had a quickness of step.'[7]

## STABLES BUILT BEFORE 1800

Three stables found on the survey, in Hethel, Fritton and Shelfanger, dated from pre-1700, and all of them had one early feature in common: a hay loft over the stable. Up to about 1800 hay lofts over stables were thought to be a good arrangement. Not only was it convenient to keep hay there and to push it down through hatches in the floor above the hayracks as it was needed by the horses, but it also helped to keep the horses warm. Coming in, hot from work, sudden cold could well cause a chill. Of the 190 stables seen on the survey, nearly all those without hay lofts were built after 1800. One problem of the early arrangement was that the hay chamber floors rotted extremely quickly, presumably as a result of a combination of the damp rising from the hot horses and the weight of the hay stored above. The Gunton estate accounts of the 1820s are full of sums spent on mending hay chamber floors. Marshall saw some floors being made of clay puddled with straw and laid over rods. He thought this was better than planked wood as there were no gaps for the grass seed to fall down and irritate the horses.[8] Unfortunately, none of these clay floors have survived. Stables with hay lofts were not found in the areas where there was considerable late nineteenth-century rebuilding, such as the Duke of Norfolk or the Hare estates. There were a few in the north-west of the county, but they were mostly in mid-Norfolk, on the Gunton estates and in the Broads.

Another feature of the early stables was their distinctive internal arrangement. As in other parts of the country, such as Wales and Staffordshire, the horses in the early stables were stalled along the axis of the building with two rows of stalls facing the opposing gable walls. The trouble with this was that four horses were about the maximum that could be housed across the width of an unaisled building. Most of the stables arranged in this way are smaller than the later ones where the horses stood across the axis of the building parallel with the gable wall.

In his *Treatise on Building*, written shortly after his completion of Rougham Hall, Norfolk, in 1698, Roger North criticized the layout of stables that he thought typical at that time. 'I mean the laying all in one long range, without breaking the file of horses by partitions or making several stables. This looks great, but the master's ostentation is not for the horses' health; the place is cold and noisy, nothing stirs but the whole room is disturbed and an horse is a watchful creature, and hearkens after all that passeth.'[9] He thought that horses were happier if they could see each other and in his stables at Rougham Hall, the horses face each other, four on each side, across a central gangway.

Of the three pre-1700 stables surviving, two are freestanding buildings and one is built in the end of a barn. One of the two, built mainly of wattle and daub within a timber frame, but with some brick and non-original weatherboarding, stands at Church Farm, Hethel. Its jowled wall posts and chamfered beams suggest that it is pre-1700, and a sixteenth-century barn is also part of the same complex. There is an internal staircase at one end leading to the hay loft, but the stable divisions and harness posts are probably not original. A far less complete freestanding building, which may have been a stable, survives at Fritton, and the third pre-1700 example, still in the south of the county, was at Limetree Farm, Shelfhanger.

Half of the pre-1800 stables surviving are not in fact freestanding but abutting or part of barns, and the Shelfhanger example is of this second type. The barn of which it is part is seventeenth century, but the building of the stable involved the demolition of part of the barn, probably at the end of the seventeenth century. It was not clear how much of the internal arrangement was original. Two small rooms had been partitioned off in the corners of the stable, one for harness and one for feed. There was a hay loft with hatches above the troughs. The most striking thing about this altogether unusual building was the decorative carved wooden pediment over the stable door (illus. 13), which appeared to be in its original position and was an indication of the esteem in which horses were held.

About 40 of the stables visited were built before 1800. They are scattered fairly evenly across the survey area, but there were none on the fen edge. Half had a hay loft over the stable, while some of the others may have been lofted originally. About half were either built on the end or were an integral part of barns. In fact, there appears to have been a long period of overlap in stable design and a great variety of types was found in the stables dating between 1700 and 1800.

Stables on the end of barns usually ran the full width or nearly the width of the barn, and therefore, as at Neache's Farm, Felmingham, the horses would stand with their heads towards the gable ends and their backs to a central passage. In this way five or six horses could be housed on either side. There would be a door in the centre of the side wall, a pitching hole in the gable, and sometimes a door in the gable end, often leading into a tack room alongside the stalled horses. Sometimes, but not always, there was a door leading into the barn, an arrangement which would reduce the carting involved in moving the threshed straw from the barn to the stable.

There are some very substantial eighteenth-century examples of freestanding stables. At Beeches Farm, Fritton, and Algarsthorpe Farm, Great Melton, the horses stood across the width of the building in a long stable providing stalls for ten horses, with a separate harness room. There was a hay loft above with decorative ventilation bricks to keep a flow of air through the hay. Long ranges, lacking the height of lofted stables, were also being built by the late eighteenth century and many long unlofted ranges survive, particularly on the LeStrange estates, some with a tack room on the end. There do not seem to be any regional variations. The type built is more likely to have been governed by the size of the farm than its region; where more than half a dozen horses needed to be housed a long range, lofted or unlofted, was more suitable.

It is not clear how many of these early stables were originally part of a yard complex. At Algarsthorpe Farm and Courtyard Farm, Ringstead, the stable and yard arrangement appears to be eighteenth-

101 The stables at Bridge Farm, Bradfield survive in a particularly complete form.

(*left*) Tack room with harness pegs. (*right*) Ladder leading to hay loft. This early nineteenth-century stable is a late example of a stable with a hay loft.

century and original. The turning out of horses at night became more usual in the nineteenth century, and so some of the horse yards may not have been created until then.

## CHANGES IN STABLE DESIGN AFTER 1800

A change in stable design is obvious from about 1800. The agricultural improvers were advocating better ventilation. It was claimed that horses were more healthy in stables without lofts,[10] and so they became single storey with ventilation, either in the roof or gables. Only eighteen of the 135 stables within the survey built after 1800 had hay lofts. This change of design was not universal across the United Kingdom. In north-east Wales they remained mostly lofted, the upstairs often being used for farm servant accommodation.

Stables also became larger and the arrangement of stalling along the length of the building more usual. The provision of tack rooms and a feed store were by no means universal; often, where the horses were stalled along the length of the building, the hooks for tackle were along the opposite wall between the doors. Opinion as to the value of a tack room was divided. Some felt that it was better to have pegs near where the horses were groomed as the harness was more likely to be hung up if it did not have to be carried far. Others felt it was harmful to both the metal and the leather for the harness to be hung up in the stable and advocated a separate tack room. The position of this tack room varied. At Bridge Farm, Bradfield, and Manor Farm, Southborough, amongst others, the tack room was in a lean-to on the side of the stable, while often it is at one end. The gutting of many stables makes it impossible to say how frequently tack rooms were provided but that they were not an unusual feature is shown by the descriptions in the sales catalogues. Two-thirds of those farms sold in 1919 on the Gunton and Evans-Lombe estates and half of those on the Letton estates had harness rooms. They were therefore more widespread than in Staffordshire and Wales, particularly on the larger farms.

In contrast to the period before 1800, very few stables built later are either part of or abutting the barn. Instead, they are mostly freestanding or part of a livestock range. The clay lump stable at Limetree Farm, Forncett End, is a very substantial two-storey building built in 1840. It is a late example of a stable with a hay loft. There are four stable doors, two opposite each other, leading into stables at either end where the horses stood facing the gables. In between the two stables are the tack and chaff rooms and behind the building is a horse yard. These well-built stables incorporate early as well as more progressive features and illustrate the overlap often found in stable design.

It might be expected that with the increase in the amount of machinery available to the farmer after 1850 the number of horses

102 Ventilator/window in stable at Park Farm, Stow Bardolph, probably built in the 1870s.

kept would increase, and so additions to the eighteenth-century accommodation would frequently be found. This is not the case. On only 20 farms do two separate stable blocks survive and in only a few cases could one be dated to the eighteenth and the other to the late nineteenth century. On many of the farms with eighteenth-century stables, this accommodation remained adequate throughout the next 100 years. On farms where the only stable is nineteenth century it is most likely that this is a replacement of an earlier one of unknown size; but it has to be said that there is no real evidence for an increase in stable accommodation between 1800 and 1900.

As well as the general increase in the number of freestanding stables and the decline in the popularity of the hay loft, there are several developments in the detail of construction during the nineteenth century. Cobbled floors were replaced by hard black engineering fabrics. Very few cobbled floors have survived modern phases of alterations, but those that did are in eighteenth-century stables. In many buildings semi-circular lunette windows, sometimes but not always with cast-iron

103 This riding-horse stable at South House Farm, Fleggburgh with its lunette windows, is typical. The chimney is above a fireplace in a groom's room.

window frames, had replaced square or rectangular ones by the early nineteenth century, and these have come to be recognized as a distinctive and almost universal feature of stable architecture; however, no reason for this design can be suggested. Elaborate systems of ventilation, often involving cast-iron work, were also developed. On the Evans-Lombe estate rectangular grilles, about the area of two bricks, are to be found just below eaves level and a round grille is often built into the gable wall. On the Hare estate sliding wooden shutters are provided and on many farms sliding cast-iron shutters are found in riding-horse stables.

Buildings specifically designed for riding-horses are not found on all farms. They are usually near the house and often contain elaborate fittings. The horses always have separate stalls, and there is always a tack room and sometimes a grooms' room with a fireplace.

One feature that seems to be confined almost entirely to Norfolk stabling is the lack of partitions between the horses. All farm designers recommended wooden partitions between the horses to prevent them kicking each other. However, even where the original fittings survive, this was not generally the case in the survey area. Often there was one partition at the end of the building to house the 'stingy' or difficult horse (every farm had one!). Otherwise the building was open. Stalling may have been unnecessary because horses rarely spent the night indoors. Most stables adjoined yards and the horses were fed and

**104** Open stable at Lyng House Farm with a single stall partitioned off at the end for the 'stingy' horse.

groomed in their stalls and were then turned out for the night. When Arthur Young was writing in 1804 this seems to have been an unusual practice, confined to 'the angle of county formed by Woodbridge, Saxmundham, and the sea.'[11] By 1836 it was the normal method of looking after horses in the county and is described by Loudan. 'The Norfolk system of horse management differs materially from that pursued in most other counties in England, in not having any stall or divisions in the stables, save perhaps one for a vicious or troublesome horse . . . the horses are not confined to the stable, except at feeding and cleaning times, when they are tied up; at other times they are turned into a dry, well-littered straw yard.'[12] By 1840 this sytem was far more widespread and was described by Denton in 1864 as 'the midland practice'.[13]

A late example of a well planned stable group is that on the newly-built farmstead of South Lopham, built in 1862. Here there are three horse yards, each serving a separate stable that housed a plough team of four horses. At one end of the open feeding area was a harness room and at the other a chaff house. There was one cutting house, for cutting straw into chaff, at the end of the range.

It can be seen that a great variety in stable design is found across the county. There seems to be little regional variation and different types were built over widely overlapping periods. There is little distinction to be made between estate and non-estate areas, although from the sales catalogue evidence available it appears that tenant farmers were, if anything, underprovided with horse accommodation.

# 14

# Livestock

## COWS

The rapidly increasing number of cattle and heightened interest in livestock husbandry from the mid-eighteenth century made good housing become increasingly important. There is no evidence for specific accommodation for cows on Norfolk farms, or provision for their inwintering in stalls as in the northern and western areas. Cattle sheds, where the stock are tied in stalls throughout the winter, which were favoured in the north and west, are not found in eastern England. It was usual in areas where there was a shortage of straw as it is more economical on bedding. Cattle are often housed for half as long again in the north as in the south and so 50 per cent more fodder will also be needed. Hay storage is therefore more important there than it is in East Anglia. Yards are a more suitable form of cattle housing in the drier east where there is plenty of straw available.[1] William Marshall categorically stated in the 1780s that 'cow houses were unknown in Norfolk farming.'[2]

Milking was usually an outside activity and milking yards are marked on several eighteenth-century plans. Norfolk was never renowned as a dairy county, and by 1804 dairies were confined to the areas around Hingham, Attleborough and Watton, 'but fewer cows than formerly'.[3] Butter from Swaffham and Downham Market was sent to Cambridge and London. By the 1840s dairies were only found in the 'neighbourhood of towns where the milk is of considerable value', and in the west of the county, providing for the London market. In the summer the cows were kept on grass and in the winter they came into the yards and were fed on hay and turnips. Most farmers had a few cows to provide for their own needs, but no more.[4]

Dairies were found on nearly all farms, however small. These were usually in the farmhouse, on the north side for coolness, and near the kitchen, but they have usually been altered beyond recognition. On one derelict farm in North Walsham only the tiled ledges for the cream crocks survived.

### Cattle housing – sheds and yards

The inwintering of cattle gradually became more widely practised from the late eighteenth century, although there are scattered references to the stalling of cattle during the winter from Elizabethan times. Nathaniel Bacon, farming about 600 acres in the north Norfolk parish of Stiffkey, was stalling his cattle in the 1580s.[5] The increasing production of turnips, followed by mangolds and swedes, plus the need for manure to keep up the increasing output of grain, meant that cattle, unlike sheep, were taken off the fields in the autumn, since in the fields there was little to eat and plenty of mud to churn up, and instead were kept in well-strawed yards where they could be fed. The straw and manure would build up and be well trodden through the winter, turning into a manageable and valuable commodity.

C.S. Read noted the rather unlikely practice of putting cattle out to root fields to eat 'small white turnips and swede-tops' by day and lodging them in yards at night. He commented in 1858 that 'this custom is certainly going out of practice and so it ought...the cattle cannot do themselves much good, during cold wintry weather, by eating dirty turnip tops off the mirey soil, and as to consolidating the land, surely a clod crusher would do that as well.' Instead, by the late 1850s almost all the roots were removed from the land and consumed in yards by cattle.[6]

By the late eighteenth century, interest in livestock housing is evident in the pages of the *Annals of Agriculture* where the method of achieving an ideal layout for ease of feeding, economy of labour and the proper making of manure was frequently discussed. William Marshall described a set of buildings he visited near Blofield in the 1780s: 'Some of their bullock sheds are large, expensive buildings. Mr Batchelor has a very good one: it consists of a centre building, thirty-six feet long, nineteen feet wide and about eleven feet high at the eaves; with a pair of wide folding doors at each end; and with a lean-to on each side, the whole length of the building eleven feet wide...The centre building is the turnip-house; the lean-tos, sheds for the bullocks; which stand with their heads towards, or rather in, the turnip house; from which they are parted by a range of mangers only;...This shed holds twenty bullocks, ten on each side, fastened by the neck, with chains, swivels and rings...'[7] Marshall visited a similar shed in Ranworth, but nothing

of this type, with a central turnip house and the animals tied, was found anywhere on the survey. C. S. Read considered that 'sheds for tying up cattle were common in this county during the last century', but implies that the system had gone out of favour by the 1850s.[8]

The most usual arrangement was a system whereby a yard was enclosed; often on the south side of the barn for warmth, the barn forming one wall. At least two walls of the yard would support a roof over an open shelter shed into which the animals would come for food and shelter. The open well-strawed yard provided plenty of room for exercise, the accumulation and the treading down of manure. There was often a turnip shed with double doors opening onto a hard road from which the tumbrils could tip their contents into the shed, and an internal door leading straight into the shelter sheds where the feeding mangers would be. These shelter sheds would be some of the only buildings on the farm to have guttering, to keep the water out of the yard and away from the previous manure.[9]

Nearly all farms must have had some sort of simple cattle accommodation to allow for the processing of straw into manure to keep the land fertile. However, they are very vulnerable to demolition. The gateways into them are too narrow for the modern tractor and the roofs of the shelter sheds are too low for the front-loaders needed for mucking out. The bases of the wooden posts holding up the roofs rot and are knocked

105 Cattle in a traditional yard, High House Farm, Thuxton.

by machinery, and soon become unsound. The yards are often next to the barn in an area needed for loading and unloading if the barn is to remain in use. It is therefore not surprising that these sheds and yards only survived on 175 of the 300 farms visited, and only 51 of these were abutting barns. Often the only sign that remains is the shadow of the shed gable on the barn wall. Nearly all those surviving were of brick or brick and flint. Clay lump was not generally considered a suitable material for cattle sheds and chalk was also too soft. Roofs were either tiled or thatched.

These types of shelter sheds and yards were built from the late eighteenth century and continued to be erected over the next 100 years. Sometimes they formed a neat, conventional E- or U-shape while often they were at an angle, filling in some awkward corner along a boundary wall or between two previously freestanding buildings, as at Green Farm, Thorpe Market. This arrangement suggests that the yards were created within an earlier arrangement as and when they were needed, rather than being part of an overall plan. At Aylsham Road Farm, Felmingham, we see the tidier arrangement with a double-sided shelter shed built at right angles to the barn, and two yards created, both sheltered from the north by the barn. Similar simple arrangements continued to be built on many farms until the end of the nineteenth century. The buildings erected on some of the newly-laid-out fen farms in Stow Bardolph and Nordelph in the 1840s contained nothing more in the way of cattle housing than shelter sheds and yards with turnip houses.

### Improved housing for better cattle and manure production

Although the surviving sample was a small one, there was enough to show the gradual sophistication in methods of housing livestock that took place through the nineteenth century alongside the survival of the simplest system.

By the 1840s there was increasing interest in improving cattle accommodation. There was a gradual change in the position of livestock within the farming economy. In the days of high grain prices cattle were seen merely as machines for making manure, but as meat prices began to rise, and the arrival of railways in Norfolk made it easier to get cattle to market, interest in the efficient fattening of cattle increased. Previous to the railway, bullocks had lost 28 pounds (13 kg) on the walk to London, which took several days. By 1850 between a third and a half of the cattle sold at Smithfield had been fattened in Norfolk.[10] The increasing availability of imported cattle feeds such as linseed cake allowed more animals to be kept, and therefore more housing was needed. The expense of the cattle cake heightened the demand for housing which in turn provided for the efficient conversion of feed into

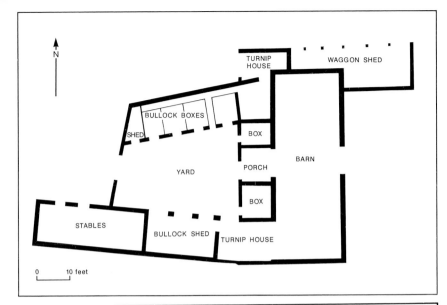

**106** Plan of Green Farm, Thorpe Market, showing bullock yard, sheds and boxes on the west side of the barn. The irregular layout is dictated by the adjacent road.

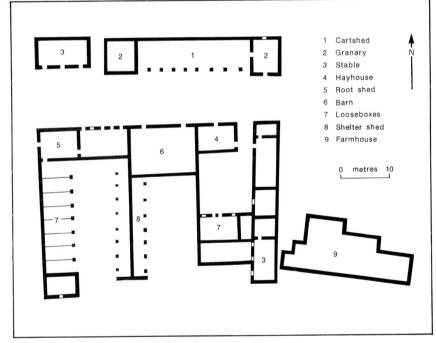

1 Cartshed
2 Granary
3 Stable
4 Hayhouse
5 Root shed
6 Barn
7 Looseboxes
8 Shelter shed
9 Farmhouse

**107** Plan of Aylsham Road Farm, Felmingham; a well-laid-out farmstead with large south-facing cattle yards.

meat and protected the manure.

The first development was the dividing up of yards so that groups of 10–12 cattle could be managed individually.[11] The new premises at South Lopham (illustration 61), erected in 1862, had four separate yards, one for cows, one for calves and two for bullocks.

Two types of improvement were being discussed and tried during the 1840s. The first and most common in Norfolk were the loose boxes. There was no doubt in C. S. Read's mind as to their value: 'Where

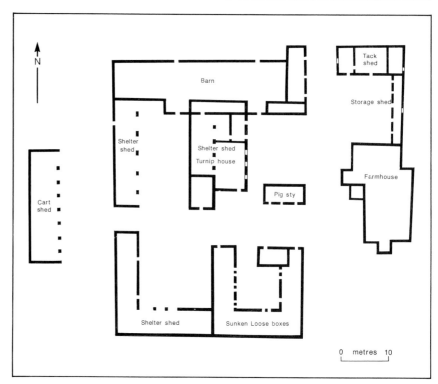

**108** Plan of Ruggs Hall Farm, Felmingham, showing the extensive cattle accommodation to the south of the barn.

landlords provide boxes, tenants are only too glad to avail themselves of the change. There can be no doubt that cattle do best in them and make the richest manure, but the first outlay entails a heavy expense on the proprietor.' These individual boxes, usually each with a door and a window and a feeding trough along the back wall, allowed for the individual feeding of cattle in the final stage of fattening for market. They were either built as individual boxes, perhaps in a lean-to on a barn, or more usually in rows with a feeding passage behind or down the centre of two rows, so the cattle could be fed from outside their pens. Often the floor of the loose box was sunken. At Ruggs Hall, Felmingham, we see both the earlier and later arrangements. To the south of the barn are two yards with shelter sheds and then at a short distance is a separate yard surrounded by sunken loose boxes and built at a later date, probably about 1850, to provide for the increasing needs for livestock accommodation. A similar range survives on another Gunton farm at Thorpe Hall, Thorpe Market. Here 30 cattle could be fattened, fifteen in loose boxes with sunken earthen floors on either side of a central feeding passage. The best examples of long double ranges with a central feeding passage were found in the Broads and were built as late as 1912. This type of sunken loose box with a feeding passage seems to be confined to the eastern survey areas of the Broads and the Gunton estates. They are, however, found in the west, on the Holkham estate, but not in the areas covered by the survey.

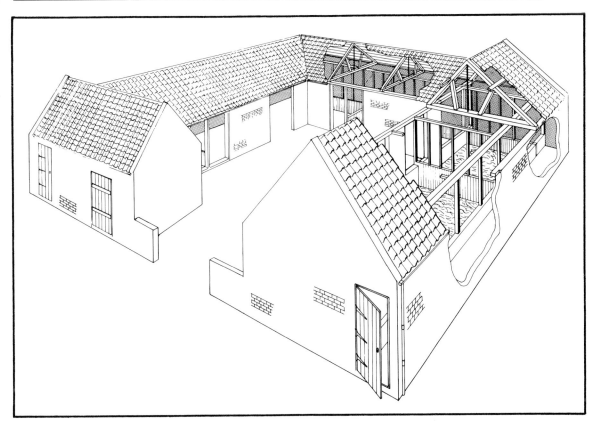

109 Drawing of the
livestock sheds at Ruggs
Hall Farm, Felmingham,
showing the loose boxes
around a yard.

More controversy surrounded the idea of building covered yards. By
the 1850s, it had been proved by agricultural chemists that the nutritional
value of manure was better preserved if it were under cover, and as
costly feeds produced richer manures, the incentive to protect them
was great. However, there was also the argument that young stock
benefited from fresh air and so perhaps the added expense of roofing
yards could not be justified. C. S. Read wrote in 1858 that covered
yards were not numerous in Norfolk and sheds with open yards were
still the most general. 'After trying all the other methods, farmers
appear to be well content with yards',[12] only two covered yards were
found on the survey.

One was a substantial farm owned by Hudson Gurney in Hethel and
the other was a pair of elaborate structures at Park Farm, Bylaugh,
built on the show farm of the Evans-Lombe estate near the entrance
to Bylaugh Hall. Unfortunately, there is little evidence on which to
date these structures. The Hethel yard was an open one in 1842 and
appears to have been roofed by 1900. This map evidence is substantiated
by the solid scissor-frame roof structure that appears to date from the
second half of the nineteenth century (illustration 45). The fact that
the yard is shown as open in 1842, and that the open sheds surrounding
it and the roof do not appear to be of one build, shows that the yard

was not originally designed to be covered and that the roof was a late nineteenth century afterthought.

The situation at Bylaugh is entirely different and it is very unfortunate that there is no record of either the architect for the yards or the date of their building. They are not shown on the 1842 map and probably date from the third quarter of the nineteenth century, which was a period of major rebuilding on the estate following the completion of Bylaugh Hall (illustration 87). Their design and construction would appear to be unique. One of the problems of covered accommodation was that of ventilation and this has been ingeniously overcome by a system of louvres, both in and below the roof itself, which can be adjusted according to wind and weather. The central yard level is slightly lower than the individual boxes around the walls, allowing for a considerable buildup of manure. There is, however, no rear passage to enable the feeding of stock from outside, which must have been a disadvantage. This very expensive and substantial design, described as a 'model homestead' in the 1919 sales catalogue, was not repeated elsewhere on the estate, suggesting that, although the farm was let, it was closely associated with the hall. Elsewhere on the estate good yard and box accommodation was built, but to a traditional design. For instance, at Field House Farm, Swanton Morley, there were eight separate enclosed yards for stock on a 450-acre farm.

The other estate with substantial post-1850 building was the Hare estate and here there are no covered yards, but again there are some very extensive ranges of loose boxes around yards, carefully designed with louvered windows to allow for ventilation.

It can be seen, therefore, that estates were providing very adequate cattle yards with loose boxes in the second half of the nineteenth century. These were often complete rebuilds with no attempt to utilize older walls or buildings. This scale of building was not found in the owner-occupier areas, or on the estates without major building programmes in the late nineteenth century, such as the Gunton or

110 Field House Farm, Swanton Morley, was one of the most intensive livestock farms found within the survey area.

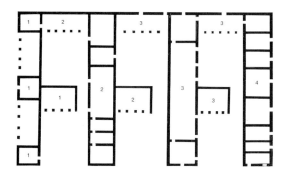
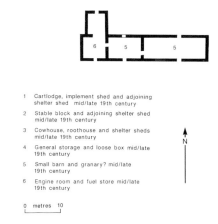

1  Cartlodge, implement shed and adjoining shelter shed  mid/late 19th century
2  Stable block and adjoining shelter shed mid/late 19th century
3  Cowhouse, roothouse and shelter sheds mid/late 19th century
4  General storage and loose box mid/late 19th century
5  Small barn and granary? mid/late 19th century
6  Engine room and fuel store mid/late 19th century

0  metres  10

LeStrange estates. Here the buildings, although adequate, were the result of a gradual accumulation.

## PIGGERIES

One type of accommodation whose survival is confined to the Fens is the pigsty. Most farms did have some sort of sty, and they are listed in sales catalogues, but they were insubstantial and probably only designed for a domestic pig eating dairy waste and household scraps. However, in the Fens they are carefully arranged for more intensive production, based presumably on potato and vegetable surpluses. Ranges of pigsties, with a steam house, were to be found on many of the farms built in the 1840s, such as Fences Farm, Newbridge Farm and Hill Farm, Stow Bardolph, and West Nordelph Farm. William Marshall in the 1780s had visited pigsties in Norfolk that he considered different to those found elsewhere. 'Instead of creeping into a pigsty, in the manner usually done, a Norfolk farmer walks into his pig house at a door similar to those of his other buildings; the building is of course higher and more expensive, but certainly more commodious than the usual form.'[13] The pigsties of the Fens had the conventional low entrances and none of Marshall's type were identified; however, this would be almost impossible to do as they would be indistinguishable from other small loose boxes on the farm.

Although Norfolk was primarily a cereal-growing county, it would be wrong to assume that the management of stock for manure and meat was neglected. Tenants wanted livestock sheds and landlords wanted their land kept in good heart. The accommodation on most farms was replaced and rationalized in the second half of the nineteenth century. Some of this rebuilding must have coincided with the period of falling grain prices after 1870, when farmers came to rely more heavily on the livestock side for their income, but the lack of dated buildings makes this very difficult to prove.

The building, although substantial, was traditional, and this style seems to have satisfied the tenants. Livestock provision was likely to be less adequate on the owner-occupier farms where generally late nineteenth-century work is less in evidence. Generalizations are dangerous though, as the finest set of loose boxes found on the survey was on an owner-occupier farm in Fleggburgh and built as late as 1900.

# 15

# Storage

## GRANARIES

Once the crop had been processed, the end products needed storing in advance either of sale or use on the farm. The straw would probably be kept in the barn until it was needed in the stable or livestock sheds and yards. The grain needed more careful storage, preferably in a granary, and there was plenty of advice available on how a granary should be built. As early as 1687 Worlidge recommended that 'bins or hutches for corn' should be built on staddle stones. However this very distinctive form of granary was rarely built in Norfolk because of the lack of suitable stone out of which to make the staddles. Cast-iron staddles survive at Old Catton Hall and may have supported a granary, but these are unusual and no granaries built on low brick pillars, which could have been used instead of stones, survive. A drawing of the farm buildings at Great Cressingham Parsonage on a map of 1776 shows what is described in the 'Explanation' as a 'granary' freestanding and on pillars, but they must have been rare and Marshall confirms this view when he states in the 1780s, 'I saw none on separate pillars.'[1] Instead, granaries were put above open buildings such as cart lodges as recommended by Waistell,[2] who also made the point that a position over cattle sheds or stables would not be suitable because of the danger of grain becoming tainted.

The main aim of granary accommodation was to provide dry, airy conditions safe from attack by vermin, and over half those remaining are over cart lodges, while others are above workshops, gig houses or inserted in barns. The walls should be smooth and clean, and many granaries have plastered interiors and close-boarded floors. The exterior walls were often weatherboard to provide some ventilation and windows were either louvered or shuttered to prevent rain getting in.

Granaries were not an essential building so long as the grain surplus was low and could be stored in the house. When the crop was threshed by hand, it could be processed as and when it was needed and so a large surplus was unlikely to build up. This explains why William Marshall saw very few granaries in the 1780s. With the introduction of machinery, and particularly contract threshing with portable steam-engines, all the crop might well be threshed at once and so had to be stored for animal feed throughout the winter or until the price was right for sale. Arthur Young thought granaries should be large enough to store two years' crop so that farmers would not be forced to sell in a year of low prices,[3] but such provision was very rare, certainly in Norfolk.

The survival of granaries in the survey areas is very patchy, with only 67 recorded on the 300 farms. More are to be found on the larger than the smaller farms. One quarter of the farms over 100 acres have a granary, while they only survive on 10 per cent of those under 100 acres at the time of the tithe survey. This figure reflects both the disappearance in general of the buildings on smaller farms as well as the fact that smaller farms did not require granaries.

The area with the fewest surviving granaries is the Walsingham estate, with only three still standing on the 23 farms surveyed. There has been a great deal of destruction on these farms in recent years and this, as much as the lack of good corn-growing land in the sandy

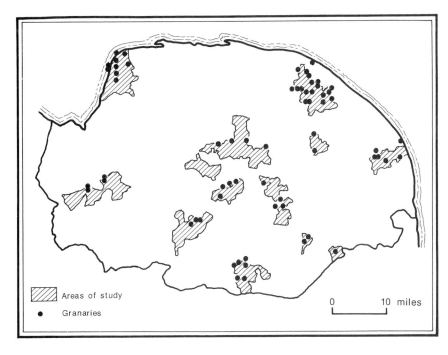

Areas of study
• Granaries

0    10 miles

III Distribution map of surviving granaries within the survey areas.

Breckland, is likely to be the explanation for want of granaries. Perhaps surprisingly, more than half the farms on the Duke of Norfolk's estates have granaries. In this heavy soil area where livestock were particularly important, much of the grain had to be kept for animal feed and so storage was necessary. This pattern of granaries in the mainly livestock areas is also found in north-east Wales where it is in the lowland areas that there are fewer granaries.[4] Only 20 per cent of the farms on the Gunton and Evans-Lombe estates have granaries, reflecting the fact that in this primarily arable area most of the grain was grown for sale.

Very few early eighteenth-century granaries survive; only half a dozen date from before 1750. We would expect granaries to be built from the late eighteenth to the late nineteenth centuries to house the increased yields of the Napoleonic War years and the grain threshed in bulk by machine.

The internal arrangements of the granaries vary considerably. In some there were separate bins, divided by the roof trusses as suggested by Waistell. 'The trusses may be arranged so as to form the divisions for the bins for different kinds of grain.' In others the grain was stored in sacks. Bins were more convenient if different types of animal fodder were being stored and measured into skeps in the granary before feeding. Otherwise, if the grain was to be moved out again in sacks, it would be better to leave the grain in them. Grain was heavy and sacks cumbersome and although most granaries had wide, often shallow-stepped external or internal staircases, a sack hoist was a very welcome labour-saving device. These are sometimes to be found above an external door, or beside a trapdoor into the cart sheds below.

Grain was the most valuable cash product of the farm and on most farms the only building with a lock was the granary; not so much, if we are to believe the oral evidence, to prevent the theft of grain for sale, as to deter the horsemen from stealing extra rations for their favourite animals. Many doors also have a cat hole, presumably as part of the effort to control vermin.

The finest granaries are to be found in the area of stone buildings on the LeStrange estates. Here they are usually over cart sheds with an external stone staircase, often with an alcove underneath, traditionally said to have been used for a dog or geese, both perfectly capable of rousing the farmer if there was a thief about.

The distribution pattern of surviving granaries is one that is filled with anomalies and may well bear little relationship to the numbers actually built. However, it would seem that they were mainly built after 1800 and are to be found particularly in the areas where livestock rather than arable farming was important. The group in the Hunstanton area on the newly enclosed grainlands of the chalk does not fit this pattern and serves as a reminder of the danger of drawing too firm conclusions from the surviving evidence.

112 This charming little chalk and carstone granary at East End Farm, Ringstead, is dated 1762. Chalk for external walls seems to have gone out of use by the late eighteenth century.

## CART LODGES

Unlike granaries, cart lodges remained on nearly half the farms visited, and although such simple structures are almost impossible to date, some must have been built in the eighteenth century. Marshall described the wagon lodges of Norfolk as 'in general commodious' and certainly 52 of those surviving have more than five bays. One would expect that the size of the cart lodge would be related to the acreage of the farm and twice as many of the larger lodges are on farms of over 200 acres. Both the scarcity of large farms and the greater importance of livestock in the south of the county is reflected by the fact that only six of the 41 cart lodges in the southern sample area have more than five bays, while nearly half those in the east are larger. The size of cart lodges, housing the vehicles needed both to bring the crop in from the fields and to take it to market, may well be a better indication of the relative importance of grain and livestock than the existence of granaries.

It was always said that cart lodges should be built facing north to prevent the paint blistering and the wheels shrinking, allowing the iron tyres to become loose. In fact, as is so often the case, the theory does not work in practice, with only slightly more cart lodges facing north, north-west and north-east (56) than face south, south-west and south-east (47). Other factors such as proximity to stables and roadways were pointed out by Waistell when he wrote, 'The cart shed or wagon hovel ought to be so placed that it might be passed in going to and from the stable; otherwise the carts or wagons will be frequently left standing out.'[5]

The difference between cart sheds and wagon lodges was not one that could easily be identified on the ground. In theory, a cart shed could be narrower than a wagon lodge, but in practice most buildings

113 A huge granary over a cart lodge was built in 1860 as part of a new set of farm buildings at Home Farm, Stow Bardolph.
(*top*) Interior view showing the huge floor space within the granary.
(*bottom*) The trap door and sack hoist.

must have been dual purpose. This is confirmed by an entry in the Gunton repair book of the 1820s, which describes repairs to a cart lodge for four carts and two wagons. Very few buildings were open on both sides, presumably because they were unlikely to open onto a roadway in more than one direction. In all but two examples the carts were parked parallel to the gable, but in two cases, both in the Broads, one two- and one three-bay cart lodge were built across the gable as lean-tos on a barn.

As the number of farm implements available increased through the nineteenth century the farmers were likely to need more accommodation and the cart sheds were used for implements as well. Rose, in his 1897 report on the Gunton estates, states that implement sheds were not to be less than 7.3 metres (24 feet) wide and tenants should not be allowed to put implements in the barn. He also said that the implement sheds were the only buildings on the farm that could be covered with corrugated iron. In fact, in Norfolk the most usual roofing material for cart lodges, as on any other farm building, was either pantile or thatch.

Very often one bay at the end of a cart shed was partitioned off and the Gunton repair book mentions dividing off one end of a cart lodge for a gig. This enclosed area could also have been used for smaller implements or those that needed full protection from the weather.

These smaller buildings, often too low for modern use, are amongst the most vulnerable of traditional farm buildings and they had already disappeared on many of the farms visited. Where they do survive, the granaries over cart lodges are some of the most attractive small-scale buildings in the landscape and the countryside is the poorer for their loss.

# 16

# The Farmstead: Layout and Building Materials

## FARM LAYOUT

Of as great interest to the agricultural writers and improvers of the day as the buildings themselves was the layout of the farmstead. By the late eighteenth century commentators were lamenting the disorganized arrangement of most farm buildings. According to Pitt, writing in *The Annals of Agriculture* in 1788, they were built 'at random, without order or method,... accumulated over generations.' Instead, writers were advocating building 'in a compact scale, and as much as possible upon a square or parallelogram'.[1] This advice was elaborated by advocates promoting the arrangement of buildings around a series of yards, one for each type of animal. The barn would form one side, usually the north, for warmth and shelter and would be flanked with shelter sheds for cattle. Cart lodges and shelter sheds, with granaries nearby, would face outwards towards the roads and the fields, often facing north to protect the wooden items stored in them from the drying and blistering sun. Stables, on the other hand, should face east, to catch the early morning light for grooming the horses. Feed stores should be near the animals whose food was kept there, hay lofts and barns near stables, and turnip houses on the end of cattle sheds.

That this advice was largely ignored, both nationally and locally, is shown by the fact that agriculturalists still had much to complain about in the 1840s. John Grey, in the *JRASE* of 1843, wrote of the 'ill-arranged and patchwork appearance of many of the farm buildings.'[3] The main problem must surely have been that very few farms were rebuilt entirely from scratch and older buildings, particularly barns, were incorporated in later improvements. The farmstead was never

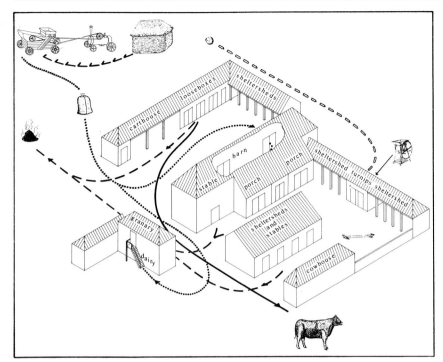

114 This diagram, based on the buildings at Bridge Farm, Bradfield, shows how a group of farm buildings might have worked in the late nineteenth century. It had not been planned as a whole – the granary, cart lodge and loose boxes to the left of the barn were added about 1850 – yet it worked quite efficiently.

static, but instead continually developed to provide for changing farming systems.

## The arrangement of buildings

Stephens' *Book of the Farm*, first published in 1844, went through three editions by 1875 and contained a section of advice on farm building. He pointed out that it was not simply the overall plan but also the relationship of the buildings to each other that was important, and he laid down general principles that should be followed. Firstly straw, being the most bulky article on the farmstead in the winter, should be housed in the centre and at the shortest distance from the stock. Different classes and ages of stock required different quantities of straw and so those requiring most straw, such as fattening cattle, should be nearest the barn, whilst those requiring least, such as horses and cows, should be furthest away.

Secondly, as sunshine was an important source of warmth, it was advisable to place the livestock yards to the south of a large building – often the barn – which could provide shelter. For this reason, Stephens recommended the building of barns on an east-west axis, with a long south wall for shelter onto which the yards could be built. The barns surveyed were fairly evenly divided between an east-west and a north-south orientation although slightly more of those built after 1800 were east-west, providing the recommended long south wall for shelter. Stephens, however, was the first to admit that 'Indisputedly correct as this statement is, it is very seldom adopted in practice.'[3]

The ideals of Stephens' plan could only be achieved in total on the rare occasions when a farm was completely rebuilt, as at South Lopham Hall in 1862 (illustration 60), and on the Hare estates in the 1840s. In all these examples, rectangular south-facing yards were subdivided to provide accommodation for horses, bullocks and cows and, at South Lopham, young stock. Turnip houses had wide doors opening onto the exterior roadway and narrower ones onto the cattle yards while chaff, cutting and hay houses were near the stables.

Infilling and modifications of old plans could result in a farmstead that worked reasonably well. The buildings were seen as links in a chain with inputs and outputs to other buildings, and so the location of each was important. The agricultural engineer G. A. Dean understood this when he wrote, 'There ought not to be the smallest convenience on a farm, down to the pigsty, that is not so precisely in the right spot, that to place it anywhere else would be a loss of labour and manure.'[4] Labour was cheap and plentiful in Norfolk before 1850, but became a more valuable commodity thereafter, and so it is perhaps not surprising that there was a rationalization of buildings between 1850 and 1900.

The diagram of Bridge Farm, Bradfield, is an attempt to understand how a group of buildings worked in 1890. The system differs from that of 50 years previously in that the crop was now threshed in the stack yard by machine rather than in the barn by flail. As the threshing was likely to be carried out all at once, possibly by a contract thresher, there would be grain to be stored, often in the barn as well as the granary. The barn's function had changed by 1890 to that of a store for straw and grain, and it would have contained a chaff-cutting machine to prepare food for the horses housed nearby. Hay was stored in a loft above the stable. Straw could easily be taken to the loose boxes, yards and shelter sheds. The cow houses, where least straw was needed, were furthest from the barn. Turnips would be stored in the turnip house to be fed in the yards. Manure would be returned to the land, whilst the cattle would go from the nearby North Walsham station to market.

## Tithe map evidence

The tithe maps of the late 1830s and 40s provide a unique opportunity to study the layout of all the farms within the survey area and from an analysis of the whole it is clear that nearly half the farms were still of an irregular layout, while only 11 per cent are classified as 'U-shaped', consisting usually of a barn flanked by livestock sheds making up three sides of a yard. Included in this type is the interestingly named 'Courtyard Farm' at Ringstead, created at the time of enclosure in 1781 and an early example of a planned layout around a courtyard. The

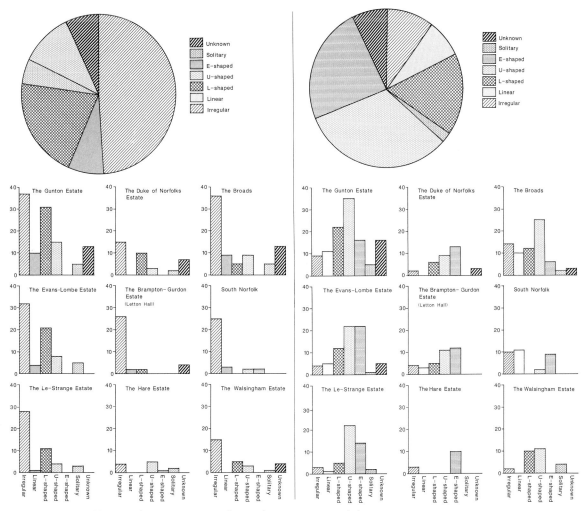

name 'may well record conscious pride in the new type of design.'[5] No farms in 1840 could be described as 'E-shaped'; that is, having the large central yard subdivided by a central livestock shed as advocated by the improvers.

When the figures are broken down regionally a great variation across the survey areas is obvious. Over three quarters of the farms in the south Norfolk sample were irregular. In this area of owner-occupiers and small landowners no farms had been rebuilt as a whole, although 12 per cent of the farms were already arranged around some sort of courtyard. In contrast, only about a third of the farms on the Gunton and Hare estates were irregular while between a third and a half were arranged around a courtyard. Both estates were ones where there was landlord interest in improvement in the early nineteenth century. Landlord influence stands out as being of particular importance in the layout of the farms in the sample areas in the first half of the nineteenth century, but even here there are only two or three farms where the

115 (left) Farm layout as shown on the tithe surveys: (above) a pie graph showing different types of farmstead layout across the entire survey area; (below) block graphs of types of farmstead broken down by survey area.

116 (right) Farmstead layout as shown on the first edition O.S. map: (above) a pie graph showing different types of farmstead layout across the survey area; (below) block graphs of types of farmstead broken down by survey area.

yard was subdivided so that smaller groups of cattle could be fed individually.

## MID-CENTURY DEVELOPMENTS

The main period of layout development for the farmsteads was the second half of the nineteenth century, which saw the recommendations of the earlier years being put into practice. When the sample is considered as a whole, it can be seen that by the second edition of the 25-inch Ordnance Survey, surveyed about 1900, only 10 per cent of the farms still have an irregular layout, whilst 56 per cent are arranged around a courtyard in either a U- or E-shaped layout. As in the 1840s the highest proportions of irregular layouts were still to be found in the non-estate regions of the Broads and south Norfolk (20 per cent), while on the Duke of Norfolk and the Evans-Lombe estates, where there was much rebuilding in the second half of the nineteenth century, only 6 per cent of the farms were still of an irregular plan. Similarly, on the Hare estates, where again there was much rebuilding, 80 per cent of the farms were of an E-shaped layout. Some 78 per cent of the LeStrange farms were modified to create regular courtyard plans, but only 34 per cent of those in South Norfolk and 42 per cent of those in the Broads achieved this layout. The relative neglect on the Gunton estate in the second half of the nineteenth century is reflected in the fact that only 45 per cent of the farms there had an E- or U-shaped plan by 1900. The contrast between estate and non-estate areas can therefore be very clearly seen throughout the nineteenth century, and is more obvious in the layout of farmsteads than in the individual buildings.

## BUILDING MATERIALS

If regional differences begin to be detectable in farm layout, they are at their most obvious when we come to study building materials. Some, such as chalk and carstone, have a very limited distribution dictated by their availability. Chalk was only found in the extreme north-west, on the LeStrange estates. Even here the easily accessible deposits of hard building blocks seem to have been exhausted by the nineteenth century and by then it was only being used to line the interior of buildings rather than for exterior work.

Carstone was used over a rather wider area and is found on both the LeStrange and Hare estates in the west. It was used in several different ways, and it was impossible to work out a chronology of types. In farm buildings it was most frequently found either as footings or mixed with chalk, brick and flint rubble. In the late nineteenth century large roughly-dressed blocks were often used alongside a continuing building tradition using smaller and narrower pieces. The use of fully-dressed stone blocks was confined to houses and not found in farm buildings.

Brick, and a mixture of brick and flint, was found across the entire area studied. The finest examples of early brickwork were found in the Broads, but its use in other areas was widespread. By 1850 the use of field-picked flints as an infill within a brick framework had increased and was particularly characteristic of the Evans-Lombe estate.

Timber-framing was a technique found over much of the area in the period up to 1800, but after that it was replaced either by brick or clay lump. Clay lump was not considered to be an ideal building material for farm buildings, particularly livestock sheds, which could easily be damaged by animals' horns. It also required frequent and regular maintenance, so, although clay lump buildings would be cheaper to erect than brick ones, their upkeep was expensive. For this reason they were more likely to appeal to owner-occupiers or tenants on estates that neglected their duties as providers of buildings. Clay lump buildings are not therefore found across all the regions of the heavy clays, but rather in the mainly owner-occupier region of South Norfolk and on the smaller Duke of Norfolk and Letton Hall estates. There were none on the Evans-Lombe estate, although much of it lay within the heavy clay belt. The cheapness of clay lump was less relevant on the estates as most had their own brick kilns to provide for estate needs. No clay lump buildings found could be dated before 1800, but as a building technique it continued well into this century.

One unusually large and impressive group of clay lump buildings built on brick plinths survives at Forncett End, south of Norwich. A wooden plaque on the gable end of the barn reads, 'H & S Coimas 1840' and all the buildings probably date from this period. The barn is a large one with two pairs of threshing doors and is divided internally into two equal parts by a clay lump wall. This is one of the latest dated barns in Norfolk and was built for hand-threshing, a practice being superseded by machinery at this date. On the end of the barn is a clay lump lean-to with a small store above which appears to be contemporary. Perhaps it contained machinery for working in the barn. Clay lump is too clumsy a building material to allow for the insertion of small and decorative ventilation holes, so on the east side of the barn, just below the eaves, there is a row of small rectangular slatted window openings, which were one way of solving the problem. To the west of the barn are open yards and loose boxes, built mostly of brick, probably at the same time as the barn.

A second clay lump building is the stable. Two open stables are separated by a tack room and chaff box. A staircase from this central area leads up to the hay loft, and hatches along the gable ends of the hay loft floor allow hay to be pushed through to the hay racks below. An outside door at first-floor level allowed hay to be loaded in from a

117 The distribution of clay lump, chalk and carstone buildings within the survey areas.

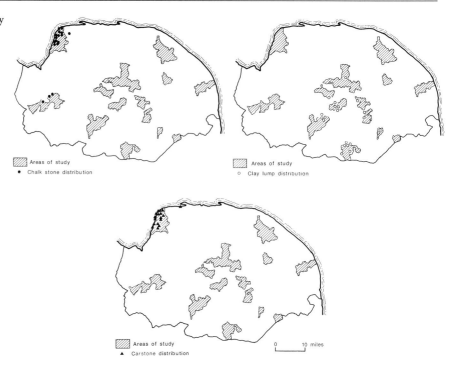

wagon outside. Two small internal doors, about 80 cm (31.5 inches) above floor level, open from each of the stables into the central chaff box, from which chaff could be scooped out and put in the troughs.

A third substantial building was a three-bay cart lodge with a granary above. Until 1988, this unique group remained, almost unaltered and with their internal fittings intact. They are now converted for housing.

Thatching had been the main method of roofing across the county until the early nineteenth century, and many seventeenth- and eighteenth-century roofs are steep-pitched to allow for the draining of water off thatch. By the 1800s, however, pan-tiles could be produced by machine and they began to replace straw thatch, which has a relatively short life. The longer-lasting reed thatch continued to be used in the Broads and is still to be found on many traditional farm buildings.

The railways were opening up Norfolk to imported building materials from the 1840s and Scandinavian softwoods were increasingly used for roof construction and weatherboarding, but in general, local building materials continued to be of paramount importance into this century, and it is the survival of this great variety, rather than anything else, that gives the regions of Norfolk their distinctive appearance. It is just this regionalism that is in danger of disappearing under modern mass-produced buildings for the agricultural industry.

# 17

# The Role of the Landlord

One of the most significant findings of the survey as a whole was the increasing distinction to be made between estate and non-estate farms throughout the eighteenth and nineteenth centuries. There was a very definite coincidence of farm building as an estate activity with the period of mid-nineteenth-century High Farming rather than with the earlier periods of improvement.

## THE LANDLORD AND
## THE 'FIRST AGRICULTURAL REVOLUTION'

F. M. L. Thompson was the first to attempt a division of the period generally described as 'the agricultural revolution' into two phases, which he called the first and second agricultural revolutions.[1] Characteristics of the 'first agricultural revolution', beginning perhaps as far back as the early seventeenth century, included new crops, particularly improved grasses, and also turnips, the introduction of crop rotations, livestock breeding and, most importantly, enclosure. It was in the enclosing of the countryside that the landlord would play the most important part. In Norfolk, much of the open field land was already enclosed, mainly by private agreement, before the great period of parliamentary enclosure during the Napoleonic Wars. Between 1796 and 1844 over 80 per cent of the commons disappeared, and most of this enclosure was landlord-inspired and financed.[2] Frequently this did not involve the erection of new farms so much as the adding of new arable fields to already existing farmsteads. Although the initial enclosure was landlord-financed, it was usually the tenant's responsibility to hedge and marl his new lands. In many cases, as at Antingham, (illustration 79) the landlord would take this opportunity to rationalize old field boundaries and improve the field layout on his farms. One might expect that the opportunity to modernize farm buildings as part of the same improvement package would be taken, but this was not usually the case.

It is true that at Redbrick Farm, Thompson, a new set of buildings was built at the time of enclosure when new fields were added to the farm (illustration 69), and the enclosure of commons in the north-west of the county in the late eighteenth century resulted in Courtyard Farm, Ringstead, but these are exceptions. More usual is the situation on the Gunton estate, where there is little correlation between farms where new buildings were erected and those that were reorganized between 1784 and 1835. Earlier barns and stables are as likely to survive on farms rationalized between these dates as those rationalized earlier. It is clear that only rarely did the enclosure and land reorganization of the 'first agricultural revolution' go hand in hand with building development.

If we look generally at the owner-occupier and tenanted farms in the

118 Some owners used their farm buildings to make political points. Mr Phillipo, a small landowner in north-west Norfolk, resented the local influence of his larger neighbours and put their busts on his barn at Severals Farm, Wood Norton. Phillipo was no respecter of persons. The inscription under one head reads 'Billy' for William Norris, the squire of Wood Norton, and under the other 'Jacob', for Lord Hastings of neighbouring Melton Constable.

survey areas before 1840 there is very little to distinguish them from each other. Both types had large barns, and some of the finest examples are on the fertile owner-occupier farms of the Broads and the heavier soils of the south. There was certainly no lack of capital amongst owner-occupiers from the late Middle Ages through to the eighteenth century.

There are, of course, estates that were erecting expensive 'model' farmsteads in the eighteenth and early nineteenth century, and J. M. Robinson regards this period as 'The great age of model farm building', citing the work of a dozen or so of the wealthiest landlowners in Britain and including the royal estates of George III. Holkham was the most conspicuous Norfolk example in this category.[3] However, the fact that Coke's improvements there, often regarded as extravagant, excited so much comment suggests that they were unusual. When Coke's new agent, Francis Blaikie, arrived in 1816, he was very critical of the improvements in buildings that had taken place. In 1827 he wrote, 'such buildings are not only attended with uncalled for expense to the landlord in the first instance, but entail a lasting encumbrance on the estate. For every particle of building not absolutely wanted is an encumbrance to the estate and a deterioration of the property. These remarks apply more immediately to Mr Coke's estate than any other in the kingdom.'[4] There was certainly much advice available to would-be farmstead builders in the form of pattern books. Although the practicality of the courtyard layout was almost universally recognized, these pattern books contain many picturesque rather than functional designs where Classical vies with Gothic and ornate with simple. If these plans were followed at all they tended to be built on the home farm next to the great house, and all those in Norfolk listed in Robinson's gazetteer, except for the Holkham examples, are beside the owner's residence.

## THE LANDLORD AND THE 'SECOND AGRICULTURAL REVOLUTION'

F. M. L. Thompson, when he listed the essential differences between the first and second agricultural revolutions, included in the second the introduction of artificial fertilizers and animal feeds resulting in a capital-intensive, scientifically-based agriculture known by contemporaries as High Farming. This broke down the 'closed-circuit system' where the farmer had relied primarily on manure and fodder crops produced on his own farm. While this is essentially true, to this list should be added the building of palatial farm buildings by the landlords on a scale that very few owner-occupiers could emulate: the confidence of the farmers is reflected in the buildings that their landlords erected.

Built on scientific principles with little regard for either Gothic or Classical forms, they provided accommodation that would allow for the best growth rates in livestock and the preservation of manure whilst applying the logic of time-and-motion studies to the arrangement of the buildings. The size of the agricultural labour force was declining and this, combined with a rise in wages, meant that, at last, labour was a valuable commodity not to be wasted.

These mid-Victorian farmsteads are the landlords' very visible contribution to the High Farming of the second agricultural revolution. It is clear that landlord investment was by no means confined to years of depression, but was important in the years of optimism as well, something that has not always been evident from the documentary evidence. In Wales there are hardly any farm buildings built before the nineteenth century and nearly all farms completely rebuilt were on estates; 'clearly owner-occupiers could not afford to build on such a scale. Small owners had to be content with replacing some of their worst buildings.'[5] C. S. Read in his survey of Norfolk agriculture in 1858 recognized this development. 'Many existing farm buildings have been much improved and several new farmsteads erected during the last 15 years...all over the county there are excellent new premises to be seen and the general aspect of the old ones is better than 15 years ago.'[6] Other Norfolk estates were now catching up with Holkham, and the finest examples within the survey areas were to be found on the Evans-Lombe and Hare estates, whilst even at Gunton, where expenditure was tailing off by the 1860s, ranges of sunken loose boxes were added to many farms. The LeStrange estate saw some substantial developments, but the solid old stone buildings of the area were often incorporated in the new work. Where estate accounts survive, as at Holkham, they confirm the very high levels of investment obvious from the buildings themselves. At Holkham the highest levels of expenditure were between 1850 and 1880.[7] These massive injections of capital on the estates helped to increase the divide between them and the owner-occupiers.

Occasionally, as at Water Lane, Oxwick, a field complex might be built by an owner-occupier. Here, in 1860, James Day built a couple of cottages and beside them a range consisting of a double row of twelve loose boxes with a central feeding passage on the south side of a yard. Two impressive timber louvers above the range made sure there was enough ventilation. Shelter sheds made up the east and west sides of the yard, with turnip houses opening on to the fields. At some later date the whole yard was roofed over to provide even more protection. By keeping the cattle in an outyard or 'field barn', the cartage of turnips and manure would be reduced. Field barns were a feature of many large farms by the late nineteenth century. However, such buildings on owner-occupier farms are unusual and were particularly unlikely to

**119** Buildings at Waterlane farm, Oxwick.
(*top*) Cattle yard, later covered, from the south.
(*centre*) The complex from the north, showing ventilation louvres and entrances to the six loose boxes on the north side of the double row.
(*bottom*) Datestone in the south gable wall of the eastern shelter shed.

have been built once the depression set in by 1880 when the contrast between landlords and owner-occupier farms increased even more.

## THE EFFECTS OF THE 'GREAT DEPRESSION'

Whilst owner-occupiers could no longer afford improvements, landlords often found it necessary to improve and extend their buildings, particularly livestock accommodation, to keep tenants. 'The confident assertion of mastery over the forces of agriculture had been replaced by the more sober stamp of pragmatism and caution.'[8] The increasing divide between landlord and owner-occupier farms can be seen when we look at farmstead layout in 1840 and 1890. One third of South Norfolk examples and a fifth in the Broads were still irregular, whilst on the estates the figure is nearly always below a tenth (illustrations 115 and 116).

The role of the landlord in farm building development can be seen to have been an increasing one as the nineteenth century progressed, from a situation where the buildings on most estates were indistinguishable from those on many owner-occupier farms, to one by the end of the century where there was virtually no new building except on the estates. Whilst there is no evidence that estates other than the very largest were leading the field in barn development and design in the eighteenth century, they certainly were responsible for most of the livestock systems being developed by the late nineteenth century. 'Nowhere is the legacy of the Victorian period more pronounced than in the area of farm buildings...the construction of new farmsteads and the modernization of existing ones, was a consuming interest of those landlords who were of an improving mind.'[9] There were more such landlords in Norfolk than has previously been supposed. No longer was it only the very largest who built model farms, but also smaller landowners such as the Hares of Stow Bardolph, who were deeply committed to improvement.

How far these buildings generally were the result of tenant pressure on their landlords and how far they were a spontaneous response to the High Farming spirit is very difficult to tell when so little estate correspondence for any but the largest estates survives. The fact that much of the most impressive building was still to be found on home farms such as Longlands at Holkham and Park Farm at Bylaugh suggests that, in fact, the landlords were leading the way in farm building improvement in the second agricultural revolution as they had been the pioneers of enclosure in the first.

# 18

# Regionalism and Farm Buildings in Agricultural Change

## FARM BUILDINGS AND IMPROVED FARMING

It remains to consider how far farm buildings were responsible for encouraging improved agriculture and how far the regional differences in buildings can be said to reflect regional farming practices.

The importance of improved farm buildings to the encouragement of better farming was a question on which contemporaries were divided. The art of farm building design was a new one at the end of the eighteenth century and interest in it was taken up by landlords for a variety of reasons, from the romantic to the practical.[1] One of the most famous of the more practical exponents was Thomas William Coke at Holkham. Arthur Young obviously approved of this high expenditure, whilst there were others who saw it as unnecessary extravagance. Nathaniel Kent, himself a land agent, writing of Norfolk in the 1790s thought that long leases were more important in the encouragement of good farming than the buildings.[2] Even at Holkham, the letter books show that it was up to the tenant to ask for new buildings and his proposals were then either rejected, modified or accepted. New farm buildings were normally the result of tenant interest in improved farming.

The rather scathing attitude of contemporaries to expensive building schemes gradually changed through the first half of the nineteenth century, until, by the JRASE's farm building competition of 1851, the value of improved buildings was fully recognized. As cattle increased

**120** Buildings such as those at Leicester Square Farm, South Creake were criticized by Arthur Young for their size and unnecessary architectural pretensions. These stables and hay loft were designed by Samuel Wyatt.

in importance and labour became more expensive, interest in design and mechanization increased, and the new Holkham agent, William Keary, took a very different attitude from his predecessor, Francis Blaikie. He was responsible for expensive developments at Holkham in the 1850s and criticized the state of the buildings on the Duke of Norfolk's estates in his report on them, written in the 1860s. It was clear to him that here at least, 'buildings were lagging behind farming practice', suggesting that even on these heavy clays in south Norfolk farming practice was in fact advancing somewhat in spite of the state of the buildings. He goes on to say that there was a surplus of barns, but not enough bullock sheds and yards to make the manure needed on the farms. Neither was he impressed by the tenantry who were 'not very intelligent or enterprising'. What he does not do is make any connection between the tenants and the buildings. Would a more intelligent tenantry have demanded change, or would better buildings have attracted better tenants?[3]

As foreign competition continued to grow during the second half of the nineteenth century it became clear that it was only through efficient and labour-saving improvements to livestock farming that farmers would continue to make profits, and so the connection between good buildings and better farming became more obvious. Cereal farming did not rely on buildings in the way lowland fattening did, and so it was with the shift in balance from cereals to animals that the link between good buildings and improved farming became closer.

Stephens stated clearly in his *Book of the Farm* that well-designed buildings were needed to help beat the depression. By this he meant a homestead 'so arranged that the labour of attendance is reduced to the minimum and where the requisite amount of labour is furnished at the least possible cost consistent with economy and stability.'[4]

By the 1890s, when Mr Rose surveyed the Gunton estate, the value of good buildings to progressive farming was fully understood. Building work was not something that should be left to the tenants, who 'as a rule, have no practical knowledge of this work and no idea of plan.' He went on to say, 'Buildings should not be built solely for individual or sitting tenants, but with a view to the general requirements and for the improvement of the estate.' By this date it was very much a tenant's rather than a landlord's market and landlords often had to offer to build new stockyards to keep tenants; a complete turnaround from the situation one hundred years previously.

## REGIONAL VARIATION IN FARMING PRACTICE AND BUILDING

One of the joys of conducting a Norfolk survey of farm buildings was the great variety of building styles across the county, but what was not clear is how far this reflected regional farming patterns. That there were widely differing farming regions in Norfolk had long been recognized; but the evidence for these was based on a limited number of sources.

Firstly, there were the descriptions of the various agriculturalists Arthur Young and William Marshall were particularly familiar with limited areas of the county, Young with Holkham and Marshall with Gunton. Later in the 1840s R.N. Bacon relied heavily on the answers to his questionnaire, which, inevitably, was only filled in by the more progressive farmers. Probably the least biased of the writers was Clare

Sewell Read. His writings were based on a lifetime in farming and some years representing the interests of the tenant farmer in Parliament.

Secondly, there are agricultural statistics. Although at first sight these would appear to be a reliable source, there are some doubts about their accuracy. Those of 1854 were divided up by Poor Law Union, and these are not always the most useful divisions when trying to isolate farming regions. The statistics gathered as part of the tithe survey are parish by parish and should therefore be more helpful.

None of these sources allows us to look at the regions, farm by farm, and it is for this reason that the study of farm buildings is particularly valuable.

Firstly, there is the prosperous north-west; a landscape of large fields created by the enclosure movement where careful farming in which crop rotation, allowing for the folding of large flocks of sheep on fodder crops in the field, was the key to success. Here, on the LeStrange estates, the survey found many very extensive groups of farm buildings, with spacious porched barns, some dating from well before the introduction of the new breeds of sheep that thrived on turnips. There can be no doubt that this was an important grain-producing region even before the eighteenth century.

The explanation for the very large barns in the infertile Brecks is a different one. All of them, built by Lord Walsingham when grain prices were at their highest during the Napoleonic Wars, are an indication of his confidence that with enormous dressings of marl this area could be made productive. They probably tell us more about the character of Lord Walsingham than about local farming practices. When prices fell, efforts at reclamation ended and these great barns remained as monuments to an ill-founded optimism on the part of the landowner. They are also a warning to farm building historians against equating large barns with high grain output.

The farms in the south of the county are a great contrast to those in the west. Small, often early barns are an indication of a low grain output. By the time underdraining became widespread, allowing for more cereals to be grown, the heyday of the barn was over and the early barns were still adequate. There are puzzling exceptions to this general rule with some very large pre-eighteenth-century barns surviving, particularly in the Hethel area. As in the Hunstanton region, it would seem that more grain than we have been led to expect was being produced on some of these farms.

Although hedge removal has destroyed the regional character of much of the area, there are places where the small fields and untidy hedgerows described by Read in the 1850s still survive. Although most of the farms had cattle yards, the owner-occupiers and small landowners of this region did not have the capital for the grand schemes, found in areas to the north.

By far the greatest number of farms visited were in the large area of mid and east Norfolk and included a great variety of buildings. The substantial eighteenth- and early nineteenth-century farms of the Gunton estate and the fine barns in the Broads are an indication of the area's early prosperity and natural fertility. In both these areas there was ample provision for the stall-fed cattle mentioned by Read in the 1850s. Sunken loose boxes were found on the Gunton estate and the Broads while the grandiose livestock accommodation built on the Evans-Lombe estate is an example of what a wealthy landowner could provide.

The farm buildings go some way towards confirming the agricultural regions described by the writers, although they do suggest that their views on the backward regions in the south and on the lack of cereals in the west before enclosure may be exaggerated. Mesmerized as they were by the improvements at Holkham, the nineteenth-century commentators failed to appreciate the work being carried out by other landowners such as the Hares, the Evans-Lombes and the Suffields, or indeed the fine barns built in the owner-occupier areas such as the Broads and country around Hethel. With these provisos, however, it is true that the traditional divisions between the regions that could be seen so clearly by contemporaries can still be seen by those today who, looking at the remaining historic farm buildings, have eyes to see and a desire to understand.

Every group of farm buildings is unique. They have been built as a result of a variety of highly individual, personal and localized developments and decisions, although those on estates may have more in common as the result of a single management plan. Because of the available documentary evidence we may well be able to learn more of the estate policy of which they are part. For these reasons estates provide an obvious unit for studying the historical development of groups of farms, often on similar soils and under similar management.

We have attempted to combine, in a unique way, the study of estates and owner-occupier farms in selected areas, to piece together the development of buildings and, through them, farming in one part of East Anglia. The identification of both common and divergent features indicates both regional unity and diversity. Comparison between the landowner and owner-occupier areas enables the consideration of the role of the landlord and the individual in building development. Comparison of buildings with documentary evidence for agricultural progress has enabled an analysis of the importance of buildings in the development of farming techniques.

The putting of this material in a national framework has been hindered by the lack of comparative material from other regions and if this book has done nothing more than to show the value of such studies and so to encourage others to attempt similar surveys before the information is lost for ever, it will have achieved its purpose.

# 19

# The Future: Problems of Conversion and Conservation

## THE PROBLEMS

'The concept of redundant historic farm buildings has not been fully acknowledged as a problem until comparatively recently.'[1]

The past 40 years have seen greater changes in the agricultural industry than any of the earlier periods of 'revolution' described in this book and, as in the past, this has meant a change in the types of building needed to serve it.

New methods have been entirely geared towards increasing efficiency, which has resulted in a decline in the number of people working on the land. Farms that employed up to 40 men in the 1930s now make do with two or three alongside specialist contractors. This has radically altered the life of rural communities. With more and more people having to find work outside the villages, the very reasons for their existence have gone. Local ties and loyalties are weakened and the sense of belonging lost. This change is accelerated by the movement of outsiders, often with different expectations and interests, into small communities.

Increased efficiency means larger farms and fields. Larger farms are the result of farm amalgamations: in the last 30 years the number of farm holdings in Norfolk alone has dropped by nearly a third. Over 13,000 km (8080 miles) of hedgerows were destroyed in Norfolk between 1946 and 1970, particularly in the areas of heavier soils. In the north and west of the county, the large regular fields of the enclosure movement required little amalgamation to suit modern needs.[2]

We have all benefited from these changes. In the 1940s Britain grew less than a third of the food consumed by her population of 38 million, produced in a way little changed since the nineteenth century. Nowadays Britain's 56 million people are two-thirds self-sufficient.

Change has not been confined to the landscape of the farm, but has greatly affected the farmstead itself. Farm amalgamations mean that one set of buildings is almost automatically redundant. The end of horse power in the 1950s meant that stables and horse yards no longer had a function. As farm machinery has grown in size, tractor cabs are now too high to be stored in cart sheds, and entrances are too narrow for combine harvesters and the wide beams of farm machinery.

It is not only the fieldwork that has become mechanized. The management of livestock has also intensified. Old cattle sheds, yards and loose boxes cannot be mucked out mechanically and more intensive feeding systems for high-density production have been introduced; it is only rarely that old buildings can be adapted for these purposes. One of the few sample studies so far carried out, in Grampian, showed up the extent of change. In almost every instance, steadings had been completely or partially gutted. 'The degree and rapidity of change in rural buildings was one of the major lessons driven home time and time again.'[3]

The most recent change is the introduction of 'set-aside'. As a result of overproduction of cereals, one-and-a-quarter million acres are likely to go out of cereal production and even more out of grassland over the next few years. Although this may well leave more farm buildings redundant, it may also emphasize the need for the farmer to diversify. Most old farm buildings have already changed their use several times and are far more versatile than modern specialist ones whose design is often obsolete after ten years.

121 Field barns are particularly vulnerable to neglect. This remote example in Barrett Ringstead is some distance from the main farmstead and is of little use to the modern farmer.

122 This cart shed at Elsing is 'semi-redundant'. Although it is used for storage of mainly redundant equipment, it will not be worth repairing.

A Ministry of Agriculture, Fisheries and Food survey of 1985 covering 90 farms visited from three regional offices in the Midlands, the North and Wales, showed that only half of the old buildings were in good condition and only 20 per cent had adequate access for modern tractors. Whilst only 10 per cent were not used at all, 15 per cent were semi-redundant, and it can be assumed that as they deteriorate, they will not be worth repairing and so a quarter of the old stock of old farm buildings is at risk. 'Any traditional building with structural movement or failure, as 25 per cent of the study sample, or roof and walls in bad condition as 12 per cent, would probably require too much work to allow economic conversion for continuing agricultural use.'[4]

The reason that so many pre-First World War farm buildings have survived at all is that there was little capital or incentive to improve them during the years of depression that lasted, with only temporary let-ups, from the 1870s to 1939. According to National Farm Buildings Surveys carried out between 1941 and 1943, only a third of farms were satisfactorily equipped with buildings. Today, almost a third of the building stock on farms dates from before 1900, but many of these older buildings only play a very subsidiary farming role. As a result 90 per cent of working buildings are post-1918.

The changes that have been seen on the farmstead in recent years are therefore not only the result of very rapid technical developments over the last 30 years, but also of the long period of neglect that went before.

In the past the value of scientific and technological progress has never been questioned; nowadays we are a little more cautious, appreciating the problems unwittingly created by the headlong enthusiasm for increased productivity that are now coming home to roost. The effects of nitrates and various food scares of recent years have increased our appreciation of the values of traditional methods and processes, developed over many generations of working with the environment. In an era of food over-production we are becoming more concerned with quality and sufficiency than quantity and surplus. Although organic farming will probably never be practised on more than 20 per cent of our farmland, less intensive systems, relying on mixed husbandry and the keeping of more animals, may well be able to make more use of traditional buildings. Alongside the monster tractors, many firms are now producing mini-versions, such as the skid-truck, which can turn and work in the confined spaces of old buildings.

We now think twice before destroying our past in our efforts to build for the future, and this problem of retaining our cultural as well as our natural heritage is nowhere more obvious than in our treatment of the traditional buildings of our farming countryside. Several changes in public attitudes are converging: a concern for food quality and the quality of life, alongside care for the historic landscape and the aesthetic quality of our surroundings.

Concern for farm buildings is relatively new. Whilst the earliest large-scale survey, in East Lothian, was carried out as long ago as 1968, it was not until the mid-70s that the interest of conservationists was fully aroused. Previously, farm buildings were 'unnoticed or taken for granted by the majority of the general public'.[5] Gradually by 1980 an awareness of the problem of redundant farm buildings was apparent, but an understanding of the opportunities for solving it was by no means clear. In the late 70s, for instance, indiscriminate conversion of all kinds was encouraged, and only later were the destructive consequences for many historical buildings realized.

Once buildings have outlived their usefulness they are very vulnerable to decay, and most of our older ones are now suffering from 100 years of neglect. Statistics show that listed farm buildings (listed by the Department of the Environment for their historic and architectural value), are the most at risk of all types of listed buildings (606 were demolished in 1987). Any attempt to preserve them is liable to be very expensive and the question of whether they are worth preserving becomes all the more urgent.

## THE OPPORTUNITIES

Farm buildings are a major feature of the countryside and are an essential part of its variety and regional identity. Individual characteristics resulting from the use of localized materials and styles have developed over long periods to serve a particular function within the limitations imposed by the environment. As a result, they seem to blend easily with the landscape, appearing to have grown from the very fields around them. This timeless quality lulls us into a false sense of security about their future. We do not miss that crumbling ivy-covered barn until, one day, we turn the corner and it has gone; instead we are faced with a heap of sugar beet making use of the hard standing that was once the threshing floor.

New buildings, although still primarily functional, largely ignore the former disciplines set by availability of local materials and the need for sheltered sites that resulted in 'a rapport between traditional farm buildings and their landscape'. Instead, their replacements 'stand obtrusive, alien and independent. The farmed landscapes we inherited from earlier generations were, by general consent, beautiful landscapes, and although they were to a very large extent man-made, the harmony between man's own and nature's work was such as to blur the distinction between one and the other and produce a deeply satisfying landscape in which we could take pride and pleasure.'[6]

This very personal view of a landscape architect is one with which anyone who has watched with dismay some of the changes in the countryside over the last twenty years can hardly disagree. It is fair to say, however, that in the ten years since Paul Walshe wrote some landowners and farmers have begun to make an effort to site and colour their new buildings to blend as far as possible with their surroundings. Yet there are more than aesthetic reasons, important though these are, for preserving farm buildings; there is also their historic value to be considered. Early grain silos and pioneer examples of the use of concrete have little aesthetic, but much historic interest. 'Conserving historical evidence has nothing to do with aesthetics.'[7]

Farm buildings, as this book has endeavoured to show, record the changing farming practices on every farm and it must be the concern of historians to see that evidence is not lost. It is not their business to judge whether a conversion is tasteful or not, but they should be interested in whether the previous uses of the building are so masked by the alterations that they are no longer obvious.

Farm buildings are, first and foremost, working agricultural buildings and to convert them for any other purpose leaves them as ghosts of their former selves. A future within farming is by far the best use for them. Any necessary alterations, whilst respecting the historic value of the existing building, only serve to add yet another layer to the palimpsest of change that it records. Modern grain silos can be put within barns, often requiring very little structural alteration to the building.

Livestock are more difficult to keep in any but the largest nineteenth-century systems. At Egmere, yards that housed about 50 cattle 100 years ago have been altered to house in the region of 120. They are fed and mucked out using the most mechanical of modern techniques, whilst the traditional sunken loose boxes stand alongside, untouched;

a structural record of a phase in the intensification of livestock husbandry.

The value of keeping historical farm buildings in agriculture has at last been recognized by the Ministry of Agriculture, Fisheries and Food. From April 1989, grants of up to 35 per cent have been available for repairs carried out in traditional materials, achieving a 'sympathetic result'. It is hoped that this will encourage farmers to try and find ways of keeping buildings in agricultural use. It is the responsibility of local government to act as a watchdog over both the historical and aesthetic legacy of our countryside, and if local authority grants for listed buildings can match those provided by MAFF, then a useful package can often be put together to save a building. Providing they are kept weathertight, some sort of low-level use can often be found. Although the new grants must be welcomed, there is always the fear that it is already too late. Many buildings are suffering from a long period of neglect and farmers may be unwilling to find the necessary 65 per cent of the costs for a building that may, at best, be semi-redundant. Although the stipulation that only traditional materials should be used is desirable, it may not be realistic. Sometimes a holding operation with corrugated iron is worth encouraging.[8]

In many cases, however, particularly in lowland intensive systems, use in agriculture is more difficult. Even low-intensity use will not be attractive to farmers where there is the tantalizing possibility of a quick capital gain from selling the building for domestic or other conversion.

123 The very fine barn at Paston, Norfolk, dated 1581, after restoration.

Over the years, in an effort both to prevent demolition and to encourage more employment in the countryside, there has been much interest in the use of farm buildings for light industrial or tourist use, and this is usually preferable to full domestic conversion. Barns can provide large airy workshops with very little alteration to the original building. Viscount Raynham, who produces high-quality hand lacquered furniture at his Raynham Workshops in traditional farm buildings at Pattesley, Norfolk, believes that the best policy is to interfere as little as possible with the fabric of the building; an attitude that would be applauded by conservationists. He has created offices and workshops within the shell of the barn and shelter shed walls by using movable wall divisions. Any alterations are in keeping with agricultural buildings; for instance, wood is creosoted rather than painted. 'You don't want it to look too smart.' Because the buildings were in relatively good repair when he began, the conversion has not been expensive, but there are other advantages in working from a farmyard. People like the environment. They prefer working in the countryside to a workshop on an anonymous industrial estate. It also has good publicity value and makes an attractive advertising line. It is a better address than Unit 102, Milton Keynes!

Not far away from Pattesley, at Letheringsett, near Holt, Peter Roberts runs a firm of cabinet-makers employing seven people in a converted barn that has won several conservation awards for the standard of the work. Its greatest merit is that, from the road, the barn looks nothing other than a traditional flint agricultural building.

In contrast to these craft workshops, Office Furniture Systems is a 'high-tech' industry based in a barn at Methwold, Norfolk. Micro-computers sit on desks fitted between old beams and a winch, designing office layouts for a worldwide market.

Other schemes have involved the creation of a series of workshops in extensive farmsteads in the hope that small industries would be encouraged to rural areas. Grants of up to 25 per cent are available from the Rural Development Commission for the conversion of redundant buildings for light industrial use. More than 2,000 buildings, mostly agricultural, have been converted with the help of such grants, and many of their enterprises are providing employment opportunities in the countryside that would not otherwise exist. The famous sixteenth-century brick and thatched Paston barn in Norfolk is to be used for a hi-tech industry for which the large open space with very little natural light is well suited.

There are, however, problems. Tenants are not always easy to find and as soon as their businesses expand they tend to move away to the towns. Small-scale 'light' industries have a habit of growing to such an extent that they need large-scale lorry deliveries and bigger machinery, which involves further, perhaps unacceptable, alterations to buildings.

The more individual units into which the buildings are divided, the greater the level of alteration and the more the historic value of the building is obscured. Neither is workshop conversion practical where the buildings are part of a working farmyard used by agricultural machinery. There is often local pressure against industrial use, and planning committees have in the past turned down workshop schemes against the advice of their officers on the grounds that the workshops are likely to increase noise and traffic. However, if the present trend from town to rural living continues, and if the cost of transport increases, there could well be more demand for office development in rural areas and farm buildings could be ideally suited to open-plan office use.

Another possibility is to take advantage of the growing tourist

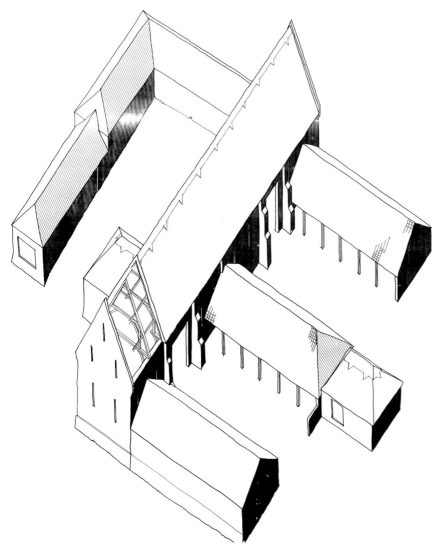

124 Plans for conversion of the Paston barn for hi-tech industry. No new window openings will be required as this work is better carried out under artificial light.

industry which is now to be found in a much wider area than just the traditional holiday resorts. Many farm buildings are used for craft, antique and farm shops as well as galleries, restaurants and coffee shops. Holiday cottages can be less disruptive to the original structure than full domestic conversion. They can be smaller and simpler in design. One-storey units set around a cattle yard can often retain many original features whilst the barn remains as a communal room, perhaps even containing a swimming-pool. However, again there is the problem of dividing up what was originally a single-purpose structure. It is always true that the less alteration there is, the more of the historic interest of the building will be retained. This adds to the attraction of 'stone tents' pioneered in the early 1970s in the Peak District National Park. Here, in conjunction with Derbyshire Historic Buildings Trust, four isolated field barns were renovated as 'stone tents' for the Girl Guides. The advantage of this was that, because the buildings were not for general public use, many of the public health requirements that might otherwise have applied could be avoided and the number of alterations needed could be reduced. Similar schemes have been tried elsewhere, such as in the Yorkshire Dales. The Countryside Commission has now formed a partnership with the Youth Hostels Association and hopes to convert about 75 barns by 1993 at a cost of only about £10,000 per barn. Only the very minimum of facilities are provided for walkers, and for the conservationist this is certainly a very satisfactory solution.

There is no doubt, however, that the most lucrative option from the farmer's point of view, and the most disruptive from the historian's, is the conversion to domestic use. Conversion for housing does not usually have the social advantages that conversion for light industry can have in the community. To justify the great expense of domestic conversion the resulting houses are usually far too highly priced for local buyers.[9]

William Morris, the Victorian founder of the Society for the Protection of Ancient Buildings, said he 'would like a house like a big barn, where one ate in one corner, cooked in another corner, slept in a third and in the fourth received one's friends...'[10] Although this is undoubtedly the best way to treat a barn conversion, there are few modern barn dwellers who would be happy with such an arrangement!

In fact the type of buyer that the barn converter will hope to attract demands very high standards of comfort and luxury: he certainly does not want to live in 'a barn of a house'. This inevitably means that the basic simplicity of the barn is lost under a smart veneer. Cheaper houses are sometimes created by converting a farmstead into a large number of separate dwellings. One farmsteading near Dunbar in East Lothian has, with the support of the district council, been made into 'a delight-ful courtyard development of 15 cottages', but here again there are problems. Even though, in this case, the conversion has been achieved without the insertion of any domestic chimneys, a minimum of alterations to the exterior and the preservation of the engine house, the unity of the building is completely broken. The greater the number of separate units into which a farmstead is divided, the greater is the destruction of the historical evidence. The central covered yard with its complex arrangement of feeding passages and pens has been dismantled to provide a green and pleasant central court.

## THE CHALLENGE

The degree and scale of these problems began to be recognized by local planning authorities in the late 1970s and many, particularly in the areas most affected by the barn conversion craze, have laid down strict guidelines as to when conversion should be allowed, in their county *Structure Plans*; and districts have produced their own advice leaflets as to types of conversion that will be acceptable. Their aim must be to preserve as much of the historic and landscape value of traditional farm buildings as possible, whilst allowing the developments in the countryside that the rural community needs. These need not necessarily be conflicting aims, but there is a very fine balance that has to be achieved, and it is here that the challenge lies.

The first planning authority to produce a planning guide for conversion was Essex.[11] This was quickly followed by similar publications in other areas, particularly in the south and east, where the pressure on housing and so the interest in sales for conversion was at its greatest. Most of this literature accepted that pressure for conversion was for residential rather than light industrial use, and that it was here that the greatest problems for sympathetic treatment were likely to be. These local initiatives were followed by responses at a national level, from The Society for the Protection of Ancient Buildings in 1984, and SAVE Britain's Heritage, The Council for the Preservation of Rural England and The Council for British Archaeology, all in 1988. These reports make similar points, but generally, the more recent the publication, the greater is the note of caution.

All agree that conversion for domestic use is the most damaging of all. The original Essex County Council report saw conversion as one way to halt the loss of farm buildings from a county renowned for the standard of its early timber barns and where only between a third and a half of those that once existed were still standing in 1979. A few years later, however, *Supplementary Planning Guidance* was produced and stated, 'The recent spate of residential conversion of historic barns has only been a partial success . . . the results have been hybrid buildings of very limited visual appeal, frequently unrecognizable as barns.' In 1985 North Norfolk District Council's publication went even further in stating, 'Experience has shown that the conversion of buildings to residential use does not in general retain the character of the building in its traditional surroundings'.

Basic design standards are suggested in all the publications. They agree on the importance of preserving the character of the building, allowing the 'strength and robustness of its original form to remain predominant'. This can be achieved by keeping external alterations to a minimum. The existing roof line should be unbroken, and the opening of the double threshing doors should be retained. Ventilation slots can be used as light sources and other windows must respect the timber-framing and be as inconspicuous as possible. The particular quality of the barn is the contrast between large unbroken areas of wall and a few large openings and this must not be lost. Extensions should not be allowed and conversion into more than one dwelling discouraged. Internal features are as important historically as the exterior. Here the 'quality of internal space' must be retained. The building must remain open to the roof, at least for part of its length and the roof structure must be visible.

The surroundings too must be treated sympathetically. 'Externally, domestic paraphernalia such as porches, conservatories, washing lines, dustbins, ranch-style fencing or exotic planting can change the down-to-earth, honest relationship that is expected between a traditional agricultural building and the surrounding buildings and landscape.'[12]

North Norfolk's newest publication (1989) is a step forward from earlier advice available in that it relies heavily on illustrations to show the historic features of all types of buildings from chapels through cottages to farm buildings and so is much easier for the general public to understand. It is at present out of print because of the high level of demand and has proved extremely helpful in explaining the value of maintaining points of interest in any conversion work. Its success is shown by the number of requests for advice received by the conservation officer, even in cases where he need not necessarily be involved.

Shropshire County Council is the most recent to respond to the problem, with its *Guidance Notes* (1990), which include detailed drawings of a group of traditional brick farm buildings followed by ones showing a successful and unsuccessful conversion. Ingenious ways of keeping historic features, such as feeding troughs as plant containers, the retention of boarded high-level hoist doors, pitching holes and the great threshing doors as either internal or external shutters, and the preservation of external staircases, are all advocated in an effort to get away from mock-Georgian doors and windows and over-fussy, disruptive detailing.

Yet, in spite of all this very laudable advice available, and the necessity for submitting detailed plans before outline planning permission is granted, a large proportion of the resulting conversions, even in what would appear to be the most vigilant districts, fall far short of the

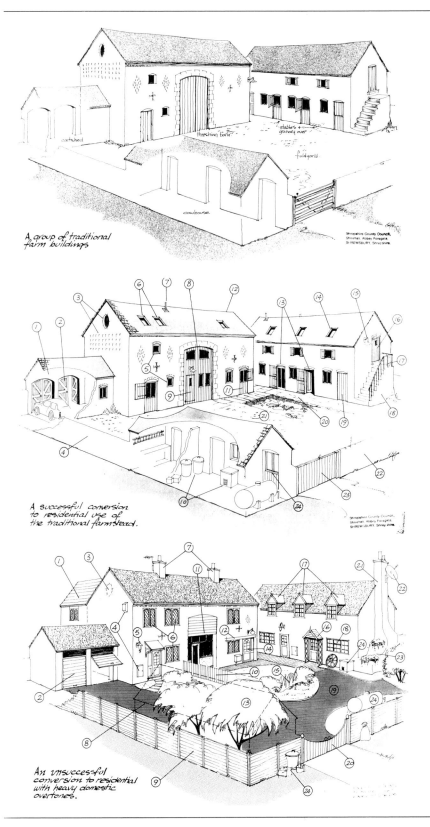

A group of traditional
farm buildings

A successful conversion
to residential use of
the traditional farmstead.

An unsuccessful
conversion to residential
with heavy domestic
overtones.

125 Three diagrams from
Shropshire County
Council's *Guidance Notes*
for farm building
conversion. Much of the
'character' and more
importantly, the historical
evidence of the original
farmstead is retained in the
'successful' conversion.
However, even here many
of the internal fittings that
are so important in the
interpretation of buildings
are inevitably lost. It is easy
to confuse retaining
historical evidence with
good taste. The dormer
windows and the enlarged
openings in the stable block
of the 'unsuccessful' scheme
are a loss of historical
integrity, while the satelite
dish, although unsightly,
has not affected the
historical significance of the
building. There is a narrow
line between the two, but the
historian must be careful to
keep his side of it.

POINTS FOR A SUCCESSFUL CONVERSION TO
RESIDENTIAL USE

1. Good use of cartshed for garaging
2. Sturdy ledged and braced doors
3. Retention of elevational detail
4. Use of foldyard wall for containment
5. Respect of original 'haphazard' openings
6. Minimum use of rooflights
7. Simple metal flues
8. Threshing doorway retained with vertical emphasis
9. Well designed, simple, postern door
10. Useful storage of domestic clutter
11. Successful infilling of unwanted opening
12. Unbroken ridge lines
13. Two examples of door/shutter treatment
14. Rooflights of correct size
15. Sensible outdoor lighting
16. Retention of loft door
17. Sturdy metal handrail detail
18. Retention of original steps
19. Simple boarding-up of unused doorway
20. Respect for original raised walkways
21. 'Hard' surfacing material of texture
22. Walling retained
23. Gate design reflects original use
24. Boarded height to retain cill line

POINTS FOR AN UNSUCCESSFUL CONVERSION TO RESIDENTIAL USE,
WITH HEAVY DOMESTIC OVERTONES

1. Extensions should be unnecessary
2. Metal up and over modern garage doors
3. Blocking-in of original barn feature
4. Domestic 'clutter' on elevation
5. Over-ornate lighting
6. Standard narrow framed windows and lead applied
7. Chimney stacks breaking ridge
8. Demolition of one of farmbuilding group
9. Excessive use of larch-lap fencing
10. Attempt to subdivide plots
11. Horizontal 'panel' detail and mixed infill
12. Ugly lintel detail
13. Inappropriate 'ornamental' trees
14. Standard door and side panel to fill gap
15. 'Soft' planting
16. Elevation broken by 'cottage' style porch
17. Breaking eaves line with too many dormers
18. Window proportion alien to original format
19. 'Sea' of tarmac (an eyesore in any rural development)
20. Unsuitable and useless gate design
21. Tall outside stack ruins plain gable
22. 21st Century tatt!
23. Over-twee detail hiding original steps
24. Domestic clutter on ground area

**126** Detail showing the attractive use of galleting in the mortar, at Lestrange Estate, Norfolk.

standards set down in the various *Guidelines*. It is often difficult to understand how some monstrous schemes were ever approved, but the truth is that modifications creep in at a later stage and alterations such as the replacement of a plain plank door by a mock-Tudor one do not need planning permission once the scheme is finished.

A final problem with the production of *Guidelines* is that their very existence can be seen as encouragement to potential converters who feel that as long as their schemes come up to the recommended standards they should be permitted, while in fact no conversion at all would still be best. Checklists of 'OK details' may not be the way ahead. Instead there needs to be an overall view in which the building and its environment are seen as a whole.

If it is almost impossible in practice to control what really goes on after planning permission is granted, the number and type of sites where conversion is permitted can be limited. In the early 1980s conversion was often seen as the solution to the problem of redundant farm buildings. South Norfolk District Council declared in 1980, 'Modern methods are making them (old farm buildings) redundant in increasing numbers and in many cases only a change of use can ensure their future retention ... in many cases the only viable use is residential.' In the past, the preconditions for eligibility were often rather loosely interpreted. These in many cases were laid down in *County Structure Plans* and *District Guidelines* and usually stated that only in exceptional circumstances would conversion for residential use be allowed outside the specified housing envelopes around existing settlements. The first essential was that the farmer could prove that the building no longer had any agricultural use. This is in fact very difficult to demonstrate. If there was not the possibility of very substantial financial gain, most farmers would find some, if rather limited, use for their buildings. Once a redundancy, however phoney, has been established the other criteria must be satisfied. These include the 'exceptional landscape or architectural value' of the building. This was occasionally more precisely defined as including most pre-eighteenth-century buildings and the more distinctive early nineteenth-century examples. 'Group value' and 'occupying a prominent and attractive position in the landscape', were two other possible criteria that were open to very wide interpretation, but still did not take account of factors that the historian would consider important. Historic value has little to do with age (nineteenth-century cattle sheds can be as valuable as eighteenth-century barns), nor with an 'attractive position'. One of the main results of this policy has been the demolition of the shelter sheds around the barns, regarded as unattractive accretions, and the preserving in isolation of eighteenth-century barns. There is a danger that future generations will gain the impression that agriculture was served by a few isolated barns and perhaps occasionally a granary, but little else. Barns most likely to get planning permission are those within housing envelopes and along village streets. Yet the historic interest of these buildings, perhaps dating from the period before enclosure when the farmer went out to his fields from a farmstead within the village, is as likely to be as great if not greater than anywhere else. Whilst 'landscape' and 'community' interest have rightly always been important in shaping planning policies, 'historical' concerns have been rather low down the list. It is clear that planners and local authorities frequently do not appreciate the value of these buildings and need educating themselves, or to take historical advice where it is locally available.

As a result of these rather ambiguous conditions, there has been a

127 A barn in south Norfolk (*top*) before and (*bottom*) after conversion. Although the outline of the buildings is preserved and many of the openings are original, the resulting external appearance is very 'un-barn-like'.

**128** There is very little to indicate that this mid-Norfolk home was ever a barn.

rash of applications as farmers see their neighbours making windfall profits and at the same time ridding themselves of rather expensive white elephants. These applications increased greatly during the boom years for property in the mid-80s, the number usually being directly related to the rise in house prices in a particular area. In Norfolk, for instance, applications in South Norfolk were generally running at a rate ten times higher than in the more remote Breckland District. South Cambridgeshire District developed a much stricter policy after a parish inventory showed that 40 per cent of the district's listed barns had been converted by the mid-1980s.

As residential development outside village envelopes is very strictly controlled, the only way around these restrictions is through farm building conversion. One example will serve to illustrate this point. 'The poor state of repair of the disused barns at Arminghall, near Norwich, which were sold at auction on October 30th for £100,000...with consent for conversion to two houses, shows that what is really being sold is the right to build a house in the country.'[13] A thumb through any local paper shows the number of barn conversions that have taken place and the number of barns for conversion that are still becoming available. The craze for them is even shown in advertisements for 'brand new barn-style residences!'. The illustrations show how planning guidelines have been disregarded. There are chimneys, rows of dormer windows, Georgian-style doors and internally far too many room divisions and inglenooks. What, one wonders is a 'continental-style barn conversion' that was advertised recently?

The level of applications does not seem to have dropped greatly with the recession in property prices, but the level of approvals has, as doubts about the success of conversion as a way of preserving historic buildings have arisen.

In two extreme examples, Canterbury District Council declared a year's moratorium on residential development while Babergh District Council in Suffolk has introduced very strict controls. In order for a building to be accepted as redundant, and eligible for residential conversion, an owner must firstly prove that the building is no longer required for agriculture and provide specialist evidence from MAFF to prove his case. He must then put the building on the market for six months for industrial, agricultural, office, community, recreational or tourist use at the appropriate price and the building must be included in the 'Vacant Employment Land and Premises Register' for at least six months. If all this fails to produce a non-residential use, then the planning application will be considered.

Loss of faith in conversion to residential use has been balanced by growing interest in change of use to light industries as a better possibility. Certainly it is likely to be better for the building, and one Conservative candidate in the recent county council elections (May 1989) included in her manifesto for a Norfolk constituency, the promise that she would, 'support the creation of new jobs...in carefully converted farm buildings'. However, progress in this direction is slow and some of the problems of this type of development have already been discussed.

One of the most recent publications on the conversion of farm buildings, and also one of the most depressing, is that by The Council for the Preservation of Rural England (Watkins & Winter 1988). Although based on a very small sample, its findings coincide in many respects with the Norfolk experience. The authors suggest five justifications for conversion:

1. The provision of employment
2. The supply of rural housing
3. Farm incomes support
4. Preservation of traditional and historic buildings
5. The encouragement of farm diversification and new land uses,

and then manage to prove that none of these things did in fact happen.

Unfortunately it is true that many conversions for industry do not provide work for locals but for skilled craftsmen, technicians and professionals from outside. They do not help those made redundant on farms.

Conversion for housing will involve the greatest destruction of the historic evidence. It is usually very much for the upper end of the market and not for locals. The exceptions to this are when dwellings for members of the farmer's family, either a son or a father on retirement, are provided.

Selling a building for conversion simply provides a one-off cash

**129** Smaller buildings can often be converted more successfully than barns. It is clear that this house was originally a cart lodge with a weatherboarded granary above. The granary stairs and owl hole above the door still remain.

injection for the farmer, while letting does create some income support. Conversion for tourism allows for much needed diversification on the part of the farmer and may well provide some employment and be a stimulus to retail trade in the area.

These findings are on the whole, disturbing, particularly as they come at the end of a period in which the number of planning permissions granted has been increasing dramatically, especially in the areas affected by the rapid rise in house prices in the south.

Conversion which, it was hoped a few years ago, might prove to be the answer to many of the problems of the countryside as well as the only way to keep up buildings, has proved to be a two-edged sword and the disastrous results of these policies from the historic and landscape points of view are only now coming to be appreciated. In many areas, barns that were listed buildings are now, after conversion, being de-listed.

Conversion to dwellings is not always as satisfactory for the farmer or new owner as might at first appear to be the case. Although the farmer will gain a large single payment when selling his barns for conversion, he could well be better off in the long run keeping control of the buildings and gaining a regular rent from workshops. Barn conversions introduce a new type of person onto the farm, often very unsympathetic to and ignorant of the needs of modern farming. He may well object to the noise of grain driers 24 hours a day at harvest and tractors with headlights working in fields well into the evenings. Mud on a shared drive and the noise and smell of animals in adjoining sheds can be another bone of contention. The truth is that suburbs rather than farmyards are the quietest places to live.[14]

There is a demand for farmhouses with barns and outbuildings and in some ways this is the best way for the farmer to sell. That the tide may well be on the turn is suggested by the East Anglian press in an article printed in October 1989. Whilst in 1988 a barn or outbuildings in a small plot of land with planning permission could be sold for development for approximately 45 per cent of the anticipated final resale value, by late 1989 this figure was reduced to 25 per cent of the final price. This figure has itself been reduced by the prevailing depressed market. Selling barns separately also reduces the value of any neighbouring property. 'There is a scarcity of well-located farmhouses available with traditional barns and buildings, and with evidence of prospective buyers seeking such premises as an entire unit, owners may do best to keep their farmhouses and adjoining properties as one and sell them as an unbroken unit.'[15]

There can also be financial worries for the barn dweller. Whilst barns in East Anglia have been selling for between £100,000 and £200,000, it costs at least another £100,000 to convert. The resulting house is usually highly individual in character and can prove difficult to sell. Barn living may be a passing fashion and future home buyers may not want to live on the edge of a busy yard near the site of early morning milking. There can be even greater problems in selling a property in close proximity to neighbours. The prospective buyer may baulk at paying a sizeable sum for what is in effect a semi-detached or terraced house. Patrick Ramsey, head of the country house department of Knight, Frank and Rutley, was quoted as saying 'Buyers are being more timid about the privacy factor of courtyard developments.'[16]

## BLUEPRINT FOR ACTION

The first problem is a lack of knowledge. Very few planning departments know exactly what their stock of historical buildings is. This means that each of the planning applications that comes into district offices has to be considered on its own merits and within the guidelines set by the *Structure Plan* rather than within an historical context. The *Norfolk Structure Plan*, for instance, requires that domestic conversion should be very much a last resort, conversion for light industrial use being better both for the retention of the historic features of the building and for the community as a whole. As residential development is now restricted to tight housing envelopes around existing villages, the conversion of a barn to a house can be seen as a way of creating a residence in the open country where it would not otherwise be permitted. Recently, however, such applications have been more and more difficult to get through planning committees in much of Norfolk.

Previously, permission could only be granted if the buildings concerned are 'of particularly high architectural or landscape value and if their retention could only be assured by a change of use.'[17] There are several problems with this statement of policy. Firstly, it makes no mention of 'historic value', which should be as important as architectural or landscape considerations. Only by including buildings of historic interest can we be sure that the mundane and typical as well as the unusual will survive. Secondly, it is in fact precisely those outstanding buildings where conversion should *not* be allowed, but which should be preserved in their entirety.

Some district councils have gone some way to acknowledging the shortcomings of this part of the policy statement and will not grant permission for the conversion of listed buildings, thus putting the onus on the owners to find some agricultural use for them, however limited. The problem of keeping them in repair if they remain within agriculture is helped by the new MAFF 35 per cent grants. It is encouraging to find that the officers of district planning departments are being pushed into a more restrictive position by public opinion in the form of the elected committees, which are granting fewer permissions than in the past. However, if decisions are to be made on anything other than an *ad hoc* basis, some assessment of the stock of traditional farm buildings and their relative historic, landscape and architectural interest needs to be made on a national scale, based on county planning departments.

A second problem of this policy was that only the architecturally interesting buildings in the group, usually the barn, would be preserved. The later shelter-sheds and loose boxes, deemed to be less interesting, were often demolished. In fact it is the whole group that illustrates the development of agriculture, and so they should all be kept together.

It has to be accepted that it is pie-in-the-sky to imagine that all traditional farm buildings can remain in agricultural use or in their original form for posterity, and one of the aims of a survey of the existing stock would be to assess priorities and establish a select group of buildings where no alteration would be permissible and where farmers could be encouraged to keep them in low-intensity use.

An example of a major initiative to save a unique landscape is the creation of a conservation area to cover 70 sq. km (27 sq. miles) of the Yorkshire Dales National Park, taking in almost 800 stone barns. These barns are simple, functional buildings with no architectural pretensions and very difficult to date. Very few were regarded as of listable quality, yet historically their very number is evidence of a farming system that from the Middle Ages to the recent past relied on cattle being housed in these small barns amongst the fields in the winter and fed from the hay loft above. Less cartage but more human effort was involved in the keeping of between six and ten cattle in scattered field barns than if the hay and manure had been carted to and from a large central point. Grants of up to 80 per cent will be available to repair barns and stone boundary walls using traditional methods and materials. Here it is the preservation of a large number of these small buildings rather than a few typical examples which is important.[18]

The majority of buildings would probably come below this category, where conversion to light industrial or tourist use, which damages the buildings least whilst helping to diversify the farming enterprise and create jobs in the countryside, would be acceptable. The interest of these buildings is likely to be that they are typical of their region or of a prevalent farming system rather than that they are of great landscape or aesthetic value.

Only in very few cases would conversion to a dwelling be an option. Barns rarely make good houses. Some can bear more conversion than others. Large Cotswold stone barns, for instance, can be easier to convert than small cob or half-timbered buildings. Conversion into several dwellings, which immediately destroys the unity of the farm-stead, should not be permitted. A house and workshop or storage is always a far better solution. As fewer planning permissions are granted residential conversion will cease to be considered as a viable option by farmers, who will then seek other uses for their buildings, perhaps even within agriculture, and with the aid of grants they will be kept in good repair.

In cases where planning permission for conversion to a non-agricultural use is permitted, one of the conditions of the permission should be that a plan and photographs of the building before conversion be deposited with a local Sites and Monuments Record, usually located either in the county planning department, museums or archaeological service. However sensitive the conversion, much historical evidence is inevitably lost and it is important that a record of the building as it was is kept.

These should be more than the usual architect's drawings that are presented when planning permission is sought. They should include fully measured and annotated ground plans and elevations, not only of the barn, but also the outbuildings, at least one major section with internal elevations, a full set of photographs of internal and external details and notes on the materials of which buildings are constructed and previous uses of the building remembered by the farmer.

An example of such a group of buildings is a cattle range and covered yard at Oxwick, in north-west Norfolk (see chapter 16). Described by the house agent as 'an unusual single-storey barn complex', it proved on investigation to be a cattle yard with a row of loose boxes on the north side of the yard, served from a central passage and ventilated through elaborate roof louvers. Here we have a rare example, noted quite by chance, of an owner-occupier providing himself with the sort of buildings we often associate with the improving landlords. These late nineteenth-century buildings are unspectacular architecturally, but of great interest historically. They might well deserve a place in a list of buildings where no alteration should be allowed; if not, then how much better that plans and photographs showing clearly how the buildings had been used are deposited with the local Sites and Monuments Record.

In summary, there needs to be a complete review of policies that affect the historic farm buildings stock. The guidelines that lay down when planning permission for conversion should be granted already exist in many counties and districts. They need enforcing in a strict and uniform way. There needs to be urgent clarification of the present confused situation as to whether conversion of listed buildings is to be discouraged or encouraged, and if discouraged, there needs to be more financial aid for keeping them in repair. English Heritage is at present addressing itself to the problem, and the final statement is eagerly awaited. Planning authorities need to know what their stock of historic farm buildings is and to have an overall policy rather than assessing each individual case as it comes up, as the Oxwick example shows.

A much greater emphasis needs to be placed on the recording of buildings before conversion and enforcing a strict code of practice as to what alterations are permissible. Here again many very valuable advice booklets have been produced by district and county councils, but one would not think so; looking at many of the conversions in their areas. More vigilance is needed on the part of planning and conservation officers as well as their elected masters and those who vote for them.

The new countryside of the twenty-first century may well be one of less intensive farming in which a wider variety of farm buildings could remain in agricultural use. It will be one in which inevitably only a minority of the population will be engaged in agriculture, but in which, as suggested by the new 'Business in the Community' initiative, an increasing number could find employment locally, perhaps in industries and offices in old farm buildings, rather than joining the ever-lengthening queues into the local towns and cities.

Finally, it is not in the end the methods of the police state that will preserve our landscape and its varied legacy of regional and individual building styles; it is the interest and concern of those who live there that is needed. Information on the buildings' history as well as how to tackle the problems of repairing historic buildings should be easily available through, for instance, historic buildings services operated by county archaeological or planning departments. The success of North Norfolk's approach shows that if the guidance is available it can be very willingly received.

Not only architects and planners, but also every owner of an historic farm needs to understand the intrinsic value of the small but unique piece of agricultural history with which he has been entrusted and to treasure it for those who come after him.

# Appendices

## I   RECORDING AND SURVEYING

One of the main reasons for setting up a farm building survey in Norfolk was the speed at which buildings were being demolished, converted or were simply decaying beyond recognition. It was essential therefore that any survey created a record that would be useful to researchers in the future, when the buildings themselves had gone, and so, ideally, nothing less than the most detailed and exhaustive survey would be adequate.

To be balanced against this, however, was the sheer size of the problem and the time available, so some sort of compromise had to be reached. The level at which the buildings should be studied provoked a great deal of discussion in the first few months of the survey. In the event just over 400 sites across varied and representative regions within the county were investigated in two years; the recording system finally adopted is described below.

### Archive research

The records for each farm fall into four categories. Firstly and very importantly, there is the archive research which was always completed before a farm was visited. The amount of information varied greatly from farm to farm with most to be found for farms that had been part of large and well-run estates. Here, as well as estate maps and plans, occasionally dating back to the late seventeenth century, there could be accounts, audit books and written surveys of the estate at various dates. Many of these estates were finally sold up in the early years of this century and often the last piece of archive evidence available was the sales catalogue. From all these sources it was often possible to ascertain the estate policy on farm building and the motives behind it. They were also an important means of dating buildings still standing. When the survey team went out into the field, it took copies of plans of the farm and its buildings at different dates, costs and descriptions of new buildings and

FULL REFERENCES OF DOCUMENTS CONSULTED
· James Wright : Survey of the Gunton Estate Vol. I. 1835.

**RESEARCHER** J.Nixon.
**DATE** January 1986.

**MODERN NAME OF FARM** Church Farm TG 252 329

**FORMER NAME OF FARM** Church Farm.

**PARISH** Antingham

**CENTRE OF EAST ANGLIAN STUDIES FARM BUILDINGS SURVEY** summary of documentary evidence

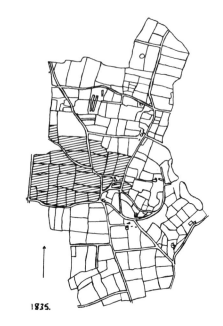

1835.

1835 Acreage: 244 acres

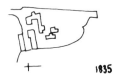

8 chains to 1"

1835

Repairs book c1825 Gunton Estate
Thomas Coleman        £130
Walls to fence in bullock yards.
Bullock shed against new walls.
Turnip house, wall from turnip
house to hedge. Gable end of small
barn repaired. Both barn doors
repaired. New barn floors (clay).
New barn floors (boarded).Add to
porch of small barn 9". New
boarded gate. Hay chamber floor
repaired. Off barn wall round door
repaired. Off barn brick floor
repaired. Boarded door into sheep
yard. Off stable door put out where
wichet now is. New stable door and
fences. 30 yards fencing for a colts
yard off barn.

Survey of the Gunton Estate T.Rose 1894
Tenant: Herbet Gaze.  130 acres 22/6d p.a.
Roof of gig house and riding horse stable wants to be put in proper repair.
There are 2 good barns, both of which are thatched. All in fairly good repair.
Several new roofs in the previous 15 years. They are far too straggling and
more than required for this acreage.There is an old implement shed standing at
the back of the bullock boxes which should be cleared away entirely, also the
high stone and brick wall round the chaft cutting works. There are 2 cart horse
stables while only one is required. "I should think the present tenant is not
a very energetic man".

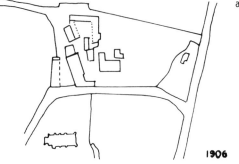

1906

FURTHER INFORMATION FILED AT:

Sheet no.1...
of.1........

repairs, descriptions of the farmstead and its condition at different periods, the most recent often being an extract from a sales catalogue.

Even if there were no estate documents to help, all farms were marked clearly on tithe maps drawn in the years following the 1836 Tithe Commutation Act, which replaced the paying of tithes in kind by fixed annual payments in cash. These large-scale, detailed maps are accompanied by a written apportionment giving, field by field, the land use, the owners and the occupiers throughout the parish, resulting in a remarkable picture of land use, ownership and farm layout in the mid-nineteenth century.

Finally, the documentary evidence included a copy of the second edition 25-inch Ordnance Survey plan of the farm buildings, revised about 1908. No building that post-dated this map was included in the survey.

### Written description

Once on the site, recording in the three remaining categories of a written description, photography and a plan could be undertaken.

The written description combined some of the features of a structured form of questionnaire whilst also allowing enough scope for more flexible recording in depth. Each building was given a number and described on a separate sheet. The first section gave essential information such as the name of the farm with a grid reference, the number allocated to the building and its original function, with some assessment of the condition and present use of the building as well as its likely date. Although its relationship to the rest of the farmstead could be seen from the accompanying plan, this was also noted on the sheet, indicating whether it was isolated and therefore perhaps a later addition, or part of the main-core original buildings.

These general remarks were followed by more detail about the wall and roof construction. Building materials could indicate the status of building. In the heavy clay regions, for instance, clay lump was often used as a cheap substitute for brick. Building materials can also indicate date. No clay lump buildings have as yet been dated before 1800. The roof construction was described in some detail because of its significance in trying to date the building. Internal divisions and features, whether they were original or not, as well as the construction of the floor and any external additions were noted in later sections as they may indicate any changes of use that took place.

Finally on this survey sheet, the dimensions of the barn were noted in an attempt to determine whether there was any relationship between the size of the barn and the acreage of the farm or the importance of arable crops in the region.

On a separate sheet, all the openings such as doors, windows and pitching holes, whether still open, blocked in or inserted, were recorded and this information could prove very important in working out how the buildings were originally used and any subsequent changes.

### Planning

The whole farmstead was recorded on a 1:500 plan that had been enlarged from the latest 1:2500 Ordnance Survey map and was then annotated in the

130 (*opposite*) A completed documentation sheet for Church Farm, Antingham. For this farm there was a map of 1835 and 1906 as well as a description in 1825 and 1894.

| | |
|---|---|
| **FARM:** Church Farm | **PARISH:** Gt. Hautbois   **GRID REF:** TG 261 208   **DATE:** 5.3.86 |
| **BUILDING NO:** 1 | **FUNCTION:** Barn       **SURVEYOR:** |

| | |
|---|---|
| **GENERAL** | **DATE:** c. 1700 <br> **CONDITION:** Good <br> **USE:** Being converted in near future to residential use <br> **RELATIONSHIP TO FARMSTEAD:** |
| **WALL CONSTRUCTION** | **MATERIALS:** Brick. Flemish bonding ( Brick size = 2 × 4½ × 9" ) <br><br> **PLINTH/BASAL COURSES:** Brick plinth with a brick and flint footing. <br> **DETAIL:** Tumbling-in brickwork at gables. Raised gables indicate roof originally thatched. |
| **ROOF** | **SHAPE:** Gable-ended N—S <br> **CLADDING:** Probably originally thatched, present covering-corrugated iron. <br> **STRUCTURE:** Principal rafter <br> **PURLINS:** Two butt-purlins, morticed into principal <br> **COLLARS:** One, morticed into principal <br> **BRACING:** Arched braces on tie-beams. Straight bracing over entrance <br> **COMMON RAFTERS:** Five in each roof bay    **ROOF BAYS:** 10 ( 8 to south of dividing ) wall <br> **TIE BEAMS:** Six, two of which define entrance bay. <br>      — Unrelated to principals. <br> **TIMBER:** Adze-cut and pit-sawn. |
| **INTERNAL DIVISION(S)** | North end of barn is divided by a roof-height inserted brick wall, forming a stable area at this end. Stable area lofted, the joists being integral with the lower wall. Integral porch area on east wall which is 3.3 m deep and recessed 0.2 m symmetrically. |
| **FLOOR** | Concreted, with some stone threshing floor surviving-extends to porch. |
| **INTERNAL FEATURES** | Carpenter's marks on ties begin at north end. Slit ventilation in East and West walls, Lozenge-shaped ventilation in both gables. Owl hole in south gable. Walls of stable area are whitewashed. |
| **EXTERNAL BUILDINGS** | Late c. 19th. cartshed butting onto east wall. <br> Late c. 19th. shelter sheds butt onto west wall. |
| **DIMENSIONS** | **LENGTH:** 26.5 m   **WIDTH:** 6.3 m   **HGHT TO WALL PLATE LEVEL:** 3.9 m <br> **STEAD LENGTH:** (south) 9.2 m      **ENTRANCE/BAY WIDTH:** 3.2 m |

field. Each building was numbered as in the written description and opening marked. The position of internal walls and the posts holding up the roof of open sided sheds were marked. This annotated field plan was redrawn in the office and a summary interpretation of the buildings and the development of the farmstead indicated in the key. Some buildings merited more detailed treatment and a second visit was then made to the farm to take measurements.

## Photography

The photographic record was as full as possible. Every building was photographed from each side with detailed shots of significant features, both internal and external. The position from which each photograph was taken was marked on a plan. Although it might appear that a good photographic coverage makes a written description and detailed drawings unnecessary, this is certainly not the case for two main reasons. Firstly, even with a variety of sophisticated wide angle and telescopic lenses, buildings within a group and surrounded by farmyard clutter are notoriously difficult to photograph, and secondly, it is only when buildings are carefully studied in the way necessary to produce a written description, using the prompts on the questionnaire, that some of the significant features will be noticed.

## Oral evidence

A final very important source of information was the farmer and those who had worked on the farm for many years, perhaps seeing the change from horse to tractor in the 1950s. They were often able to help discover the original, or at least the previous uses of buildings and to explain details of design. Sometimes their observations only added to the confusion, when for instance, they pointed out small features that might have gone unnoticed, and had always puzzled them, such as the inexplicable trap doors in some barn walls that may have been used for belting. Memories, however, are rarely reliable before the First World War and most of the buildings studied went back several generations before 1914. There was little in the oral evidence that could help explain the use of buildings in the years of 'High Farming' and before.

It was not only in the interpretation of the buildings themselves that the oral evidence was important; it also helped to build up a picture of life on the farm before tractors, combine harvesters and intensive battery livestock production. The fact that cattle really did do better in south-facing yards was confirmed again and again; it was not just a theory put forward by the authors of farming textbooks, but was true in practice. It was only the problem of tractor access and mucking out that prevented many of these yards still being used. Information such as where cattle, grain and fertilizer were bought and sold, how much grain and unthreshed crop there was in a stack and how long it took to build, all helped to give a much more detailed picture of farming whilst at the same time increasing understanding of the buildings and how they were used.

By using these survey methods, it was usually possible to visit two farms a day. Sometimes it was clear that a particularly interesting building merited

131 (*opposite*) Record sheet for the barn at Church Farm, Great Hautbois, as filled in in the field.

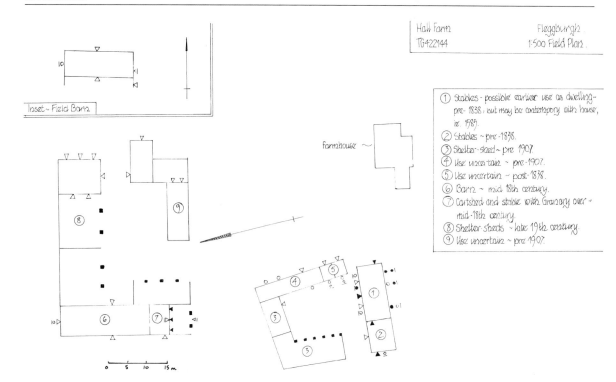

Hall Farm        Fleggburgh
TG422144        1:500 Field Plan.

Inset ~ Field Barn

Farmhouse ~

① Stables - possible earlier use as dwelling-
   pre- 1838, but may be contemporary with house,
   ie. 1589.
② Stables ~ pre-1838.
③ Shelter-shed ~ pre 1907.
④ Use uncertain ~ pre-1907.
⑤ Use uncertain ~ post-1838.
⑥ Barn ~ mid 18th century.
⑦ Cartshed and stable with Granary over ~
   mid-18th century.
⑧ Shelter-sheds ~ late 19th century.
⑨ Use uncertain ~ pre 1907.

0   5   10   15 m

**132** Annotated field plan of Hall Farm, Fleggburgh. The triangles on the drawing represent doors and the circles, windows. Blacked-in symbols are openings that are blocked, while unshaded symbols represent openings still open. A line beside the symbol means that the opening is at first-floor level.

more detailed measured drawings and in several cases these were undertaken; some appear in this book.

### The final record

It is always the case in surveys of this kind, that as much time is spent back in the office writing up the day's work as in the field, and this is something frequently forgotten when time and resources are being allocated. Field notes have to be typed up (in this case, onto a word-processor, so information is stored on disc as well as in the farm files), plans redrawn, photographs labelled and catalogued and information filed so that it can be retrieved. Most of the data collected on this survey was also computerized, which enabled the interrogation and retrieval of specific information. A copy of the written and drawn records was deposited with the country Sites and Monuments Record and of the photographic record at the National Monuments Record.

It is very much to the credit of the teams working on this survey that they seem to have struck a good working balance between recording of detail and covering a wide enough sample of buildings.

# II FARM MUSEUMS AND HISTORICAL FARM BUILDINGS OPEN TO THE PUBLIC

## Buckinghamshire
Chiltern Open Air Museum, Newland Park, Gorelands Lane, Chalfont St Giles. *Cruck barn, eighteenth-century granary on staddles.*
Bradwell Abbey Field Centre, Milton Keynes. *Medieval barn.*
Pitstone Green Farm Museum, Pitstone.

## Cambridgeshire
Wimpole Home Farm, Wimpole, Cambridge. *Farm buildings designed by Sir John Soane* (NT).

## Cheshire
Tatton Park, Knutsford (NT).

## Cleveland
Newham Grange Farm Agricultural Museum, Coulby Newham, Middlesborough.

## Clwyd
Erdigg, near Wrexham. *Eighteenth-century dovecot and other farm buildings* (NT).

## Cornwall
Lanreath Mill and Museum, Looe, Cornwall. *Tithe barn.*
Cotehole House. *Late fifteenth-century barn and dovecot* (NT).

## Derbyshire
Elvaston Castle Museum, Borrowash Road, Elvaston, Derby. *Estate yard, restored as it was in 1910.*

## Devon
Alscott Farm Museum, Shebbear.
Morwellham Quay Open Air Museum, Tavistock. *Part of a traditional farmstead.*
Buckland Abbey. *Eighteenth-century farm buildings and fifteenth-century barn* (NT).
Hound Tor, Manaton. *Ruins of thirteenth-century longhouses.*

## Durham
North of England Open Air Museum, Beamish Hall, Stanley. *Farmstead, c.1800.*

## Dyfed
The Shire Horse Centre of Wales, Vayner Isaf, nr. Puncheston, Dyfed. *Housed in traditional vernacular buildings.*

## Essex
Hayes Hill Farm, Stubbins Hill Lane, Crooked Mile, Waltham Abbey, Essex. *Sixteenth-century barn in Lea Valley Park.*
Grange Barn, Coggeshall, Essex. *Twelfth-century aisled barn* (NT).
Cressing Temple barns, Essex County Council. *Two early thirteenth-century aisled barns. Limited opening during the summer.*
Upminster Tithe Barn Agricultural and Folk Museum, Hall Lane, Upminster, Essex. *Fifteenth-century barn.*
Priors Hall Barn, Widdington. *Aisled barn, c.1400 (English Heritage).*

## Gloucestershire
Ashleworth Tithe Barn. *Early sixteenth century.*
Smerrill Farm Museum, Kemble, near Cirencester. *Cotswold barn.*

## Gwent
Model farm, Wolvesnewton, near Chepstow. *Nineteenth-century farmstead. Cowhouse and stables in the form of a St Andrew's cross. Now museum and craft shop.*

## Hampshire
Hampshire Farm Museum, Botley.

## Hereford and Worcester
Avoncroft Museum of Buildings, Stoke Heath, Bromsgrove, Worcestershire. *Granary, cartshed, windmill, barn, stable.*
Bredon Tithe Barn, Bredon, Worcestershire. *Thirteenth-century stone aisled barn* (NT).
Middle Littleton Tithe Barn, near Evesham, Hereford. *Thirteenth-century stone barn* (NT).

## Highland Region
Highland Folk Museum, Duke Street, Kingussie, Invernesshire.

## Humberside
Hasholme Carr Farm, Holme-upon-Spalding Moor, Humberside. *Nineteenth-century farmstead, open two weekends a year.*

## Kent
Museum of Kent Rural Life, Lock Lane, Cobtree Manor Park, Sandling, Maidstone. *Oasthouse*

and dairy buildings.

Whitbread's Hop Farm, Beltring, Paddock Wood. *Museum with oasthouses.*

Wye College Agricultural Museum, Brook, near Ashford. *Fourteenth-century barn, nineteenth-century oasthouse.*

## Leicestershire

Rutland Farm Park, Catmose Farm, Uppingham Road, Oakham. *Mid-Victorian farm buildings.*

## Lincolnshire

Church Farm Museum, Church Road, Skegness. *Nineteenth-century farm buildings.*

## Norfolk

Wroxham Barns. *Restored nineteenth-century buildings used for open days and events.*

Alby Crafts. *Restored nineteenth-century buildings used as a craft centre.*

## North Yorkshire

Ryedale Folk Museum, Hutton-le-Hole, North Yorkshire. *Longhouse, wheelhouse.*

## Oxfordshire

Manor Farm Museum, Cogges, Witney. *Traditional farmstead with buildings sixteenth–nineteenth century.*

Great Coxwell Tithe Barn, near Farringdon. *Thirteenth-century aisled stone barn* (NT).

Vale and Downland Museum Centre, The Old Surgery, Church Street, Wantage, Oxfordshire. *Three barns.*

## Shropshire

Acton Scott Working Farm Museum, near Church Stretton. *Model farmsteads, 1769.*

## Somerset

Somerset Rural Life Museum, Glastonbury. *Fourteenth-century stone tithe barn.*

Somerset farm park, Bossington, Porlock. *Traditional farmstead.*

Stoke-sub-Hamdon. *Medieval farm buildings* (NT).

## South Glamorgan

Welsh Folk Museum. *Longhouses, circular pigsties, barns, etc.*

## Staffordshire

Museum of Staffordshire Life, Shugborough Hall, Great Haywood. *Model farm built by Samuel Wyatt, early nineteenth century.*

## Suffolk

Easton Farm Park, Model Farm, Easton, Woodbridge. *Model farmstead, c.1870 with an ornate dairy.*

Museum of East Anglian Life, Abbots Hall, Stowmarket. *Medieval timber aisled barn.*

## Sussex

Weald and Downland Open Air Museum, Singleton, Chichester, West Sussex. *Wide selection medieval–nineteenth-century buildings.*

## Warwickshire

Baddesley Clinton. *Mid-eighteenth-century barn* (NT).

## West Yorkshire

East Riddlesden Hall, near Keighley. *Two barns, one medieval* (NT).

Pennine Folk Museum, Ripponden. *Early nineteenth-century Pennine farmstead.*

West Yorkshire Folk Museum, Shibden Hall, Halifax. *Seventeenth-century Pennine barn.*

## Wiltshire

Lackham Agricultural Museum, Lacock, Chippenham. *Granaries.*

Museum of Wiltshire Folk Life, Avebury, Marlborough. *Seventeenth-century barn.*

Bradford-on-Avon Tithe Barn. *Large medieval stone barn* (English Heritage).

Avebury. *Late seventeenth-century great barn* (NT).

## Worcestershire

Avoncroft Museum of Buildings, Stoke Heath, Bromsgrove.

*Note* NT indicates a building owned by the National Trust.

# NOTES

## Chapter 1

1 Wade Martins, S. 1980

## Chapter 2

1 Wade Martins, P. 1980b. 114–122
2 Yaxley in Wade Martins, P. 1980a, 624–5
3 Lake, 1989, 67
4 Harvey, P. in Hooke, 1985, 41
5 Davenport, 1967, 21 & 49
6 Holkham MS
7 NRO, Barnes, 1/5/86
8 Beresford & Hurst, 1971, 106–12
9 Dyer 1986, 25
10 Wiliam, 1986, 18
11 Wrathnell, 1989, 249
12 Jarrett & Wrathnell, 1977, Evans & Jarrett, 1987, Evans, Jarrett & Wrathnell, 1988
13 Beresford & Hurst, 1971, 106–111
14 Nankervis, 1989
15 Thirsk, 1985, 719
16 Smith, P. in Foster & Alcock, 1963, 435
17 Grundy, 1970, 1
18 Barley in Thirsk, 1985, 670
19 Beresford & Hurst, 1971, 115
20 Wiliam, 1986, 180
21 Rigold, 1971, 10–11
22 Lake, 1989, 156
23 Bloom, 1843, 259
24 Lake, 1989, 62
25 Clarke, 1972, 25–6
26 Lecture by J. Smith summarized in the Historic Farm Buildings Group *Newsletter*, 8 January, 1989
27 Colvin & Newman, eds. 1981, 97
28 Alcock, 1981
29 Robertson, 1793
30 Alcock, 1981
31 Jenkins, 1961

## Chapter 3

1 Fussell, 1947 and Thirsk, 1985, 534
2 Overton, 1985, 205
3 Jones, Bell & Martin, 1988
4 Hansell, 1988
5 Hoskins, 1964
6 Brunskill, 1982, 20
7 Thirsk, 1985, 246–7
8 Griffiths, 1987
9 Wiliam, 1986, 42
10 Lecture by Susan Denyer, summarized in Historic Farm Buildings Group *Newsletter*, 8 January, 1989
11 Brunskill, 1982, 112–14, Tyson, 1979–82
12 Lecture by Tim Whittaker, summarized in Historic Farm Buildings Group *Newsletter*, 8 January 1989
13 Holderness, 1976, 73
14 Young, 1804, 31
15 Wade Martins, S. 1987, 37–40
16 Brunskill, 1982, 110
17 Wiliam, 1986, 70

## Chapter 4

1 Thirsk, 1985, 165
2 Wiliam, 1986, 43
3 Mingay, 1963, 166
4 Robinson, 1983
5 Messenger, 1975
6 Robinson, 1983, 65
7 Marshall, 1804, 160
8 Robinson, 1983
9 Robinson, 1983, 30
10 Kent, 1796, 113
11 Fussell, 1954
12 Robertson, 1793, 30–31
13 Hepburn, 1794, 56
14 Hepburn, 1794, 49
15 Hepburn, 1794, 56
16 Donaldson, 1794, 21
17 Leslie, 1794, 23
18 Fenton & Walker, 1981, 209
19 Robinson, 1983, 17–25
20 Johnstone, 1794, 74–5
21 Johnstone, 1794, 15
22 Beaton, 1988 and Slade, 1978
23 P. de la R. du Prey, 1979
24 Robinson, 1983
25 Fenton & Walker, 1981, 174
26 Fenton & Walker, 1981, 161
27 Macdonald, 1975
28 Hutton, 1976

29 Fenton & Walker, 1981, 167
30 Wade Martins, S. 1988, 38
31 Hellen, 1972
32 Wade Martins, S. 1980, 143
33 Wade Martins, S. 1980, 143–4
34 Wade Martins, S. 1980, 150–3
35 Robinson, 1983, 67
36 Robinson, 1983, 68
37 Loudan, 1844, 450
38 Sutherland collection, Stafford Record Office, quoted by Richards, 1973, 26
39 Robinson, 1983, 9, 141 and 169
40 Macinnes, 1988, 70–87
41 Loch, 1820, Appendix 1, 17
42 Loch, 1820, Appendix 1, 21

Chapter 5

1 Rosselli, 1971, 42–64
2 Wade Martins, S. 1980, 120
3 Read, 1858, 265–311
4 Stirling, 1913, 1, 269
5 NRO Bacon MS 4363
6 Brigden, 1986, 188
7 Brigden, 1986, 202
8 Holland, 1989
9 Jenkins, 1869
10 Thompson, 1850, 186
11 Dean, 1851 and Wade Martins, S. 1980, 169–70
12 Denton, 1863, 61
13 Taylor, 1973, 204
14 Bedford, 1897, 50
15 Smith, 1856, 359
16 Orwin & Sellick, 1970 and Harvey, N. 1989
17 Gray, 1971

Chapter 6

1 Wade Martins, S. 1988, 41–3
2 Brown, 1988, 33
3 Brown, 1988, 37
4 Brown, 1988, 50
5 Brown, 1988, 46
6 Wade Martins, S. 1980, 183
7 Course & Moore, 1984
8 Moscrop, 1890
9 Wade Martins, S. 1980, 124–5

10 Rew, 1896, 35
11 Brown, 1988, 24
12 Brigden, 1986, 71
13 Harvey, N., 1984, 175
14 Curtis, *Farm Buildings*, 1912, quoted by Harvey, N., 1984, 195–6

Chapter 7

1 Peters, 1988, 24–31
2 McCann, 1987
3 Smith, 1985, 69
4 Wade Martins, S. 1980, 181
5 Wade Martins, S. 1980, 229

Chapter 8

1 Bacon, 1844, 13
2 Marshall, 1787, 1
3 Thirsk, 1987, 15
4 Kain & Prince, 1985
5 Young, 1804, 26
6 Read, 1858, 265–311
7 Marshall, 1787, 1, 2
8 Overton, 1985
9 Roe, 1975, 223–9
10 NRO LW 1559

Chapter 9

1 Marshall, 1787, 1, 2
2 NRO MC70/17/5
3 I & ESRO HA/54/8/160/164–7
4 Roe, 1975, 209
5 Kain, 1986
6 Roe, 1975, 229
7 NRO MC 150/12
8 Kain, 1986, 80
9 Young, 1771, 2, 111–14
10 Wiliam, 1986, 152

Chapter 10

1 Marshall, 1787, 1, 2
2 NRO WLS XXIX/2/19 416x4
3 Armstrong, 1963, 116
4 Roe, 1975, 168
5 Postgate, 1962, 94
6 NRO WLS XXIX/2/10

7   Postgate, 1962, 87
8   NRO WLS LXVIII 478x9
9   Kain, 1986, 82
10  NRO WLS XXIX/2/10/416x4
11  NRO WLS XXIX/7
12  NRO WLS XXXIX/2/10/416x4
13  NRO WLS XLVI/4
14  NRO WLS LXVIII/1 487x9
15  NRO WLS XVII/7/23
16  NRO WLS XVIII/7/23
17  NRO WLS LXVIII/9/1
18  Wiggins, J. *Survey, terrier and valuation 1849.*
    MS in possession of Sir Thomas Hare
19  NRO Hare 541 222x2
20  Kain, 1986, 80
21  NRO Hare 541, 222x2
22  NRO Hare 5370, 221x6
23  NRO Hare 5370, 221x6
24  NRO LeStrange MSS, Boxes 5–12
25  Roe, 1975, 208
26  Kain, 1986, 78

## Chapter 11

1   Marshall, 1787, 1, 2
2   Suffield, 1913, 75
3   NRO Bacon MS 4363
4   Read, 1858, 263–311
5   Young, 1771, 2, 137
6   Marshall, 1787, 1, 2
7   Young, 1771 2, 140
8   Young, 1771 2, 138

## Chapter 12

1   Colvin & Newman, 1981, 97
2   Kent, 1796. 110–1
3   Kent, 1775, 152
4   Marshall, 1787 1, 81
5   Young, 1804, 20
6   Wade Martins, S. 1980, 137
7   Yaxley in Wade Martins, P. 1980b, 604
8   Yaxley, 1984, 89
9   NRO MS 22095
10  NRO MS 22095
11  Wiliam, 1986, 107
12  Young, 1804, 19–20
13  Marshall, 1787 1, 84–5
14  Raynbird, 1849, 21

15  Marshall, 1787 1, 81
16  Rose, 1937, 69
17  Robinson, 1983, 82 quoting *Transactions of
    the Society of Arts* XIV (1790), 290–304
18  Marshall, 1787, 1, 82
19  Kennedy, 1988, 19–23
20  NRO WLS XXIX/2/10
21  NRO Bacon MS 4363
22  Hudson, 1850, 282

## Chapter 13

1   Hudson, 1850, 283
2   Harvey, N. 1984, 137
3   Young, 1804, 479–80
4   Young, 1804, 481
5   Young, 1804, 481
6   Bacon, 1844, 317
7   Bacon, 1844, 306
8   Marshall, 1787, 2, 23–5
9   Colvin & Newman, 1981, 95
10  Denton, 1863, 165
11  Young, 1804, 480
12  Loudan, 1831, 157
13  Denton, 1864, 165

## Chapter 14

1   Grundy, 1970, 3
2   Marshall, 1787, 1, 83
3   Young, 1804, 446
4   Bacon, 1844, 301–3
5   Smith, 1989, 17
6   Read, 1858, 269
7   Marshall 1787, 2, 274–6
8   Read, 1858, 295
9   Read, 1858, 295
10  Caird, 1851, 170
11  Read, 1858, 295
12  Read, 1858, 295
13  Marshall, 1787, 1, 83

## Chapter 15

1   Marshall, 1787, 1, 83
2   Waistell, 1827, 36
3   Young, 1770, 52
4   Wiliam, 1986, 240
5   Waistell, 1827, 46

## Chapter 16

1  Kent, 1796, 113
2  Grey, *JRASE*, 1843, vol. 4, 1
3  Stephens n.d., 4th ed., 6, 316–7
4  Dean, 1851
5  Harvey, N. 1984, 102

## Chapter 17

1  Thompson, 1968, 62–77
2  Manning, 1988
3  Robinson, 1983
4  Wade Martins, S. 1980, 95
5  Wiliam, 1986, 259
6  Read, 1858, 295
7  Wade Martins, S. 1980, 94 and appendix 3
8  Brigden, 1986, 45
9  Brigden, 1986, 23

## Chapter 18

1  Robinson, 1983
2  quoted by Bacon 1844, 27
3  NRO Keary 1861
4  Stephens, 1844, 312

## Chapter 19

1  Essex County Council, 1979
2  Baird & Tarrant, 1973, 14
3  Fenton & Walker, 1981, 205
4  MAFF 1985, 25
5  Wilkinson, 1987, 257
6  Walshe, 1979, 21
7  Carole Ryan, Conservation Officer, Shropshire County Council, personal correspondence
8  For a full discussion of the implications of the grant, see SPAB *Newsletter* 10, 2 and 3 (spring and summer, 1989)
9  Watkins & Winter, 1988
10  Yeats, 1926, 180
11  Essex County Council, 1979
12  MAFF 1985, 27
13  Hanson, 1987
14  Collier, 1989
15  *Eastern Daily Press*, 13 October, 1989
16  *Eastern Daily Press*, 13 October, 1989
17  *Norfolk Structure Plan*, 3.4.26, policy H.11
18  Noble, 1989

# BIBLIOGRAPHY

ALCOCK, N.W., *Cruck Construction*, Council for British Archaeology Research Report, 42, 1981.

ARMSTRONG, B.J., *Norfolk Diary*, Hodder and Stoughton, 1963.

BACON, R.N., *Agriculture of Norfolk*, London, 1844.

BAIRD, W.W., and TARRANT, J.R., *Hedgerow Destruction in Norfolk 1946–1970*, Centre of East Anglian Studies, University of East Anglia, Norwich, 1973.

BEATON, E., 'The Sandside Kiln Barn, Caithness', *Caithness Field Club Bulletin*, spring 1988, pp. 1–4.

BEDFORD, Duke of, *The Story of a Great Agricultural Estate*, London, 1897.

BERESFORD, M., and HURST, J.G., eds., *Deserted Medieval Villages*, Lutterworth, 1971.

BLOOM, J.H., *Notices, Historical and Antiquarian of the Castle and Priory at Castle Acre*, Richardson, London, 1843.

BRECKLAND DISTRICT COUNCIL, Norfolk, *Conservation Advice Sheet, 4, Barn Conversions*, n.d.

BRIGDEN, R., *Victorian Farms*, Crowood Press, 1986.

BROWN, J., *Agriculture in England. A Survey of Farming 1870–1947*, Manchester University Press, 1987.

BRUNSKILL, R.W., *Traditional Farm Buildings in England and Wales*, Gollancz, 2nd ed., 1982.

CAIRD, J., *English Agriculture, 1850–51*, London, 1851.

CARTER, A., and WADE MARTINS, S., *A Year in the Field*, Centre of East Anglian Studies, University of East Anglia, Norwich, 1987.

CLARKE, D., 'Pennine aisled barns', *Vernacular Architecture*, vol. 4, 1972, pp. 25–7.

COLLIER, D., 'Beware the Barn Dweller', *Farmers Weekly*, 27 January, 1989, p. 72.

COLVIN, H., and NEWMAN, J., eds., *Of Buildings: Roger North's Writings on Architecture*, Oxford University Press, 1981.

COUNCIL FOR BRITISH ARCHAEOLOGY, 'A policy for the countryside', *British Archaeological News*, vol. 3, no. 6, August, 1988, pp. 57–61.

COURSE, E., and MOORE, P., 'Victorian farm buildings in Hampshire', *Proceedings of the Hampshire Field Club and Archaeological Society*, vol. 40, 1984, pp. 107–14.

DARLEY, G., *A Future for Farm Buildings*, SAVE, 1988.

DAVENPORT, F.G., *The Economic Development of a Norfolk Manor 1086–1565*, Frank Cass reprint, 1967.

DEAN, G.A., *The Land Steward*, London, 1851.

DENTON, J.B., *The Farm Homesteads of England*, London, 1863.

DONALDSON, J., *General View of the Agriculture of the Carse of Gowrie in the County of Perthshire*, London, 1794.

DYER, C., 'English peasant buildings in the later Middle Ages', *Medieval Archaeology*, vol. 30, 1986, pp. 19–43.

ESSEX COUNTY COUNCIL, *The Essex Countryside, Historic Barns, A Planning Appraisal*, 1979.
*Residential Barn Conversion, Supplementary Planning Guidance*, n.d.

EVANS, D.H., and JARRETT, M.G., 'The deserted village of West Whelpington, Northumberland, third report, part one', *Archaeologia Aeliana*, fifth series, vol. 15, 1987, pp. 199–209.

EVANS, D.H., JARRETT, M.G. and WRATHNELL, S., 'The deserted village of West Whelpington. Northumberland, third report, part two', *Archaeologia Aeliana*, fifth series, vol. 16, 1988, pp. 139–93.

FENTON, A. and WALKER, B., *The Rural Architecture of Scotland*, John Donald, 1981.

FOSTER, L.I. and ALCOCK, L., eds., *Culture and Environment*, Routledge & Kegan Paul, 1963.

FUSSELL, G.E., *The Old English Farming Books, from Fitzherbert to Tull, 1523–1730*, Lockwood, 1947.
*More Old English Farming Books, 1731–1793*, Lockwood, 1950.
*The Farmer's Tools*, Mebrose, 1952.
'Reclamation of the Yorkshire Wolds', *Journal of the Land Agents' Society*, vol. 53, April 1954, pp. 159–61.

GRAY, J.R., 'An Industrial Farm Estate in Berkshire', *Industrial Archaeology*, vol. 8, 1971, pp. 171–83.

GREAT YARMOUTH BOROUGH COUNCIL, *Barn Conversions For Residential Use*, 1980.

GREY, J., 'On Farm Buildings', *Journal of the Royal Agricultural Society of England*, vol. 4, 1843, pp. 12–3.

GRIFFITHS, E., *The Management of two East Norfolk Estates in the 17th century*, Unpublished U.E.A. Ph.D. thesis, 1987.

GRUNDY, J.E., 'Note on the relationship between climate and cattle housing', *Vernacular Architecture*, vol. 1, 1970, pp. 1–5.

HAMPSHIRE COUNTY COUNCIL, *Saving Old Farm Buildings*, 1982.

HANSELL, P. and J., *Doves and Dovecotes*, Millstream Books, 1988.

HANSON, M., 'Lowly Cattle Sheds', *Country Life*, 17 December, 1987.

HARVEY, N., *A History of Farm Buildings in England and Wales*, 2nd ed., David and Charles, 1984.

'The farmsteads of the Exmoor reclamation', *Journal of the Historic Farm Buildings Group*, vol. 3, 1989, pp. 45–58.

HELLEN, J.A., 'Agricultural innovation and detectable landscape margins: the case of wheel houses in Northumberland', *Agricultural History Review*, vol. 20, 1972, pp. 140–54.

HEPBURN, G.B., *General View of the Agriculture and Rural Economy of East Lothian*, Edinburgh, 1794.

HOLDERNESS, B.A., *Pre-industrial England*, Dent, 1976.

HOLLAND, R.A., 'Fertilizers, Farming and Philanthropy – the Proctor Story', *Chemistry and Industry*, July, 1989, pp. 415–20.

HOOKE, D., ed., *The Medieval Village*, Oxford University Committee for Archaeology, 1985.

HOSKINS, W.G., 'Harvest fluctuations and English economic history, 1480–1619', *Agricultural History Review*, vol. 12, part I., 1964, pp. 28–46.

HUDSON, J., 'On the construction of farm buildings', *Journal of the Royal Agricultural Society of England*, vol. 11, 1850, pp. 280–2.

HUTTON, K., 'The distribution of wheel houses in the British Isles', *Agricultural History Review*, vol. 24, 1976, pp. 30–5.

JARRETT, M.J., and WRATHNELL, S., 'Sixteenth- and seventeenth-century farmsteads: West Whelpington, Northumberland', *Agricultural History Review*, vol. 24, 1977, pp. 108–19.

JENKINS, H.M., 'Lodge Farm, Castle Acre', *Journal of the Royal Agricultural Society of England*, 2nd series, vol. 5, 1869.

JENKINS, J.G., *The English Farm Wagon*, Oakwood Press, 1961.

JOHNSTONE, B., *General View of the Agriculture of the County of Dumfries and Galloway*, London, 1794.

JONES, BELL and MARTIN, 'Oasthouses in Ewhurst parish, evidence for the history of an industry', *Sussex Archaeological Collections*, vol. 126, 1988, pp. 195–224.

KAIN, R.J.P., *Tithe Atlas*, Cambridge University Press, 1986.

KAIN, R.J.P. and PRINCE, H.C., *The Tithe Surveys of England and Wales*, Cambridge University Press, 1985.

KEARY, H.W., 'Description of the Duke of Norfolk's Norfolk estates', 1861, MS in NRO.

KENNEDY, A.T., 'The influence of wind on the orientation of threshing barns', *Vernacular Architecture*, vol. 19, 1988, pp. 19–23.

KENT, N., *Hints to Gentlemen of Landed Property*, London, 1775.

*General Survey of the Agriculture of the County of Norfolk*, London, 1796.

LAKE, J., *Historic Farm Buildings*, Blandford Press, 1989.

LESLIE, W., *General View of the Agriculture of Nairn and Moray*, Edinburgh, 1794.

LOCH, J., *An Account of the Improvements of the Estates of the Marquis of Stafford*, London, 1820.

LOUDON, J.C., *Encyclopedia of Agriculture*, 2nd ed., 1831.

McCANN, J., 'Is Clay Lump a Traditional Building Material?', *Vernacular Architecture*, 18, 1987, pp. 1–16.

MACDONALD, S., 'The progress of the early threshing machine', *Agriculture History Review*, vol. 24, 1975, pp. 63–77.

MACINNES, A.I., 'Scottish Gaeldom, The first phase of Clearance', in *People and Society in Scotland*, vol. 1, 1760–1830, T.M. Devine and R. Mitcheson, eds., John Donald, 1988, pp. 70–87.

MANNING, M., ed., *Commons in Norfolk*, Norfolk Research Committee, 1988.

MARSHALL, W., *Rural Economy of Norfolk*, 2 vols., London, 1787.

*The Landed Property of England*, London, 1804.

*The Review and Abstracts of the County Reports of the Board of Agriculture for the Several Agriculture Departments of England*, vol. 3, Eastern Department, London, 1811.

MESSENGER, P., 'Lowther Farmstead Plans', *Transactions of the Cumberland and Westmorland Antiquarian and Archaeological Society*, vol. 75, 1975, pp. 327–51.

MINGAY, G.E., *English Landed Society in the Eighteenth Century*, Routledge and Kegan Paul, 1963.

MINISTRY OF AGRICULTURE, FISHERIES AND FOOD, *Redundant Farm Buildings in England and Wales, a Pilot Study*, 1985.

*Farming and Conservation Grant Scheme*, 1989.

MOSCROP, W.J., 'Covered cattle yards', *Journal of the Royal Agricultural Society of England*, 3rd series, vol. 1, 1890, p. 473.

NANKERVIS, J., *The Traditional Farm, Wicca, Zennor, St Ives, Cornwall*, MAFF 1989.

NOBLE, G., 'Barns and walls in the Yorkshire Dales', *English Heritage Conservation Bulletin*, Issue 8, June 1989.

NORTH NORFOLK DISTRICT COUNCIL, *Planning and Design Guide*, 1989.

ORWIN, C.S. and SELLICK, R.J., The Reclamation of Exmoor Forest, David and Charles, 1970.

OVERTON, M., 'The diffusion of agricultural innovation in early modern England, turnips and clover in Norfolk and Suffolk 1580–1740', *Transactions of the Institute of British Geographers*, vol. 10, 1985, pp. 205–21.

PERRY, P.J., 'High Farming in Victorian Britain', *Agricultural History*, vol. 55, 1981, pp. 156–65.

PETERS, J.E.C., *The Development of Farm Buildings in West Lowland Staffordshire up to 1880*, Manchester, 1969.

'Post-Medieval roof trusses in some Staffordshire farm buildings', *Vernacular Architecture*, vol. 19, 1988, pp. 24–31.

POSTGATE, M.R., 'Field Systems in Breckland', *Agricultural History Review*, vol. 10, 1962, pp. 80–101.

RAYNBIRD, H., *Agriculture of Suffolk*, London, 1849.

READ, C.S., 'Recent improvements in Norfolk farming', *Journal of the Royal Agricultural Society of England*, vol. 19, 1858, pp. 265–311.

'Agriculture in Norfolk' in WHITE, W., *Norfolk Directory*, London, 1883, pp. 69–76.

REW, H., 'Report on Norfolk', *Parliamentary Papers*, 1896, vol. XVII, pp. 596–7.

RICHARDS, E., *The Leviathan of Wealth*, Routledge and Kegan Paul, 1973.

RIGOLD, S., 'The distribution of aisled timber barns', *Vernacular Architecture*, vol. 2, 1971, pp. 20–2.

ROBERTSON, G., *General View of the Agriculture of Mid Lothian*, Edinburgh, 1793.

ROBINSON, J.M., *Georgian Model Farms*, Oxford, 1983.

ROE, P., *The Development of Norfolk Agriculture in the nineteenth century*, unpublished U.E.A. M.Phil. thesis, 1975.

ROSE, W., *The Village Carpenter*, Cambridge University Press, 1937.

RUFFINIERE DU PREY, P. DE LA, 'John Soane, Philip Yorke and their quest for primitive architecture', *National Trust Studies*, 1979, pp. 28–37.

RURAL DEVELOPMENT COMMISSION, *Old Buildings, New Opportunities*.

ROSSELLI, J., 'An Indian Governor in the Norfolk Marshland: Lord William Bentinck as Improver, 1809–27', *Agricultural History Review*, vol. 19, 1971, pp. 42–64.

SHROPSHIRE COUNTY COUNCIL, *Planning Guidance Notes – Farm Building Conversion in Shropshire*, 1990.

SLADE, H.G., 'Rothemay: An eighteenth-century kiln barn', *Scottish Vernacular Building Group Newsletter*, 4, 1978, pp. 21–30.

SMITH, A.H., 'Labour in late sixteenth century England: a case study from north Norfolk', *Continuity and Change*, vol. 4, 1, 1989, pp. 11–52.

SMITH, L., *Investigating Old Buildings*, Batsford, 1985.

SMITH, R., 'Bringing Moorland into Cultivation', *Journal of the Royal Agricultural Society of England*, vol. 17, 1865, pp. 356–62.

SOUTH NORFOLK DISTRICT COUNCIL, *The Conversion of Farm Buildings to Residential Use*, 1980.

STEPHENS, HENRY, *The Book of the Farm*, 4th edition, 1844.

STIRLING, A.M.W., *Coke of Norfolk and his Friends*, 2 vols., John Lane, The Bodley Head, 1913.

SUFFIELD, LORD, *My Memories, 1830–1913*, London, 1913.

TANCRED, T., 'Essay on the construction of farm buildings', *Journal of the Royal Agricultural Society of England*, vol. 11, 1851, p. 192.

TAYLOR, C., *The Cambridgeshire Landscape*, Hodder & Stoughton, 1973.

THIRSK, J., ed., *The Rural Economy of England, collected essays*, Hambledon, 1984.

*The Agricultural History of England and Wales*, vol. 5, 11, 1640–1750, Cambridge University Press, 1985.

'English Agricultural Regions and Agrarian History, 1500–1700', in *Studies in Economic and Social History*, THIRSK, J., ed., Macmillan, 1987.

THOMPSON, H.S., 'Farm Buildings', *Journal of the Royal Agricultural Society of England*, vol. 11, 1850, pp. 185–7.

TROTTER, J., *General View of the Agriculture of the County of West Lothian*, Edinburgh, 1793.

TYSON, B., 'Low Park Barn, Rydal: The reconstruction of a farm building in Westmorland in the seventeenth century', *Transactions of Cumberland and Westmorland Antiquarian and Archaeological Society*, vol. 79, 1979, pp. 85–98.

'Rydal Hall farmyard – the development of a Westmorland farmstead before 1700', *Transactions of the Cumberland and Westmorland Antiquarian and Archaeological Society*, vol. 80, 1980, pp. 113–130.

'Skirwith Hall and Wilton tenement (Kirkland Hall), The rebuilding of two Cumbrian farmsteads in the eighteenth century', *Transactions of the Cumberland and Westmorland Antiquarian and Archaeological Society*, vol. 81, 1981, pp. 93–112.

'Some traditional buildings in the Troutbeck valley', *Transactions of the Cumberland and Westmorland Antiquarian and Archaeological Society*, vol. 82, 1982, pp. 151–76.

WADE MARTINS, P., 'Excavations in North Elmham Park', *East Anglian Archaeology*, vol. 9, 1980a.

'Village sites in Launditch Hundred', *East Anglian Archaeology*, vol. 10, 1980b.

WADE MARTINS, S., *A Great Estate at Work*, Cambridge University Press, 1980.

*Norfolk, A Changing Countryside*, Phillimore, 1988.

'Farm buildings, some basic questions', *Journal of the Historic Farm Buildings Group*, vol. 1, 1987.

ed., *Farm Buildings, A Resource Pack for History and Environmental Studies*, Centre of East Anglian Studies, University of East Anglia, Norwich, 1988.

WAISTELL, C., *Designs for Agricultural Buildings*, London, 1827.

WALSHE, P., 'Conserving traditional farm buildings', *Landscape Research*, vol. 4, part 3, 1979, pp. 20–1 and p. 27.

WATKINS, C. and WINTER, M., *Superb Conversions?* CPRE, 1988.

WILIAM, E., *Traditional Farm Buldings in North-east Wales, 1550–1900*, National Museum of Wales, Welsh Folk Museum, 1986.

*The Historical Farm Buildings of Wales*, John Donald, 1986.

WILKINSON, P., *Alternative Uses for Redundant Farm Buildings*, Reading College of Estate Management Centre for Advanced Land-Use Studies, 1987.

WRATHNELL, S., 'Peasant Farmsteads and Villages in North-east England', in *The Rural Settlement of Medieval England*, Aston, M., Austin, D., and Dyer, C., eds., Blackwell, 1989, pp. 247–67.

YEATS, W.B., *Autobiographies*, Macmillan, 1926.

YAXLEY, D., ed., 'Survey of the Houghton Hall Estate by Joseph Hill, 1800', *Norfolk Record Society*, vol. 50, 1984.

YOUNG, A., *The Farmer's Guide*, London, 1770.

*A Farmer's Tour through the East of England*, 4 vols., vol. 2, 1771.

*A General View of the Agriculture of the County of Norfolk*, London, 1804.

# Index